PATHS NOT TAKEN

PATHS NOT TAKEN

BRITISH LABOUR AND INTERNATIONAL POLICY IN THE 1920S

HENRY R. WINKLER

THE UNIVERSITY OF NORTH CAROLINA
CHAPEL HILL AND LONDON

The paper in this book meets the guidelines for permanence and durability of the Committee on Production Guidelines for Book Longevity of the Council on Library Resources.

Library of Congress Cataloging-in-Publication Data

Winkler, Henry R. (Henry Ralph), 1916–

   Paths not taken: British labour and international policy in the 1920s / Henry R. Winkler

     p. cm.

   Includes bibliographical references and index.

   ISBN 0-8078-2171-3 (cloth : alk. paper)

   1. Great Britain—Foreign relations—1910–1936.   2. Labour Party (Great Britain)—History.   I. Title.

DA578.W475   1994

327.41–dc20   94-4590

                                                    CIP

98 97 96 95 94   5 4 3 2 1

Published with the help of the Charles Phelps Taft Memorial Fund, University of Cincinnati.

FOR BEA

CONTENTS

Preface

ix

Introduction

1

1. The Background

7

2. Labour and the Paris Settlement

26

3. The Aftermath of War

59

4. The Beginnings of Change

92

5. Labour's Uneasy Success

124

6. Alternatives to Locarno

155

Conclusion

192

Notes

199

Bibliography

227

Index

237

PREFACE

Many years ago, I tried to suggest in a couple of articles the process by which the British labor movement transformed a set of foreign policy attitudes that were the propaganda of a tiny minority group into positions that, however controversial, were the program of a party prepared to face the responsibilities of government and of international diplomatic intercourse. My intention then was to flesh out what were essentially shorthand sketches in a fuller investigation of the step-by-step interplay among Labour's policy makers and the handful of organs of Labour opinion that served them with their rank and file.

For a variety of reasons not particularly relevant here, I was diverted from those intentions and spent the better part of three fulfilling decades in administrative responsibilities at Rutgers University and the University of Cincinnati. As an aside, I tend to think that those responsibilities in public institutions helped give me a better sense of the political process and of how the politicians' world of compromise and give-and-take must of necessity operate. Now, in retirement, I have turned to an unfinished task. My intention is not to reproduce once again the story of Labour's foreign policy after the First World War. That has more than adequately been done. Instead, I have wanted to follow the emerging and conflicting patterns that characterized Labour's discussion of policy in the twenties and that resulted, by the end of the decade, in what might have been a viable and reasonably responsible posture had not all the assumptions of the twenties been quickly shattered in the tragic dissolution of European order during the thirties.

As is always the case, my obligations are many. I am grateful to the University of Cincinnati for giving me a sabbatical year at the end of my tenure as president, to its Research Council for a generous grant to facilitate my work, and to its Charles Phelps Taft Memorial Fund for aid in publication. Librarians at the Public Record Office, the divisions of the British Library, and the various college and university depositories listed in my bibliography have been invariably helpful. I am especially beholden to Dr. Angela Raspin of the Manuscript Room of the British Library of Political and Economic Science at the London School of Economics, to Stephen Bird, Archivist at the Labour party headquarters, to Norman Higson, Archivist of the Brynmor Jones Library of the University of Hull, to Sally Moffitt, Associate Librarian of the Walter Langsam Library of the University of Cincinnati, and to my Assistant, Mrs. Marie Ludeke. All of them provided help substantially beyond the call of academic duty.

I have had the great good fortune to number my most perceptive critics among the members of my family. My daughter, Karen J. Winkler of the *Chronicle of Higher Education*, and my son, Professor Allan M. Winkler of Miami University of Ohio, have read and corrected the manuscript and, perhaps even more important, have encouraged me to complete it at every step of the way.

Above all, my wife, Bea, worked with me in libraries and archives, reminding me from time to time how fundamentally absurd politicians—like the rest of us—often are. Her judgments from the perspective of a lay person frequently compelled me to reconsider my assumptions and always added pleasure to the satisfaction of rediscovering my academic roots. This book is dedicated to her with thanks and with love.

INTRODUCTION

After the First World War, the British Labour party engaged in a decade-long debate on international policy. As the party struggled to establish its credibility in domestic affairs, it also developed positions that demonstrated its readiness to take over the conduct of foreign policy whenever that became possible. Over the years, a small group of moderate internationalists gradually advanced a number of alternatives to the more traditional insistence on protecting national interests by national rather than international means. They argued increasingly that the fledgling League of Nations must become the essential mechanism in the search for international peace and security. Their position encountered fierce resistance from a wide spectrum of Labour's policy makers and opinion shapers whose disillusionment in the postwar period was bitter and intense. By the end of the decade, the gradual acceptance of the "League of Nations" outlook marked a significant shift in Labour's approach in the international area and reflected its growing maturity as an international force.

During the 1920s, most Conservatives deprecated the attempt to develop a system of collective security in place of an almost exclusive dependence upon national armaments. They feared any closer integration with other states, especially in Europe, and rejected reforms of the new League of Nations Covenant that might curtail in any way the principle of national sovereignty. For their part, while the Labour party was attempting to establish its plausibility as a responsible force in national politics, many in the labor movement refused to accept that responsibility required accommodation and compromise. They repudiated the notion that even the flawed international body born of the peace settlement could be employed to ensure a more peaceful and a more secure world order. As the outline of that settlement became clear, an almost root-and-branch repudiation of the aims of "capitalist" and "imperialist" governments swept across all but a small segment of the Labour party and its affiliates. Suspicion of France in particular was endemic. It led to an unwillingness, or an inability, seriously to consider France's fears of a resurgence of German power and her concern for the security that had twice been imperiled in less than half a century. A substantial group within the ranks of Labour viewed postwar Germany as the aggrieved nation and often ignored the growing strength of revisionist nationalism in the Weimar Republic. Many—perhaps most—within the labor and trade union movements looked with considerable skepticism at the infant League of Nations. To them, the League was merely an instrument of capitalist governments determined to preserve their position in the world of power politics no less than their primacy over working people at home. It required long discussion, as well as the experience of office in 1924, to persuade many within the mainstream of Labour that the simple expression of international goodwill by British socialists was an unrealistic foundation upon which to base a responsible foreign policy.

The move away from the bitter disillusionment of 1919 and 1920 was never smooth and often acrimonious. In a sense, as some of Labour's standard-bearers attempted to wean the movement away from the protest of the immediate postwar years, two foreign policies, personified by two dominant figures, came into being. The differences between Arthur Henderson, the solid, steady secretary of the Labour party, and Ramsay MacDonald, its most colorful and glamorous figure, were as much a matter of style and personality as of substance, but on one issue they were poles apart. MacDonald, despite his pragmatic approach to policy when he became prime minister and foreign secretary, was never persuaded that any international organization would have to rely upon arms to enforce agreements and ensure the peace. Instead, he placed his trust in the gradual development of an international spirit of goodwill. Henderson, even when he made compromises to accommodate Labour's widespread misgivings about the use of arms, nevertheless came increasingly to be the leading spokesman among all major British politicians for the support of international institutions backed by international force. He made effective use of the policy papers produced by members of Labour's newly formed Advisory Committee on International Questions, where the small group of advisors who shared his enthusiasm for a moderate "League of Nations" policy came to dominate. As the years passed, these advisors came to forge a moderate policy urging the fullest possible use of League agencies in the day-to-day conduct of international affairs. They provided data for supporting the work of such bodies as the International Labour Organization and the Mandates Commission of the League. Above all, they helped Henderson argue the case for the use of the League, backed by a measure of force, to uphold international agreements and even, if the circumstances made it possible, to encourage peaceful change.

Differences within the very top ranks of Labour were never fully reconciled before the disintegration of the second Labour government, and the near collapse of the Labour party, in 1931. During the tenure of that government, MacDonald kept the control of policy toward America firmly in his own hands and often appeared to be less than enthusiastic about the determination of his foreign secretary, Henderson, to strengthen the machinery of the League of Nations. For the most part, however, he accepted the direction in which the latter was attempting to steer his colleagues. In Henderson's hands, Labour's policy stressed the importance of limiting national armaments, emphasized initiatives such as arbitration or other pacific techniques to eradicate the causes of international differences, and advocated arrangements for pooled security against aggression. In sharp contrast to the Conservative party, Labour came to regard the League of Nations as a central institution in a new world of international cooperation. Henderson in particular championed the League's role in cultivating substitutes for war while he recognized somewhat reluctantly that the international body must have available the sanction of collective force if it were to resist attacks upon the international order of the future. Whatever the reluctance, it is clear that by the close of the 1920s the principal architects of Labour policy accepted that their hopes for security and stability rested not on some idealized and theoretical blueprint of a brave new world, but on the existing international institutions of the world in which they lived. And it is possible to argue that, in struggling to strengthen the institutions of international intercourse during their brief tenure of office, they were substantially more realistic than were the more traditional builders of the gimcrack international structure that fell apart so tragically in the thirties.

My purpose in the pages that follow is to examine the halting and sometimes contradictory steps by which mainstream Labour leaders, constantly barraged with advice from their various constituents, persuaded their followers to abandon the angry rhetoric sufficient for a small minority sect and to accept the fact that a responsible British policy could only be shaped by negotiation and compromise with other governments and by the level-headed use of the existing international system. The Labour party was less than two decades old when the First World War erupted. It had come into existence to promote the Parliamentary candidacies of Labour representatives, primarily for the purpose of dealing with bread-and-butter issues having to do with working conditions and labor relations. A few spokesmen such as Keir Hardie, mainly affiliated with the relatively feeble Independent Labour party (ILP), articulated a somewhat theoretical internationalism, but there is little to suggest that the rank and file of Labour paid much attention to international issues before the coming of the war.

All that changed as the horrors of the world conflagration impelled some within the labor movement to question the policies that had brought on the crisis. During the war, both the Labour party and the ILP developed elaborate schemes for international organization when peace was restored. In both cases, the proposals envisaged an international body that would have wide-ranging functions in the everyday conduct of international affairs.[1] The rhetoric of Allied statesmen, in particular Woodrow Wilson but even David Lloyd George, stimulated the hope that alternatives to systematic carnage might yet be found, but in fairly short order that hope was shattered as the makers of the peace settlement severely limited both the powers and the possibilities of the new international bodies that they created. Labour as yet did not have the power to influence significantly the shape of the world that emerged in the aftermath of hostilities. The result was an angry wave of frustration and disenchantment that swept over all sections of Labour in the immediate postwar years. Even moderate leaders, in the trade unions as well as in the political branches, shared the feeling of hopelessness and suspicion that welled up in reaction to the settlement hammered out by the governing classes of the Allied nations.

The fact that a new party, formed to promote other purposes, should have moved, however hesitatingly, away from the dead end of sterile criticism toward a constructive, if controversial, foreign policy stance requires explanation. Disapproval is an easy posture for a party out of power. It is even easier if that party, like the Labour party until after World War I, has no realistic anticipation of having to form a government in the near future. The most extreme of positions seems plausible so long as it does not have to be put into practice. When a political movement approaches the possibility of office, at least in a democratic society, then it must face up to the question of how its opinions and demands can be translated into action. In the field of foreign affairs, the policies of other governments, their fears and ambitions and postures, can no longer be ignored. The result, more often than not, is likely to be a tempering of stridency and an attempt to work effectively within existing institutions in pursuit of the broad aims of the party's constituencies. That is precisely what happened in the twenties as Labour made its circuitous progress toward a viable international policy.

Within Labour's ranks, the interplay of public dialogue and private deliberation was often disorderly and sometimes disorganized. But the process gradually shifted the labor movement from an almost total refusal to countenance any action of British governments or their allies to a grudging acceptance of the need to work within the existing international system in order to achieve a more peaceful and more humane world. In dealing with this shift, I have attempted to parallel the considerations of the key figures in the movement with the perceptions that were aired in the important organs of labor opinion at the same time. Sometimes they differed sharply; sometimes they agreed; but always in this period there was a vigorous debate out of which the changing shape of Labour's international policy emerged. Participants in the debate reflected the long-standing spectrum of interests that made up the labor movement—the Independent Labour party, Fabians, trade unions—but also included new recruits to Labour, mainly from the Liberal party, who most frequently had changed allegiance because of their disgust with traditional British foreign policy both before and after the war. These newcomers were by no means all of the same mind. Some adopted and continued to support the most extreme positions; others soon found themselves ranged with the few Labour leaders, like MacDonald and Henderson, who gradually became the voices advocating one form or another of constructive moderation.

Step by step, with many setbacks, the advocates of international cooperation came to the fore. The diehards, particularly within the Independent Labour party that was moving rapidly toward disaffiliation from the Labour party, were increasingly isolated on issues of foreign policy as they were on domestic questions. Among the advisors who prepared countless policy papers for the leadership of the Labour party and the Trades Union Congress, and among those leaders themselves, arguments for making the fullest use of new international institutions, above all the League of Nations, to a large extent prevailed.[2]

The attempt to achieve peace and security after World War I is a chronicle of failure. But it is too often forgotten that the decade of the twenties appeared to offer the hope that Europe and the world could settle down to a peaceful future. For the advocates of conventional approaches to foreign affairs, the signature of the Locarno treaties in 1925, guaranteeing the critical frontiers of western Europe and providing for arbitration agreements between Germany and some of her eastern neighbors, promised stability and a return to normality. Germany's entry into the League of Nations seemed further evidence that the aftermath of war was gradually disappearing. For a brief period of time Europe experienced a measure of economic prosperity that augured well for the future. But the Great Depression soon changed the hopes of the twenties into the fears and tensions of the thirties. The economic collapse created circumstances in France and Britain making it difficult for those countries to take a firm lead when complete rethinking of previous policies was essential. Unrest in Germany, a hazard that influenced all policies in the twenties, reached new heights and finally brought Adolf Hitler into power.[3]

It is tempting to speculate on what might have been the fate of Europe had Britain more fully adopted a policy of conciliating Germany in the twenties and helped shore up the struggling democratic republic. If, in addition, she had cooperated more fully with France in supporting a League of Nations system with effective sanctions, would such a policy have undermined the propaganda of German nationalists and given Europe as a whole the opportunity to deal with the consequences of fear and depression more adequately? There are too many variables and imponderables to warrant a confident answer. It is clear that the policies adopted by the Lloyd Georges and Curzons, the Baldwins and Chamberlains, along with their continental counterparts, failed with almost breathtaking rapidity. After one brief decade mankind again faced the threat of measureless destruction. Looking back, therefore, it seems proper to remember that there were alternative roads that might have been followed. The fact that those paths were not taken does not make them any less important. During the 1930s they pointed the way for those within the labor movement, such as Hugh Dalton and Clement Attlee, who pleaded for a policy of collective resistance to Nazi aggression and ultimately made it possible for the Labour party to play a crucial role in the great wartime coalition constructed by Winston Churchill. And today, as the world once again grapples with questions of how to legitimate the pronouncements of an international body, and with sensitive problems of sanctions and enforcement, the paths explored by British Labour in attempting to fashion a consensus on similar issues during the 1920s warrant our attention.

CHAPTER 1

THE BACKGROUND

Foreign policy was hardly the primary focus of the Labour party. But foreign affairs influenced the efforts to create a more equitable society at home, and Labour, like other groups, had to confront international issues whether it wished to or not. The account of Labour's effort to deal with the larger world is in many ways the story of its growing maturity as it gradually became a significant force in British politics.

In a few brief years after World War I, the Labour party made good its position as successor to the shattered and demoralized Liberals. Founded at the beginning of the century, it was still a relatively small third force as late as 1918, claiming to speak as the political representative of the working class, but dwarfed in the shadows of the two older parties. By 1929, its leaders had twice formed a government. Although Labour had not succeeded in winning a majority in the House of Commons, it had established itself beyond question as the constitutional alternative to the Conservative party.

The speed of Labour's emergence could hardly have been predicted by even the most optimistic of the party's managers. The electoral history of the party since its striking early success in 1906, when the Labour Representation Committee had returned twenty-nine members to Parliament, gave no hint of the possibilities of the future. While German Social Democracy, for example, seemed on the surface to be growing increasingly more powerful despite constitutional shackles, its British partner limped along without any success to match the 1912 electoral victories of the German Socialists. It was true that Labour representation in the House of Commons increased to forty and then to forty-two in the two elections of 1910. But these were hardly figures upon which to base any expectation of a rapid triumph. Indeed, in the tense period of industrial unrest between December 1910 and the outbreak of war, it seemed to some observers that the loose federation established in 1900 was in danger of breaking up completely. The appearance of syndicalism no less than the increasing turn to direct action among the trade unions challenged the tactics being pursued by the leaders of the party. In particular, a substantial minority felt frustrated by the policy of parliamentary collaboration with the Liberal government of Herbert Asquith.[1] Their exasperation was fed by the fact that during these years the party suffered several losses in by-elections and was unable to win a single additional seat. Once the war broke out the electoral truce froze the political status quo to the further impatience of certain groups within the movement, although there appears to be no sufficient warrant for believing, as some claimed, that the truce itself, rather than the general attitudes of the electorate, worked significantly to the disadvantage of the Labour party. In any case, when Labour faced the voters in Lloyd George's coupon election of 1918, at which support of the wartime coalition was the major criterion of acceptability, its final return of fifty-seven official members of Parliament was actually a smaller proportion of its candidates than had been the case in 1910.

After 1918, Labour entered upon its period of most spectacular growth. In a certain sense it may plausibly be argued that a Labour party as such did not really exist before that year. On February 26, at the annual conference, a new constitution, drafted largely by Arthur Henderson and Sidney Webb, a key figure in the Fabian Society component of the party, was accepted by the delegates. Previously a loose federation of affiliated societies, the Labour party now became a national organization, with local branches in every parliamentary constituency and open to all "workers by hand and brain" who subscribed to its program. For the first time the labor movement had the means to build up an effective electoral machine throughout the country. Equally important, the new constitution made it increasingly possible to attract recruits from among individuals, such as professional people, who had until now been largely ineligible for direct membership. The process of change, however, was slow and often contentious. Historian David Marquand has commented on how much the Labour party, in the early twenties, remained a loose federation of local bodies and special interests rather than a unitary organization with a single purpose, "full of fissures," as he put it, "between the trade unions and the I.L.P., between the I.L.P. and the Divisional Labour parties, between different unions and different sections of the same union, between 'intellectuals' and manual workers, between pacifists who had been in prison during the war and patriots who had spoken from recruiting platforms, between 'Right' and 'Left,' between respectability and revolt."[2] Despite the tension and the controversy, the years between 1918 and 1931 were years of growth and transformation for the party. As it became heir to the mantle of the declining Liberal party, Labour was forced to rethink its attitudes and reformulate its programs in terms of the realities of responsible office rather than as the propaganda of a small minority.

The reshaping of the Labour party's policy was most striking in the field of foreign affairs. Labour felt its way slowly toward a policy that was first partially tried out in 1924 when Labour was in office, was implemented with relative consistency by its second government between 1929 and 1931, and, in theory at least, was the platform upon which it took its stand in the tragic decade of the thirties.[3]

The decade after the war was generally a period of hope. To most people in Great Britain the victory of 1918 brought a sense of security and self-confidence that lasted until well into 1929. From a military point of view the postwar settlements left the British Isles as safe from any immediate threat as they were ever likely to be. Like their French counterparts, British statesmen were concerned with the exploitation of victory. Whereas France was obsessed by the fear of renewed German aggression, British planning for a time was generally based upon the thesis that no major war was to be anticipated for at least ten years. It is common to conclude that this assumption reflected a peculiarly British belief that it was unnecessary to look ahead more than a decade. In reality, whatever may be thought of their accomplishments, British policy makers attempted to take advantage of their hypothesized margin of safety to promote a relatively long-run strategy of foreign policy.

That strategy reflected notions of Britain's role that may have been suitable for a wealthy, contented power, but hardly appropriate for a nation no longer able fully to defend its stake in the external world. Despite the underlying optimism of the immediate postwar era, the United Kingdom emerged from almost five years of battle greatly weakened. On virtually every level of power—strategic, political, economic—Britain's nineteenth-century preeminence was challenged. Above all, the acceleration of prewar trends made more critical her dependence upon overseas trade to pay for food and raw materials. Because the standard of life of her people was so exposed to the vagaries of a complicated international system, the restoration of that system was judged to have crucial importance for Britain. As a result, the safeguarding of national security, particularly in relation to Europe, came to be equated very largely with policies designed to promote general economic recovery and, as a corollary, to foster the general pacification of the continent.[4]

In the 1920s, it was considered almost blasphemous to hint at the possibility of another war.[5] For a time most Englishmen took it for granted that the world was entering a new era of tranquillity, during which such international difficulties as obviously existed could be gradually reconciled by some process of peaceful adjustment. High hopes for the creation of a more secure world were not confined to a tiny minority outside the mainstream of British sentiment. "Advanced" opinion in all parties and at all levels assumed that

disarmament would systematically be achieved and that the outlawry of war
and aggression was only a matter of time. Even Conservative leaders, more
"traditionalist" in their approach, anticipated a long period of constructive
consolidation—which they thought they had achieved when they accepted
the Locarno agreements in 1925.

In this atmosphere the diverse Labour attitudes on foreign affairs were
forged into an operative program for the Labour party. There was from the
start a bitter reaction to the handiwork of the Allied statesmen who had
crafted the settlement at Versailles. But that very spirit of disillusionment
reflected the optimistic conviction that a better international order could be
achieved—and that it was being frustrated by the lack of vision of the men
who held the reins of power. This sense of the possible was of course considerably reinforced by the growing political strength of the Labour party as the
decade unfolded.

The shock of war triggered significant changes in Labour's outlook on
international matters. Before the conflict, working-class interest in foreign
affairs was sporadic and slight.[6] The workers newly enfranchised in 1867 and
1884 directed their political attention much more toward domestic issues
than toward the obscure complications of external relations. Despite the
enormous increase in British productivity over half a century, despite, indeed, the undoubted rise in the standard of life of the "average" worker,
millions on the land or in the drab industrial slums continued to live in
squalor and poverty. Of necessity working-class organization was primarily
concerned with the "condition of England" question. The new unionism,
sweeping through the ranks of unskilled and semiskilled labor toward the end
of the century, dramatized the urgency of the struggle for economic and
social advancement. It soon brought the strength of added numbers to a trade
union movement hitherto dominated by the established craft organizations of
highly skilled workers. But even when the new unionists had persuaded the
chiefs of the Trades Union Congress of the need for political action, the very
circumstances that induced the leaders of organized labor to redirect their
efforts into the channels of the parliamentary process made it certain that
they would give short shrift to questions of international consequence.

In similar fashion the socialist societies whose establishment paralleled
that of the new unionism were largely occupied with a thoroughgoing criticism of contemporary social and economic institutions. Both the Social
Democratic Federation, Marxist in its inspiration, and the Independent Labour party, deeply rooted in the nonconformist tradition, worked to arouse
the social conscience of their time to an awareness of the intolerable conditions hidden behind the facade of industrial society. Until about the turn of

the century, there is little evidence that either group, the withering SDF and the more vital ILP, paid other than lip service to an internationalism that, if genuinely embraced, might have led to a modest comprehension of foreign policy issues and their relation to domestic problems.

Not even the Fabian Society, select, small, and almost exclusively intellectual, lifted its eyes far beyond the horizon off the British shores. The Fabians gave modern British socialism much of its doctrine, but it was a doctrine whose concrete application virtually ignored foreign affairs. Organized to "permeate" the existing political parties, these middle-class intellectuals reluctantly moved toward cooperation with trade unionists and working-class politicians in the creation of a new political party. But the purpose for which such a party was envisaged remained the achievement of the "gas and water" socialism of the Fabians. Ambivalent on the issue of imperialism that came to a head during the Boer War, they tended to be silent on other international questions until the First World War made imperative some stand on the most crucial issues of the time.[7]

In large measure, the prewar Labour party inherited this indifference to the world of diplomacy and foreign policy. Formed by its constituent groups to promote legislation "in the direct interest of labour," the Labour Representation Committee of 1900 was forged into a full-fledged party on the anvil of such measures as the Taff Vale decision, which made it possible for a trade union itself to be sued for damages caused by its members in the course of a trade dispute.[8] Understandably, the new party found virtually all of its energies absorbed in the struggle to defend workers' rights through the medium of Parliament. The most prominent leaders of the Labour party, Keir Hardie and Ramsay MacDonald, each in his own way, were committed internationalists, yet neither was particularly effective in educating the labor movement to the dangers that confronted it in the years before 1914. In the House of Commons the two were the major and frequently the only spokesmen on foreign affairs for the small parliamentary Labour party, pressing for better relations with Germany, warning against being used to promote the purposes of Tsarist Russia, pleading for release from the oppressive burden of armaments that plagued every major nation.[9] As a result, while it is possible to discover occasional pronouncements by party leaders on foreign affairs, it seems clearly out of touch with the "feel" of the prewar period to emphasize their importance.[10]

This is not to say that the Labour party had *no* international outlook before 1914. Enough commentators have written about the "internationalism" of Labour's background to make it unnecessary to stress the point, but it is wise to keep the conception in proper perspective. The Labour party and some of its constituent societies were indeed members of the Second International. On occasion the party joined with its fellow members in denouncing imperialism and colonial exploitation, branding militarism, and stressing the international solidarity of the working classes. But the legend of socialist solidarity, to be broken so irreparably when the European armies marched in 1914, even before 1914 represented an aspiration rather than a reality of international life. As far as the British Labour party was concerned, it was, in a certain sense, a member of the Second International by sufferance. Non-Marxist, unwilling to subscribe to the thesis of class warfare, it was made eligible for membership by a compromise formula that hardly concealed the deep rifts separating it from its more doctrinaire fellows. Perhaps it is symbolic of the *pro forma* character of the labor movement's participation in the International that even the Trades Union Congress sent delegates for a long time, despite the fact that it can hardly be argued that the TUC treated its participation seriously. On the other hand, the theoretical position of the Independent Labour party encouraged its more prominent role in the organization, and for a time Keir Hardie's support of the general strike against war made him a leading figure, although it is difficult to discover that his position garnered any widespread support at home.[11] There is in sum little evidence of any genuine temper of working-class "internationalism" among the rank and file of the labor movement, and its presence among the leaders of the Labour party can perhaps be more plausibly related to the myths of labor solidarity than identified as a fundamental motivating force within the party before 1914.

Much more important than the influence of socialist internationalism was the heritage that the Labour party received from the liberal tradition of the nineteenth century. "That power politics are wicked and must be subjugated to the rule of law; that Britain must stand for applying morality in international affairs and, in particular, for helping small nations to achieve their independence; that rich and fortunate nations have an obligation to raise up the backward colonial peoples; that the elector everywhere wants peace if only the politicians will allow it; that what [the] British above all hate is a bully who breaks the law"—these, Labour's left-wing intellectual R. H. S. Crossman once wrote, are the essential components of that liberal tradition in foreign policy.[12] Fundamentally, he argued, such an approach was much less a policy than a moral repudiation of the evils of power politics. It was an expression of the liberal conscience, and its main function was that of protest against the excesses of traditional British policy.

In the early twentieth century the spokesmen of that conscience were as much the leaders of the Labour party as the official representatives of Liberalism. The prewar internationalists of the Labour party tended to be vague, imprecise, never really sure whether to support a policy of collaboration by sovereign states or to advocate the absorption of competing nationalisms in some broader world sovereignty. Their uncertain position almost exactly paralleled that of a minority of dissident Liberals who were moved, in the years before 1914, to reject the imperial and diplomatic maneuvers of their own party as they had opposed those of the Tories.[13] In both cases, the "liberal" protest—a kind of *cri de conscience*—stands out much more clearly than any proposals for an alternative policy.

Perhaps the most instructive example of the essentially liberal character of the influences molding Labour's attitudes toward international affairs is to be found among the currents of pacifism that ran so strongly in its ranks both before and after the First World War. It is apparent, of course, that there were advocates of a doctrinaire "socialist pacifism" in evidence before 1914.[14] It is equally clear that these advocates became more vocal and extended their sway in the first few years after the conflict. But "socialism" and opposition to "capitalist-inspired" struggles were not really the crucial determinants of the pacifism of the bulk of Labour's adherents. It may be questionable whether the political outlooks of the rank and file stemmed so consciously from their religious beliefs as Labour publicists have sometimes held.[15] Nevertheless, on issues of war and peace, the deeply religious views of the London politician George Lansbury was still much more typical than the militant industrial anticapitalism of the Clydesider James Maxton. Labour pacifism was deeply rooted in the ethical, Christian, and even Manchesterian soil of nineteenth-century British liberalism. Granted the limitations of the view that the evils of international conflict could be simply removed by an act of will, the fact remains that Labour pacifists of the early twentieth century, like their Liberal counterparts, came to this view more frequently by way of biblical injunctions and moral precepts than through systematic socialist analysis of the forces of international society. And when Labour speakers argued that expensive armaments were incompatible with an active program of social reform, they were in effect demonstrating, to personify a point of view, that they were the true heirs of the Mancusian John Bright, a John Bright translated into the collectivist world of the "New Liberalism," but a John Bright, nonetheless, shocked as much by the waste as by the immorality of war and reacting in essentially the same fashion as his later Liberal and Labour successors.[16]

Taken together, these two elements in the prewar background of Labour— the indifference of the mass of its supporters to international questions and the essentially liberal outlook that shaped whatever attitudes were in evidence—were of considerable weight in determining the course of the party in the postwar years. The very lack of interest in foreign affairs, which made the cataclysm of 1914 so totally unexpected to all but a tiny minority, bred compensating extremism once the war was over. Seen in retrospect, the international policies that had been pursued by the British and other governments appeared mean and sordid, particularly to people who had paid so little attention to them in the past. As a result, when those who had opposed the war (and some who had not) hammered home the moral that resort to arms was never a solution to international differences, that no capitalist government could be trusted, that international cooperation was a chimera until most states became socialist, and that working-class solidarity across national lines was the only hope for a peaceful world, they found substantial support for their millennialism among the ranks of Labour.

At the same time, the idealistic liberal strain in British society helped persuade the Labour party of the advantages of "practical" cooperation among the nations. The "League of Nations Policy" that emerged endorsed an international organization to help settle disputes between nations and also to regulate many peacetime activities of the world, thus making war less likely in the future. The policy offered an alternative to doctrines of class war with which British socialists were uncomfortable, however much they may have been attracted to them in their period of temporary disillusionment. And that alternative in turn was based upon more congenial conceptions of international morality, pacifism, and collaboration that represented a return to the liberal heritage upon which Labour's approach to foreign policy had originally been built.

This is not to say that the sole impact of the liberal tradition was ultimately in the direction of taming the extremism of the postwar Labour party. Indeed, the Liberal party itself contributed, at least indirectly, to virtually all the strains of doctrine that competed for Labour's attention in the 1920s. The many-sided nature of these "liberal" influences in shaping the development of Labour's foreign policy is nowhere more apparent than among the group of left-wing radicals who made their way into the new party during or shortly after the war. Increasingly dissatisfied with the outlook of the Liberal party, they entered the ranks of Labour mainly to find a platform for their views on foreign policy. During the twenties their prominence in the consideration of foreign affairs was unquestionably out of all proportion to their numbers within the party.[17] Many of their leaders were active in the Independent Labour party and their views tended to be channeled through the journals and the conference resolutions of the ILP. Most of the same individuals were prominent in the Union of Democratic Control founded in 1914 to expose the so-called secret diplomacy of the Great Powers and to argue the merits of democratic control of foreign policy. Some participated actively in the work of the Advisory Committee on International Questions, where problems were analyzed and proposals shaped for the guidance of Labour party leaders and rank and file alike. A number came to occupy positions of importance in the first Labour government of 1924.

Among this group of ex-Liberals, perhaps the most important were Norman Angell, Noel and Charles Roden Buxton, Arthur Ponsonby, Charles Trevelyan, and E. D. Morel.[18] In 1914, for example, Angell, author of the enormously popular book *The Great Illusion*, which had questioned the economic advantages of victory in war, had joined with Morel, Ponsonby, and Trevelyan to form the Union of Democratic Control. But unlike Trevelyan and Ponsonby, who were pacifists, and also unlike Morel, who mistrusted the use of coercion in international affairs, Angell from the beginning insisted on the need to develop an effective system of collective security. Frail, ascetic, almost shy, a scholar rather than a politician, Angell, once he had joined the Labour party in 1920, took to the hustings to present his case to the electorate.[19] Impatient with demagogy, refusing to talk class war, he was probably not the most effective campaigner. But in his books and within the small circle of the Advisory Committee on International Questions, his reasoned arguments for collective security were influential in at least tempering the currents of pessimism and pacifism that ran high in Labour circles in the twenties.[20]

Unlike Angell, Noel and Charles Roden Buxton virtually inherited their keen concern for public questions. Great-grandsons of Sir Thomas Fowell Buxton, the "Liberator" of the slaves in the British Empire, sons of a Liberal governor of South Australia, they brought to public affairs a sense of moral responsibility that possibly stemmed from the strong Quaker strain in their background. In the House of Commons before the war the two were connected with the anti-imperialist wing of the Liberal party. They shared an intense interest in the Near East, and as leading figures in the Balkan Committee became the virtual standard bearers of the oppressed peoples in that area. When the war came, Noel Buxton, who was never a pacifist, supported its efficient prosecution, at the same time identifying himself with those who desired a negotiated peace. His commitment to a moderate settlement and his conviction that the Labour party understood the need for a reconciliation with Germany helped motivate his shift from the Liberals in June 1919, shortly after his brother had joined the ranks of Labour. Like other former Liberals, he brought much needed experience in foreign affairs to the councils of the party and during the twenties was an active advisor to party leaders on international questions. Essentially a Fabian in outlook, he exerted his influence to try to temper the overheated ideological rhetoric of Labour's left-wingers. Even when he served as minister of agriculture in the first two Labour governments, his main interest was in foreign affairs, but after 1924 his part in the formulation of a foreign policy program diminished as he gradually assumed the role of an elder statesman.[21]

Charles Roden Buxton's impress on Labour's foreign policy attitudes took a rather different turn from that of his brother. Like so many of the ex-Liberals, he became active in the Independent Labour party after his conversion to Labour. But where many of them soon moved away from the extremism that characterized the ILP assessment of the international scene, Roden Buxton threw himself wholeheartedly into ILP causes. Much more pacifist than Noel Buxton, tending to view his pacifism as hard-headed realism, he became by the middle of the decade one of the ILP's leading spokesmen, not only in public but through such vehicles as the Advisory Committee on International Questions. Opposed to war, he was also opposed to sanctions and during the twenties gave effective expression to that point of view.[22]

Arthur Ponsonby and Charles Trevelyan were similar in many respects. Both came from families prominent in the nineteenth-century annals of British politics, and both had achieved some prominence among the radicals of the prewar Liberal party.[23] Pacifist by conviction, they opposed the war on principle and were among the five original founders of the Union of Democratic Control, which had been formed early in the war to promote the "democratic control" of foreign policy.[24] After joining the Labour party, both rose to high office, Trevelyan as a two-time president of the board of education and Ponsonby as undersecretary of state for foreign affairs in the first Labour government. Temperamentally, however, they differed. Trevelyan, grand nephew of Thomas Babington Macaulay and brother of the historian G. M. Trevelyan, was intense and impatient, and eventually in the thirties, disillusioned by his inability to win over his adopted party completely to his views on foreign and domestic policy, he retired to his estates and cultivated his private garden. Ponsonby, the son of Queen Victoria's private secretary, had served as a diplomat and then as Sir Henry Campbell-Bannerman's principal private secretary. Shocked by the extremes of wealth and poverty he witnessed around him, he nevertheless had been particularly influenced by his opposition to the foreign policy of Sir Edward Grey to move steadily toward socialism and affiliation first with the ILP and then with the Labour party. He had more staying power than Trevelyan and although his all-out and highly theoretical pacifism began to lose favor after 1924, he continued throughout the twenties to keep the arguments for unilateral disarmament and nonresistance before his fellow Labourites in a steady stream of speeches, books, and articles. Especially in the first half of this critical decade, both Ponsonby and Trevelyan were influential in making the absolute rejection of war as an instrument of national policy a significant force in the private and public councils of the Labour party.

The Union of Democratic Control, as we have noted, was one of the vehicles through which a number of the ex-Liberals circulated their views within the Labour party. For a time, its journal, *Foreign Affairs*, was the leading voice urging the revision of the postwar peace settlement. The hopes of its editor, E. D. Morel, that its three-penny cost would promote a wide readership, were never realized, and the paper required substantial private subsidies to remain alive. Under Morel, *Foreign Affairs* offered key leaders of the labor movement a highly interpretative, but also well-informed, commentary on the contemporary international scene. Ironically, when Morel's successor as editor, Helena Swanwick, raised its price to sixpence and broadened its coverage in October 1926, the change attracted some additional foreign readers but hastened the decline of the journal in Britain itself.[25]

The membership of the UDC fell off sharply from its wartime high by 1922 and its importance for Great Britain as a whole has perhaps occasionally been overstated.[26] Nevertheless, it would be difficult to exaggerate its influence on the labor movement in the early postwar years. Not only did some of the leaders of the Labour party share many of the opinions expressed by the UDC; they also took office in the organization and helped to determine its policies.[27]

But the heart of the UDC, its real founder and its constant whip, was Morel. Single-minded to the point of fanaticism, he was no stranger to unpopular causes. Before the war he had worked indefatigably to reveal the appalling slavery imposed upon the natives of the Congo, carrying his campaign for amelioration through to victory in the teeth of almost hysterical slander and vituperation. Turning to foreign affairs, he had then begun to question the secret commitments, especially to France, being undertaken by the Foreign Office and to warn that their effect would be to embroil Great Britain in a continental war. When the war broke out, he continued to attack the secret diplomacy he considered responsible and threw himself into the struggle for a negotiated peace. His activities resulted, indirectly at least, in his imprisonment, but his experience only hardened his convictions.[28] After the war, he joined the Independent Labour party and soon was repeating before prospective constituents arguments he hammered home week after week as editor of *Foreign Affairs*. Ardently sincere, with a high sense of justice, Morel from the beginning was a passionate advocate of the revision of the Versailles settlement. He was almost violent in his partisanship for the new Germany and equally violent in his opposition to French policy. His long-run impact on the Labour party is difficult to judge. In the election of 1922, it is true, he was able to unseat Winston Churchill at Dundee, in part on the issue that Churchill was a "warmonger." And in 1924, as his private papers indicate, Morel's supporters thought he had a good chance to be foreign secretary or, barring that, undersecretary of state for foreign affairs.[29] He attained neither post, but when Ramsay MacDonald took the Foreign Office himself, his undersecretary, while not Morel, was Ponsonby, a somewhat less bellicose, less dogmatic, but more pacifistic Morel. What his influence might have been had he lived is mere conjecture. It may be that Morel's sudden death in December 1924 spared him the experience of the repeated failures that subsequently so frustrated colleagues like Trevelyan and Ponsonby. In any event, Morel's point of view was not only influential but popular within the ranks of Labour during the half decade after the armistice.[30]

Of the Liberal recruits who entered the Labour party by way of the Independent Labour party, most were unquestionably attracted more by the ILP's pacifism than by its socialism. But whatever the reason, their addition to a group that included virtually every leader of the Labour party strengthened the role of the ILP in intraparty debates on foreign policy.[31] Before the war, of course, the ILP had been the most important source from which the Labour party drew ideas and enthusiasm. Now, as the Labour party broadened its base and approached closer to political responsibility, the ILP became more and more a minority movement, slowly drifting away from the main currents of Labour thought and policy. Nevertheless, in the immediate postwar period its alienation from the majority of the labor movement was not yet a fact, and its support, particularly among the newly organized constituency parties, was substantial.

Aside from the ex-Liberals already noted, the most prominent ILP interpreters of foreign affairs were Philip Snowden and H. N. Brailsford, Snowden only briefly and Brailsford throughout the twenties. Like his fellow ILPers, Ramsay MacDonald and J. R. Clynes, Snowden was one of the major political figures in the Labour party. But unlike Clynes, whose growing estrangement from the ILP soon became evident, and also unlike MacDonald, who was sufficiently flexible to delay a complete break with the ILP until almost the end of the twenties, Snowden for two or three years was the leading expositor of the ILP position in foreign affairs. Then, increasingly dissatisfied with the leftward drift of the ILP, he resigned first his treasurership and then his membership in the organization.[32] But before the break, his regular column was the outstanding feature in the *Labour Leader*, the major weekly organ of the ILP. Here, his flaming indignation at the Versailles settlement, his biting indictments of the course of postwar diplomacy, and above all his open and avowed pacifism reflected more characteristically than the work of any other single individual the ILP approach to international questions.

The *Labour Leader* was required reading for ILP activists throughout the country, but its circulation was always relatively small. When it came upon bad days in 1922, it was reorganized by Clifford Allen, renamed the *New Leader*, and placed under the brilliant editorship of H. N. Brailsford. Already a journalist of real distinction, Brailsford had acquired a reputation before the war as a sensitive interpreter of Balkan problems. During the war, he had republished among other things a scathing indictment of the imperialist rivalries of the powers and penned the most thoroughly developed left-wing project for a League of Nations to be aired in Great Britain.[33] Never an easily stereotyped commentator, Brailsford was one of the "London intellectuals" whom many of the provincial ILPers regarded with considerable suspicion. He was not an orthodox spokesman even after he took over the *New Leader*. Combining a "somewhat ambiguous Marxism" with what he called "democratic socialism," his radicalism paralleled in a sense the growing importance of the left-wing Clydesiders who, with their allies, were more and more to dominate the declining ILP in the twenties.[34] Although he was not a working politician like Snowden, Brailsford was prominent in shaping and in propagating ILP attitudes toward world affairs. Under him, the *New Leader* became one of the liveliest, as well as one of the most controversial, weeklies of opinion in the country. Through its pages, he presented his version of the ILP case a good deal more effectively than its opponents ever managed to exhibit theirs in the *Daily Herald*, the official paper of the labor movement as a whole.[35]

One of the more notable parts played by the ILP after the war was as a bridge between the ex-Liberal intellectuals and the leadership of the trade union movement. Trade unionists were inclined to be suspicious of the devotion of the "foreign legion" to the working class movement. They appreciated the prestige the converts brought to the Labour party and were willing to make use of their talents, but at the same time found it difficult to mix easily with people whose social and intellectual background was so different from their own. And yet, in the early twenties, on questions of foreign affairs, many in the trade union leadership remained closer to the radicalism of the ILP and the Union of Democratic Control than to any program of conventional and supposedly realistic moderation. This may be attributed in part to the influence of such old-line ILP politicians as Ramsay MacDonald and especially Philip Snowden, who had won the confidence of the trade unionists over the years. Sharing many of the general convictions of the ex-Liberals on international questions, men like MacDonald and Snowden helped persuade the trade unionists to accept the collaboration of the recruits in the formulation of policy.[36]

Few of the trade union leaders themselves were really prominent in the Labour party's consideration of international issues. Those who were, such as J. R. Clynes and J. H. Thomas, were frequently heeded less than were the activists in the ex-Liberal and ILP ranks. The result, in the years of disillusionment after 1918, was a spirit of all-out militancy quite out of keeping with the customary portraits of the trade unions as a bulwark of conventional nationalistic attitudes on foreign affairs. This militancy involved more than a class-conscious reaction to such policies as intervention in revolutionary Russia. Until about 1924, a general suspicion of the capitalist governments of the world and the international instruments they had devised was an ever-present theme at Trades Union Congress meetings. Then a change gradually set in. Labour's experience of office in 1924, followed by the failure of "working class" pressures in the general strike of 1926 and accompanied by a growing realization of the weakness of such bodies as the Labour and Socialist International, helped to swing the trade unionists toward the temperate program of international conciliation advocated increasingly by party leaders. The change, however, came too late and with too little preparation in the trade union movement to have been a significant factor in the approach adopted by the Labour party by the end of the decade.

Even Clynes and Thomas felt compelled on occasion to respond to the temper of the movement with slogans of pacifism and class war. But on the whole their influence was in the other direction. A leader of the National Union of General and Municipal Workers, Clynes, who had begun work as a "piecer" in a textile mill at the age of ten, remained active in trade union affairs even after he became a major political figure in the Labour party. Quiet to the point of self-effacement, in the early postwar years he was nonetheless effective in holding the small parliamentary party, composed at the time almost entirely of trade union representatives, in check.[37] With Ramsay MacDonald still in the political wilderness, with Will Adamson almost pathetically inept as leader in the House of Commons, and with Arthur Henderson absorbed in rebuilding the party on a mass basis, Clynes held the spotlight briefly as the advocate of the fullest use of international machinery and techniques to promote the foreign policy aims of Labour.[38] After 1922, when MacDonald defeated him for the leadership of the parliamentary party by five votes, Clynes tended to concern himself more and more with matters of domestic policy.

The contribution of J. H. Thomas to the development of policy on foreign affairs is somewhat more difficult to assess. The son of a domestic servant who had started work in a chemist's shop at the age of nine, he had become, as general secretary of the National Union of Railwaymen, one of the two or three most powerful figures in the Trades Union Congress during the twenties. Untroubled by the subtleties of political theory, inclined to cultivate his reputation as a man of the people motivated by "plain facts," he was nevertheless one of the more eloquent as well as astute politicians of the decade. In 1924 he served as colonial secretary and in 1931 was seriously considered by MacDonald for the post of foreign secretary. The continuing debate on foreign policy within the Labour party reveals little from Thomas in the way of ideas or initiative, but his influence within the trade union movement was so considerable and his relationship to Ramsay MacDonald so close that his response to other people's lead must be taken into account throughout the period.

To complete this catalogue of personalities, it is necessary to mention several figures who do not fit neatly into any of the categories outlined above. Leonard Woolf was not often in the public eye, but his work was crucial in the step-by-step formulation of the Labour party's approach to external relations. Cambridge-trained, associated with the Bloomsbury set, husband of Virginia Woolf, and one of the most brilliant publishers of his generation, he was essentially a Fabian in Labour politics, although vigorously anti-imperialist in outlook.[39] During the war, he had already published for the Fabian Society one of the fundamental contributions to the debate on the League of Nations, a brilliant and thorough study entitled *International Government* (1916). In the twenties his services were mainly of two kinds. As secretary of the Advisory Committee on International Questions, he acted as a catalyst, bringing into focus the diverse and often contradictory currents of thought out of which proposals for propaganda and action gradually emerged. And at the same time many of the pamphlets and manifestos issued by the Labour party were often, in their final form, the products of his pen.

While Leonard Woolf served behind the scenes, two other stalwarts of the Advisory Committee came to the fore as prominent politicians. Philip Noel-Baker, the son of a Liberal M.P., had been educated at Quaker institutions, including Haverford College in the United States. A brilliant athlete, he was a member of the British Olympic teams in 1912 and again in 1920. During the war, because his Quaker convictions forbade him to undertake active combat, he served in France and Italy in ambulance units. The experience shook him deeply and began to shape his most pivotal political views, which developed rapidly at the Paris Conference, where he served as personal assistant to Lord Robert Cecil. Increasingly convinced that disarmament required the growth of pacific institutions for helping to solve international issues, he quickly became an important member of the group closely associated with Arthur Henderson in attempting to redirect Labour's thinking away from the sterile negativism fed by the postwar disillusionment. At Geneva in 1924, in the Advisory Committee thereafter, and as Henderson's parliamentary private secretary after 1929, Noel-Baker consistently coupled his advocacy of disarmament with support for plans to strengthen existing peace-keeping machinery. His role within the Labour party in the twenties is perhaps most aptly symbolized by a description that was once given of him as "Member of Parliament for the League of Nations."[40]

Hugh Dalton rose in the Labour party even more rapidly than Noel-Baker. His childhood at Windsor (where his father was Canon of St. George's Chapel), education at Eton and Cambridge, and promising academic career at the London School of Economics all were doubtlessly of less consequence in the formation of his views than his reaction to the experience of war. Four years of Army service and the bitter loss of virtually every close friend of his university days left him with a deep concern for international affairs and a driving ambition to participate in active politics.[41] As time went on, Dalton's influence began to make itself felt from the Labour back benches, behind the scenes in the Advisory Committee on International Questions, and through a number of publications in which he outlined his approach to the problems of war and peace. By the time he became undersecretary of state for foreign affairs in the 1929 government, his position was well on its way to becoming the dominant view in the party. Like Noel-Baker, Dalton was a passionate partisan of the League of Nations. But, in contrast, he had no illusions about the League as an immediate cure for the use of force in international affairs. Not a pacifist, he had the courage, when such admonitions were unpopular, to warn his party continually that a system of international law and organization, if it were to develop, required the ultimate sanction of international force. Much more than most Labour politicians, he saw the case that could be made for the Versailles treaty. Openly anti-German because of friends who had died in the war, he was influential in breaking down the almost psychopathic suspicion of France that was such a hallmark of Labour's postwar attitudes. Altogether, the fact that the Labour party was not completely pacifist in the twenties and was able eventually to hammer out a workable conception of foreign policy owed much to the able assistance that Dalton's booming voice and fluent pen gave to the efforts of Arthur Henderson.[42]

Finally, some attention must be given in this preliminary sketch to the two most important leaders in the Labour party. It would be difficult to find a pair of more sharply contrasting personalities than Ramsay MacDonald and

Arthur Henderson. On the surface the plodding Henderson cut a sorry figure when compared with the brilliant MacDonald. In Parliament and on the platform, his speeches, however manifest their sincerity, seldom rose above the level of a dull earnestness. Constantly immersed in the details of party organization, he often appeared to contemporaries to be nothing more than an able political manager. MacDonald, on the other hand, was one of the most successful orators of his time. Stimulating and impressive, he had a flair for the dramatic that caught the imagination of the public as his undoubted intellectual gifts earned the attention of his colleagues. He was patently more interested in international affairs than in any other aspect of public life and considered himself most competent in this field. His leadership was acknowledged, and yet it can be argued that Henderson's long-run impact on Labour's foreign policy was more important and more lasting than that of MacDonald.

MacDonald held the spotlight throughout the years we are considering. Complex and enigmatic, he eludes any easy thumbnail description. During the war he suffered execration as pro-German because he was the most prominent of those who had opposed British entry into the conflict. At bottom, he was motivated by an unsparing antagonism to prewar British policy. Believing that the war could have been prevented, he also believed that Britain should have remained neutral. Once the struggle erupted, MacDonald agreed that it had to be won, but his criticism of its causes and his intimate association with the Independent Labour party's demand for a negotiated peace made it impossible for him to retain the leadership of the Labour party.

Of his courage during the war there can be no doubt. His precise point of view is more elusive. To the public he seemed an ardent spokesman for the international outlook of the ILP. But the ideological pacifism that was the ILP's most firmly held conviction touched MacDonald hardly at all. As the years passed, his temperamental inability to accept the ILP philosophy on domestic as well as international issues became evident, particularly after the ILP helped him regain the leadership of the parliamentary party in 1922. And yet, at least down to 1924, he managed to be sufficiently vague in his pronouncements to be claimed by the ILP as he was claimed by virtually every other wing of the party. He tended to display a rather tenuous reliance on the development of the international spirit far more often than he revealed any genuine willingness to hammer out the tedious details of a new approach to international politics.

MacDonald's great achievement, perhaps the climax of his career, came in his conduct of foreign policy during his first government. His success in conciliating France and in ending the Ruhr impasse was the one solid accomplishment of his short-lived government. But the tactical skill with which he carried to completion a task begun by Lord Curzon tends to emphasize the fact that MacDonald, despite the flood of words he poured out on foreign policy questions, was essentially a symbol and an executor of policy.[43] It would be misleading to deny the role of the charismatic quality of this "magnificent substitute for a leader" in winning adherence of the rank and file to the official program of the party.[44] But in the day-to-day struggle to bring the international views of the party into something like a workable focus, Henderson was arguably more effective.

The simplicity and directness that were Henderson's distinguishing marks in the eyes of his contemporaries concealed a personality almost as complex as that of MacDonald.[45] Until the war Henderson's career had glided steadily along in the grooves of trade union activities and Labour party organization. He was, in the opinion of Beatrice Webb, "a first rate manager of men—the only one in the front rank of the Labour Movement," but he had displayed little interest in and perhaps less knowledge of British relations with the rest of the world.[46] The coming of the war marked the turning point of his career. Unlike MacDonald and a sizable group within the party, Henderson supported the war actively once Britain was involved. At the same time he soon became one of the leaders in the search for means to prevent its recurrence. While his aspiration was genuine, he made it clear that he realized, as few within the labor movement did, that the organization of peace must be attempted within the limits of the possible. As a Methodist lay preacher, he was emotionally attached to the pacific ideal, but his years of experience as a trade union official and party worker offered unmistakable evidence of the practical day-to-day need for negotiation and compromise. His speeches and tactics even in this early period demonstrate that he was convinced that the will to peace was not enough, that real results must be sought within the framework of generally accepted machinery and techniques of international organization.

In this task he depended heavily upon the newly created Advisory Committee on International Questions, set up by the Labour party Executive in May 1918, with the following terms of reference: "To consider, report and advise upon International Policy and all questions of an international character, and to watch and advise upon current international developments. Further to consider and advise upon international questions of an economic character, jointly with the Committee on Trade Policy and Finance, or through a Joint Sub-Committee."[47] Not only was the committee designed to provide the Executive with data and with advice, but it also had the task of preparing propaganda materials and furnishing ammunition to Labour speakers and publicists. It was "a research bureau, a propagandist agency and a speaker's first-aid station as well."[48] Nevertheless, its role in the preliminary formulation of policy seems clearly to have been the most vital of its services to the Labour party after 1918.

From the beginning the membership of the committee was somewhat amorphous.[49] All the party's M.P.'s were entitled to attend its meetings, the work of which was of course secret, and from time to time outside experts were called in for information and advice. Thus, in going over the minutes one runs across such names as Arnold Toynbee, L. B. Namier, and James T. Shotwell. A striking proportion of the ex-Liberal recruits participated in the deliberations of the committee. But its hard core came to be composed of Leonard Woolf, who was its secretary, Noel Buxton, Will Arnold-Forster, Philip Noel-Baker, and a handful of others.[50] During the twenties, the changing composition of the committee reflected fairly accurately the growing success of the moderates within the Labour party. For example, while H. N. Brailsford became less and less prominent in its work as time went on, middle-of-the-roaders like Hugh Dalton cropped up to take his place. This would imply, and correctly, that in its early years the Advisory Committee shared much of the explosive temper of the party as a whole. Its preliminary memorandum, to illustrate, indicated that "the establishment of the Committee . . . is in particular a step in the direction of that much to be desired Democratization of Foreign Policy and a break with the evil tradition of the Foreign Office."[51] But then, in the confidential memoranda of the committee, one can trace almost minutely a growing awareness of the limits of foreign policy. And it is fascinating to see how, step by step, the deliberations of the committee were translated, particularly by Henderson, into the accepted policy of the Labour party.

Labour's international outlook by the end of the twenties struck a new note of maturity in contrast to the cry of disillusioned bitterness that was raised in 1919. Altogether, the influences that shaped that change were more than ordinarily complex. Clashing temperaments, ideological differences, and the inexperience of a virtually new national party all played their role. Little by little knowledgeable leaders faced the fact that Labour's foreign policy views might soon have to be translated into responsible action as the party took over the reins of government. As a result, they hammered out a position based upon the need for compromise and accommodation with other nations and upon the expanding use of existing international institutions in the conduct of world affairs. An account of the international policy—or policies—which emerged during the critical postwar decade makes up the remainder of these pages.

CHAPTER 2

LABOUR AND THE
PARIS SETTLEMENT

As the Great War came to an end and representatives of the victorious Allies gathered in Paris to draft the "preliminaries" of the peace, virtually all of Labour's leaders and most of its organs of public opinion became increasingly worried about the possibility for a viable settlement.[1] While many had heralded the end of the war with optimism and the hope that a new international order could be shaped, they quickly became disillusioned as the terms of peace began to emerge. Week by week, it became increasingly evident that the terms being hammered out by the tense and harried delegates had little in common with the wartime aspirations that had made the Labour party and its affiliates the leading advocate of a generous peace of reconciliation. Hope gave way to despair and despair to a bitter rejection, for a time, of virtually all that the Paris treaties embodied.

Toward the end of the war, the Trades Union Congress, the Independent Labour party, the Fabians, and the Labour party all had accepted a *Memorandum on War Aims* that may easily be labeled the first major pronouncement on foreign policy in the history of the movement. Denouncing secret diplomacy, imperialism, and conscription, it demanded that foreign policy be placed under the control of popularly chosen legislatures, advocated the limitation of armaments and their private manufacture, and argued for the need to achieve complete democratization of all countries. For a time, because they championed self-determination for disputed territories and regarded a League of Nations as central to the new world order they envisaged, many key figures within the ranks of labor came to believe that President Wilson's views were close to their own.[2]

It is doubtful, however, that this official position, championed by Ramsay MacDonald no less than by Arthur Henderson, faithfully reflected the attitudes of Labour's rank and file. For the moment, the Labour party's leaders were out of step with most of their followers. As the war drew to a close, majority sentiment was represented neither by Henderson nor by Mac-

Donald, but rather by publicists such as Robert Blatchford, the early socialist pioneer whose anti-German strictures before the war had helped estrange him from the party. Unlike some of the spokesmen for Labour's right wing, Blatchford considered it desirable to establish a League of Nations.[3] But he wished to see it made up of the Entente Powers reinforced by the inclusion of certain neutrals. He thought it right and necessary to exclude the Central Powers for a time. War, he wrote, came not so much from economic causes as from the dynastic ambitions of autocracies. Since such dangerous ambitions were to be apprehended only from the Central Powers, the first and chief duty of a League of Nations must be to protect the world's peace against them.[4] Advocates of an all-inclusive international organization denounced Blatchford's support for the "old balance of power theory," but their criticisms only highlighted the popularity of his argument.[5]

The General Election of 1918 emphasized how much closer the British public was to Blatchford's views than to those of the official leaders of the labor movement. During the election campaign, many Labour candidates made their case largely on the basis of the positions staked out by those leaders. Leaflets poured from the press attacking the past handling of foreign affairs and demanding the "democratization" of foreign policy. They hammered home the thesis that the only way to end war was through a League of Nations and insisted that a League consisting only of the present allies would be no League at all but a military and political alliance made against another such alliance and looking toward another war.[6] One such election manifesto summed up in somewhat cumbersome fashion the Labour party's appeal. It urged voters to support Labour candidates because the party was resolved that there should be no more war. It had sought a "people's peace" founded on the principles of justice and freedom, with no annexations and no indemnities. It was striving to make the League of Nations a real union of peoples and thus to establish a firm basis for international cooperation, and through Labour's own international organization it was endeavoring to unite all the workers of the world for the maintenance of peace and the development of human freedom.[7]

Lloyd George, of course, read the popular temper a great deal more accurately than the authors of these manifestos. The campaign waged by many Coalition candidates was in effect one loud cry for vengeance. The electorate, grateful to the politicians who had brought the war to a successful end, were more than willing to respond to sweeping accusations and extravagant promises. The Opposition was swept aside. Although the Labour party returned fifty-seven members to Parliament as compared with forty-two in 1910, most of its representatives came from the trade union groups whose views, imme-

diately after the end of the war, were relatively close to those of Lloyd George
and his supporters. With the exception of J. R. Clynes and J. H. Thomas,
virtually every political leader of Labour was rejected. Ramsay MacDonald,
Arthur Henderson, and Philip Snowden were all defeated. To a country
flushed with victory, their warnings that peace must be built on more than
punishment hardly seemed worthy of attention. Distrusting Lloyd George,
Labour's leaders learned that they could not yet look to the people to compel
him to work for the kind of peace they desired. Yet for a time at least they
were optimistic, counting on the president of the United States to use his
enormous prestige in behalf of a settlement they could support.

But Labour party strategists were hardly content to accept whatever lead
was furnished by Wilson. In May 1918 the first meeting of the new Advisory
Committee on International Questions had been held.[8] In the months that
followed, the committee had undertaken to analyze some of the generalizations embodied in the party's policy statements. The result was a series of
confidential briefs, marshaling information and presenting recommendations
to the Labour party Executive and the parliamentary party.

Most significant among these reports was one that discussed the party's
support for a League of Nations. The first object of such a League, it noted,
would obviously be to substitute for war peaceable methods of settling disputes. The nations must bind themselves to submit questions that they might
not have been able to settle by diplomacy either to a court of international
justice or to mediation. Any member of the League breaking its covenant
should be treated as an enemy by the other members. From this point of view
the League would be a universal alliance of all against the lawbreaker.

So far, the report was going over well-worn ideas. But in the light of the
later history of Labour party attitudes, the next section, dealing with the
sanctions of the proposed organization, is significant. The Advisory Committee raised the question of how the nations of the League might coerce an
offender if necessary. The answer depended upon whether or not the states
remained armed. If they were to disarm, retaining only police forces to keep
internal order, then a refusal of all intercourse with the offending state would
probably be enough to bring it to reason. If the nations remained armed, then
it was conceivable that one of them might make an armed attack upon another. In that case all the other members must be prepared to employ their
forces to protect the member attacked. Armed force, the memorandum admonished, must be met by armed force or it could not be met at all.

This early warning of the need for military sanctions was coupled with a
cautious approach to the question of disarmament. Granting that the smooth
working of a League would be facilitated if all states disarmed at once, the

Advisory Committee acknowledged that immediate and complete disarmament, however desirable, was hardly to be expected. Short of that, they thought it might fairly be anticipated that, as the years passed and the League demonstrated its ability to maintain the peace, the disappearance of mistrust would make possible a gradual reduction and final disappearance of national armaments.

But while recognizing the need for force, the Advisory Committee stressed that a genuine League would have to undertake positive tasks of international cooperation, for these would do more for peace than any threat of coercion. From the outset the League should coordinate such undertakings as the control of backward areas and of international communications, the development of labor legislation and the continuation of the joint purchases and distribution of materials inaugurated by the allied nations as a wartime necessity. In the long run, the memorandum concluded, the habit of cooperation might bring nations to regard international war as they viewed civil war—contrary to good morals and good policy.[9]

The implementation of Labour's demand for an idealistic peace posed serious problems. Aside from Wilson, the Allied leaders who would determine policy at Paris appeared to offer little hope. Georges Clemenceau of France was already making plain his certainty that his country required a system of alliances and strategic frontiers. Lloyd George's intransigence during the election campaign convinced Labour that he would demand a vengeful settlement, while his failure to appoint a Labour representative to the British delegation merely added to the distrust with which he was regarded.[10] Two lines of action, accordingly, were adopted in an effort to influence the forthcoming decisions. The first was a campaign in the Labour press to generate support for the socialist peace program. The second was the attempt to mobilize international socialist and trade union opinion through meetings to be held while the Paris Conference was sitting.[11] In both cases, Labour hoped that popular support for a peace of reconciliation might help to counteract the forces it regarded as hopelessly backward-looking in their approach to the problems of the postwar world.

Although Professor Carl Brand has demonstrated how fully British Labour and its allies supported President Wilson in the months that followed the Armistice, it needs to be reiterated that from the beginning support was accompanied by generous doses of skepticism about Wilson's ability to resist the forces of traditional diplomacy arrayed against him.[12] As early as November, the Union of Democratic Control, most of whose major figures were by now affiliated with the Labour party, addressed a long letter to the president urging him to insist upon the implementation of his Fourteen Points. Hailing his declaration of January 8, 1918, as one that marked a new departure in the course of human affairs, the UDC warned that his purposes would be fatally subverted if the peace conference should prevent the Russian people from determining their own form of government or if it should seek to impose crushing indemnities upon defeated peoples now striving to establish new regimes under the most difficult conditions. In addition, the UDC cautioned against the seizure of territory by the victorious powers no less than against the placing of further restrictions upon the international flow of goods. Finally, in a slashing reference to what the UDC feared was official British policy, the letter protested against any refusal to include disarmament at sea in a general program of disarmament.[13]

In much the same spirit, Labour undertook a series of popular demonstrations. The fact that many in the rank and file spurned the insistence of some of their leaders on a conciliatory peace did not prevent others from supporting the search for a better ordering of international relations in the future. On January 2, for example, at a mass meeting in the Albert Hall, leaders of the Labour party and the Trades Union Congress demanded the conclusion of a "Wilson Peace" and sponsored resolutions assuring him that British Labour stood behind his efforts to achieve it.[14] The tone of much of this agitation may be summarized in the remarks of George Lansbury, whose support for the Russian revolutionaries was already underlining his role as one of the chief critics of Allied policy. "The world," wrote Lansbury, "must have a peace based on the principles adopted by Dr. Wilson or civilization will perish. The imperialists are in their last ditch and will die fighting to the last. . . . The Americans are eager for British help. They look across the channel for a sign that our people understand that their president is the apostle of humanity."[15]

Support for the American president, then, did not mean that Labour was at all certain that his views would prevail. Indeed, even as the Paris Conference came together, there were voices cautioning that too much must not be expected of him. As Wilson made his swing through England, France, and Italy, a few of Labour's most important spokesmen increasingly began to point out the dichotomy between his principles and the plans of other Allied leaders. When Clemenceau publicly avowed his adherence to the "old system" of alliances and the balance of power, journalists and politicians, particularly those identified with the ILP, drew pessimistic conclusions. H. N. Brailsford, already an important member of the Advisory Committee on International Questions, spelled out his fears in British and American publications.[16] He warned that the kind of League of Nations to which Wilson looked forward would be impossible if the world was first to be constituted on Clemenceau's system of alliances. Such a system meant perpetual feud and the studied, deliberate, official fomentation of nationalist passions. But Wilson did not seem to realize how difficult his task really was. "Since his great achievement in imposing the nominal adoption of the Fourteen Points," wrote Brailsford, "Mr. Wilson has been silent—silent through many speeches. . . . He has moved with smiles . . . among the men who are preparing a helot's future for the German nation and neither by appeal nor by argument has he said a word to cool the fever of vengeance or abate the demands of greed."[17] Philip Snowden, who as early as October had cautioned a meeting in Glasgow against trusting in any "capitalist" League, echoed Brailsford's words in only slightly more tentative language.[18] Among those who knew President Wilson, he observed, there were differences of opinion as to whether he would be strong enough to give the world a peace in accordance with his declared aims. If he failed, then America would probably withdraw from the peace conference, enter into competition with the other European powers, challenge the naval supremacy of Great Britain, and perhaps maintain some form of military service. In the light of recent declarations by Allied statesmen, Snowden's whole tone reflected serious skepticism about Wilson's ability to carry them along with him, whatever his own beliefs.[19]

This skepticism was bolstered in some Labour circles by the conviction that the Allied governments were more concerned about crushing the Bolshevik regime in Russia than binding up the wounds of war. George Lansbury, for example, was singularly uncritical of the excesses of the new Russian leaders and perhaps equally uninformed about the thrust of their early policies. In the *Herald*, he professed to see a close connection between the wanton delay of the peace conference and plans to launch a "new and senseless and wicked war."[20] Snowden, for his part, mixed a realistic assessment of Allied actions with a less than accurate depiction of the character of the Russian regime. He charged categorically that policy in Russia was directed not against Bolshevik excesses but rather toward the overthrow of a form of government that was objectionable to the capitalist class in other countries. Such a scheme, he declared, was in reality a war upon a philosophy of social democracy. It was clearly incompatible with a real European partnership based upon the recognition of equal rights and enforced by a common will.[21]

Labour's program to mobilize international working-class pressure on the Paris proceedings contributed to the calling of the Berne socialist and trade union conferences early in 1919. Despite the opposition of the Allied governments, delegates began to meet on January 26 and the official Labour and Socialist Conference was opened on February 3.[22] Previously, when the project began to take shape for a Labour conference to be held at the same time as the official peace conference, the Advisory Committee on International Questions had undertaken to prepare recommendations as to procedure. As early as November 1918, it had circulated a memorandum, written largely by G. D. H. Cole, already one of Labour's leading younger intellectuals, outlining the elements that should appear in a Labour charter. Arguing that any international labor conventions must be supported by more binding sanctions than in the past, Cole insisted that such sanctions could materialize only if the Labour charter were made part of the fabric of an effective League of Nations. In such a League, a permanent body must be created to initiate fresh international labor agreements and to supervise the administration of those in being. The memorandum also contained Leonard Woolf's plea, doomed to disappointment, for official Labour representation at the peace conference and a series of proposals by Sidney Webb reiterating the economic demands of the *Memorandum on War Aims*. Webb urged that the peace treaty should prohibit economic discrimination against the former enemy. Further, he submitted, it should make provisions for promoting the open door, as well as for international rationing against famine, measures against unemployment, the prevention of sweated labor, and the enforcement of maximum hours in all countries.[23]

Along with proposals for international labor legislation, the Advisory Committee again tackled the problem of international organization. H. N. Brailsford drew up a report repeating demands that he and the ILP had made during the war. The report, which was considered by the Advisory Committee on January 21 and forwarded to the British delegation at the Berne Conference, rejected the concept of a League of Nations made up solely of government representatives. It was a fiction, Brailsford contended, that premiers or foreign secretaries represented a nation. They represented only the nation as power. So long as international action was entrusted exclusively to governments it was doubtful whether the world could ever escape from its obsession with force. Brailsford proposed, therefore, that the British delegation at Berne advocate the inclusion in the League's machinery of a "Deliberative International Parliament" composed of delegations chosen by proportional representation from each national parliament. Its functions should be to create an international public opinion, to influence other organs of the League, and to prepare for the governing body of the League suggestions for international legislation.[24] In an obvious effort to conciliate those to whom any League was likely to appear as a capitalist instrument, Brailsford predicted that in the future the Labour and Socialist International would remain a powerful agency of organization and agitation. It could never control the League, however, "unless indeed we look forward to the revolutionary triumph of the Soviet idea." Those who rejected that conception were bound to work for the democratic evolution of the international body on the basis of parliamentary forms. The scheme is of considerable interest, for despite its radical divergence from most of the conventional Wilsonian versions of a League of Nations, this was the project which in substance was pressed upon the Berne delegates by their British colleagues.[25]

At Berne the British delegation was a strong one. MacDonald, Henderson, Ethel Snowden, C. T. Cramp, and J. McGurk represented the Labour party, while Thomas, Margaret Bondfield, G. H. Stuart Bunning, T. Greenall, and R. Shirkie came from the Trades Union Congress. From the start they played a leading role. In the eyes of British Labour the purpose of the conference was threefold. It should suggest solutions for the nationalist problems brought to a head by the war. It had to propose an antimilitarist policy, including a scheme for a truly democratic League of Nations. And finally, it must bring into being a permanent organization to safeguard and develop international standards for labor legislation.[26] Behind all these purposes, of course, was the need to ascertain whether the International could be rebuilt upon the ruins of war and revolution.[27] While other national groups quite evidently had somewhat different conceptions of the purpose of the conference, it was within this framework that the British delegates carried on their work.

The Berne delegates, who met under the eyes of police spies and *agents provocateurs*, failed to reconstitute the Second International. It would be a mistake, however, to underestimate the significance of the gathering for Labour's creation of its postwar foreign policy. On the one hand, the conference was divided by the emotion-charged question of war responsibility, although a superficial formula of agreement was patched up. More importantly, the conferees found it impossible to reach accord on their attitude toward Bolshevism. The simmering controversy over whether socialism could only be built upon a base of parliamentary democracy, symbolized in the conflicting Branting and Adler-Longuet resolutions, erupted with a force soon to split the old International. But on the other hand, for most of the issues confronting the peace conference at Paris the Berne delegates were able to achieve virtually unanimous recommendations. We are not here concerned with the proposed Labour Charter, except to point out that indirectly at least the demands of Labour may have influenced the creation of the International Labour Organization.[28] What is germane to this study is the light that Berne throws on the emerging shape of British Labour's foreign policy. Here the questions of the League of Nations and of territorial adjustments are most revealing.

The conference report on the League of Nations was introduced by J. H. Thomas and supported by Henderson, MacDonald, and Mrs. Snowden. It is

worth noting that the orthodox trade unionist Thomas, no less than the
political pragmatist MacDonald, pressed upon his colleagues the version of a
League outlined for the Advisory Committee on International Questions by
the radical Brailsford and supported during the war by Labour's left wing.
There was, in other words, substantial agreement among the factions of British Labour. Indeed, at this stage, Henderson and Thomas, neither of whom
had ever joined the Independent Labour party, expressed views on a League
of Nations difficult to distinguish from those of their supposedly less moderate
comrades.[29]

Thomas presented the resolutions which argued that the League should be
formed by the parliaments of the various countries. Representation in its
central organ should not be by delegates of the executive branches of the
government, but by delegates representing all parties in the constituent parliaments, ensuring thus "not an alliance of Cabinets or Governments, but
a union of peoples." All nations organized on the basis of national self-
determination should be part of the League. Those peoples who had not yet
obtained the right of self-determination should be under the protection of the
League and be encouraged and assisted to ready themselves for membership.
All standing armies must be abolished and eventually complete disarmament
brought about. Until then any required armed force should be under the
control of the League, which must also have the means of economic pressure
at its disposal in order to enforce its decisions when necessary. Expanding the
conventional idea of an international court to arbitrate and mediate disputes,
Thomas proposed that the court also have the power, where it was called for,
to rectify frontiers after consultation with the peoples concerned. Next he
insisted that a major task of the League should be to promote free trade, the
open door in colonies, the international control of world trade routes, along
with the supervision of customs tariffs and the development of its power to
control the distribution of foodstuffs and materials throughout the world.
And finally, as Thomas pointed out, the resolution called upon the future
League to establish, develop, and enforce an International Labour Charter.

Ramsay MacDonald was the chief spokesman for the British position. In an
impressive speech, he emphasized that the League must rest upon general
disarmament and spoke out for an international council of representatives
elected by the parliament of each nation. His plea echoed the views of the Left
in the labor movement, which regarded national disarmament as the essential
basis for a viable international system. At the same time, it paralleled some of
the recommendations of the Advisory Committee's report without going into
the subtleties, as that document had done, of the relationship between national armaments and international sanctions. In any case, it was largely the

drive of the British delegation that moved the Berne Assembly to accept unanimously the comprehensive statement introduced by Thomas. The leaders of British Labour set their sights high in aiming at a system of international organization. Whether the more powerful conferees at Paris would aim at similar targets remained to be seen.[30]

In the debate on territorial questions MacDonald also played a leading role, and the final resolution adopted at Berne reflected the views of the British delegation fairly accurately. The Labour and Socialist Conference charged that the arbitrary and enforced union of people of different nationalities within a single state had been and always would be a cause of international disputes and a menace to peace. Accordingly, it laid down certain principles that in essence demanded self-determination for all nationalities under the protection of the League of Nations, advocated that the League guarantee the rights of minorities, and urged that the international body undertake to protect the populations of dependent areas while fostering their training toward self-government. Rejecting any territorial settlement based upon the claims of victory, strategy, or economic necessity, the conference called upon the working classes to exercise all possible pressure on their governments in order to compel them to recognize these principles as essential for lasting peace.[31]

Neither the British labor leaders nor their fellow international socialists spent much time exploring in detail the often conflicting national and ethnic aspirations that surfaced in such profusion during and after the war. The complex reality behind the territorial questions that were being raised at Paris attracted relatively little attention from much of the Labour establishment. The incantation of demands for self-determination, whatever the case, seemed more comfortable than any attempt to explore the implications of such self-determination if and where it should materialize. Long-standing historical quarrels, formidable ethnic tensions, and the clash of conflicting national dreams received short shrift from all but a few of Labour's standard bearers. Neglect, however, did not suggest simple ignorance of such differences. Rather, it reflected an almost ingenuous belief that if only a new international organization could be brought into being on the model proposed by the representatives of "international socialism," settlement of the most urgent national or ethnic or strategic issues could be left to that institution.

Meanwhile, as international labor drew up its blueprint for the postwar world, a different shape of things to come was beginning to emerge at Paris. As the peace conference entered upon its deliberations, there was some bitter criticism of its secrecy, but on the whole British Labour marked time until it

could better judge the direction in which the Paris proceedings were moving.[32] A small spasm of protest greeted the first public announcement of plans
to make the major Allied powers mandatories for the ex-German colonies,
but many Labour spokesmen still were willing to count on President Wilson
to block what they looked upon as the dangerous schemes of the Allied
leaders.[33]

The shock of disillusionment came with the publication of the Draft Covenant of the League of Nations on February 14. A few Labour commentators
greeted the draft with some enthusiasm, but as its implications began to sink
in, most of the Labour press expressed the conviction that fundamental revision was necessary.[34] Criticism was widespread, particularly on the Left.
Philip Snowden, who had never hidden his suspicions, branded the Paris
scheme a fraud, expressing amazement that President Wilson should have
given his support to such a flagrant device for constituting five great powers
the dictators of the universe. It was grotesque to exclude more than two-
thirds of Europe from the League and then to insert a condition that left it to
the one-third to refuse to admit the two-thirds. The result would be the
establishment of a counter-League and the rise of the old politics of Entente
and Alliance all over again. Such a League, he warned, could become the
most despotic instrument ever devised for crushing democratic movements.[35]

To Ramsay MacDonald the proposed League was likewise a mockery. Far
from the league of peoples responsible to democratic electorates that Labour
had envisaged, the draft that had surfaced in Paris was a "new Holy Alliance,"
whose executive was no more than an executive of the present allies.[36] Neither the "Central Democracies" nor the neutral nations had been consulted
and the terms under which they might eventually be admitted to the League
were such that no self-respecting nation could accept them.[37]

Snowden's charge of fraud and MacDonald's strictures were paralleled by
other protests. The *Herald* saw a plan not for a League, but for a "clique,"
founded on the principle of domination of the weak by the strong.[38] *Forward*
viewed the Draft Covenant as a shameless conspiracy. The Allied powers had
now appointed themselves a "League of Nations" with some outsiders like
Siam and Spain thrown in for the sake of appearances. But socialist Germany,
Bolshevist Russia, and Republican Austria were to be regarded as degenerate
pariahs. Such a League could succeed in keeping the peace, but only on
certain terms. It might be successful in the same way as the armed highway-
man who "keeps the timid old gent at peace, while he takes a gold watch and
some coins 'under his tutelage.'"[39] The Union of Democratic Control, while
welcoming the adoption of the principle of a League, regarded the Draft

Covenant as undemocratic and inequitable. Writing in the organization's journal, J. A. Hobson, while conceding that the Draft Covenant contained provisions for doing some excellent things, nevertheless condemned the whole scheme as poisoned by the vices of autocracy, chauvinism, conservatism, and futility. Its structure and its composition were thoroughly bad and nowhere in the proposals was democracy to be found.[40] In a resolution sent to Versailles on March 10, 1919, the UDC urged the British Government to work, among other things, for popular representation and control in both the main bodies of the League, the right of all civilized states to enter the League on equal terms, the general abolition of conscription, equality in the reduction of armaments, and the extension of the mandatory principle to all nonself-governing colonies and protectorates. The UDC also noted the shortcomings of the provision for unanimity in League decisions.[41]

Many in this group were pacifist in outlook and particularly disturbed that the League covenant was to make provision for forcible sanctions. One observer was discouraged to note that the League had not succeeded in rising superior to the old-time reliance upon physical force to implement its decrees. There was no awareness, argued Cyprian Bridge, that only a society of nations based upon mutual trust and moral force could be really effective for the preservation of peace and goodwill. Altogether, the proposals seemed to envisage Anglo-Saxon hegemony in world affairs. And since President Wilson must be credited with good intentions, the whole covenant seemed to resolve itself into the triumph of "Britannia über Alles."[42]

Only on the Labour Right was the Draft Covenant really accepted, and even there with little enthusiasm. The old-time *Clarion* partnership of Robert Blatchford and Alexander M. Thompson, in announcing their support, warned that any League to be effective must possess the power as well as the will to enforce peace and that in any circumstances no League could succeed unless the United States, where it was getting a cool reception, participated.[43]

Somewhat similarly, the bellicose and nationalist organ of the British Workers' League, the *British Citizen and Empire Worker*, conceded that the League of Nations would probably stop war for the present, not because of its existence, but because people were temporarily tired of war. It was well enough to accept the League, but, far from being humanity's Magna Carta, "it is mainly a patchwork of aspirations and good intentions strung together in a hurry to meet the convenience of President Wilson's domestic arrangements." As yet, the paper noted, two opposing ideas, that of a body merely to keep the peace, but passive in normal times, and the other of a League with executive powers and authority in international administration, directly contradicted each other, and no formula was capable of squaring that particular circle. Not the League, but a stiff and punitive peace represented the ideal settlement for this intransigent journal.[44]

It would be a mistake to exaggerate the importance of the Labour press. With the one exception of the *Herald*, which was soon, in a new format, to increase its numbers to about a quarter of a million daily, most of the papers noted had a relatively small circulation. But it would be an even greater error to disregard the views expressed in these organs of opinion. Major figures in the labor movement—Ramsay MacDonald, Philip Snowden, George Lansbury, others—used these papers as a vehicle for ensuring that arguments ignored by the more popular press would receive an airing. And papers like the *Labour Leader* and the *Herald* or *Forward* in Scotland appear to have been passed from hand to hand among a considerable number of readers among Labour's rank and file.

While the Labour press was airing its reactions, the machinery for official consideration of the draft treaty was set in motion. On March 4, Charles Roden Buxton and Leonard Woolf, sitting as the Advisory Committee on International Questions, resolved to document the fact that the proposed covenant did not fulfill certain vital conditions laid down by Labour in its earlier demands. In brief, they suggested to the National Executive that amendment was required on four points if the covenant were to conform to the expressed aims of the Labour party: (1) the right for all civilized states to enter the League on equal terms; (2) the establishment of a deliberative democratic assembly, representing peoples instead of governments and elected directly either from parliaments or from organized democratic bodies; (3) universal abolition of conscription; and (4) the mandatory system to be applied to all colonial possessions and protectorates instead of being confined to enemy territory.[45]

Buxton, the former Liberal, was steadily moving to the left in his new party on matters of external affairs, but Woolf had remained gradualist and Fabian in his orientation from before his publication of *International Government*. The fact that both their warnings paralleled those sounded earlier by H. N. Brailsford, from the beginning a proponent of "genuine" international institutions, is some indication of the general disappointment with which Labour greeted the Draft Covenant. On the other hand, it may be well to note that even at this early stage neither Buxton nor Woolf, in advice to the Executive, was prepared to attack the coercive features of the covenant that were anathema to the Labour Left.

Further discussion among leaders of the Labour party and the Trades Union Congress led to the acceptance of a series of twenty-two resolutions that were presented to a special congress of political and trade union representatives on April 3. With Stuart Bunning of the TUC in the chair, the meeting welcomed the publication of the Paris proposals, but endorsed all the suggested amendments. As those amendments demonstrated, the strategists of the labor movement were disturbed at the way in which the League was to be constituted. Still holding out for proportional representation from national parliaments, they also demanded that an "Executive Council" of the League be expanded to eleven members including Germany and Russia. The Labour resolutions asked for clauses in the covenant guaranteeing that no armies would be raised by conscription and providing that both the manufacture of armaments and the maintenance of forces necessary for international police purposes be under the League's direct control. Further amendments spelled out the view that the identification of aggression, application of sanctions, and declaration of war all ought to be under the aegis of a "Body of Delegates"—the later Assembly—rather than under a council dominated by the Great Powers. In other words, the Assembly, not the Council, should have final authority. Other familiar pleas appeared among the parade of amendments. One called for a declaration in the covenant urging national disarmament; another demanded that all colonies and native territories be under League mandate; a third insisted upon direct and more adequate representation for labor in the proposed new International Bureau of Labor (the future ILO). And finally, still suspecting that Allied leaders were not serious about advocating an international organization, Labour supported President Wilson in his conviction that the covenant should form an integral part of the peace treaty.[46]

This official position, which found more to criticize than to praise in the League covenant, was, if more circumspect in its choice of words, nevertheless almost identical with the more colorful reactions in the Labour press. As time went on, even some of those who had originally treated the Draft Covenant generously began to pick away at its supposed flaws. Most striking, for example, was the *New Statesman*, which came to the belated conclusion that "the lines of an international authority have not been firmly or boldly drawn; the Assembly is an unsatisfactory compromise between an Executive and a Legislature; there is only a shadow of an International Court of Justice; the problem of disarmament is shirked; the crucial sanction of the League is shadowy."[47] Altogether, virtually all elements of importance within the labor movement, whether official or not, regarded the League of Nations as a vital test of the future being prepared at Paris. Even the Allied intervention in Russia, which was to elicit a constantly growing protest during 1919 and 1920, tended to take second place to the Draft Covenant.[48] The Labour press was filled with denunciations of intervention, and a special conference on April 3 passed an angry resolution demanding withdrawal of Allied troops from Russia.[49] Yet it seems unquestionable that British Labour was at this moment most concerned with constructive plans for an international organization it hoped to see developed by the peace conference. Almost unanimously Labour's publicists found themselves seriously disappointed by the first public proposals.

In addition to their various pronouncements, British representatives continued to take a leading role in the attempt of the Labour and Socialist International to influence the makers of the peace treaty. Two days after the announcement of the Draft Covenant, Henderson, MacDonald, and Stuart Bunning were part of a delegation that waited upon Clemenceau, as president of the peace conference, to present the resolutions adopted at Berne. Clemenceau agreed to lay out the documents at the conference and referred the group to the various commissions responsible for particular problems. The interview, while cordial, was noncommittal, as was a discussion that British representatives held with Lloyd George and Lord Curzon on February 21.[50]

The delegation to Clemenceau had been dispatched by the Permanent Commission of the Labour and Socialist International, which had been set up at Berne. Henderson was named a member of the three-man Executive, while MacDonald and Stuart Bunning were the other British members of the Permanent Commission. When this commission met at Amsterdam on April 26, it was faced with a difficult situation. The Berne Conference had never really tackled the maze of territorial questions that were plaguing the peace conference. It had proposed that the various national groups in the International work out their positions in advance and then hammer out a series of demands at Amsterdam. But by the end of April much had changed. At Berne, despite fundamental cleavages on crucial issues, the overall atmosphere had been one of hopefulness. Two months later the Amsterdam socialists looked upon Paris as the graveyard of most of their hopes.

The new spirit was quickly apparent when Henderson introduced a general resolution expressing dissatisfaction with the Draft Covenant and urging disarmament. The conference decided that the resolution was not strong enough and appointed a committee, of which Stuart Bunning was a member, to study the question. The work of this committee merged with the broader consideration of territorial questions. In the final drafting the socialist peace program reflected the suspicion with which its authors viewed the work of the Paris Conference.[51]

The Amsterdam resolutions began by supporting the right of independence of Finland, Georgia, Estonia, and Armenia. They protested against intervention in the internal affairs of Hungary, demanding that the peace conference not cut up the country until the populations of the regions in question had the opportunity to express their desires in a League of Nations plebiscite. The socialists asked that the Ukrainian people be enabled as soon as possible to decide for independence or for federal union with the Russian Republic. Applying the same standard of self-determination to Austria, they declared that German Austria had the right either to preserve its independence or, as a majority of the population now demanded, to unite the whole of its Austro-German territories with Germany. The Austrians must be permitted to oppose every attempt at separating national homogeneous territories against the will of their populations. The conference refused to recognize historic or any other claims of alien nations to sovereignty over such homogeneous German districts that formed a geographical unity with other German-speaking districts. Thus, not only did this resolution approve *Anschluss* with Germany if the Austrians wished, but it took sharp exception to Czech claims that the Sudeten German districts of the Dual Monarchy must become part of the new Czechoslovak state.

While supporting the creation of the Polish state, the Amsterdam delegates suggested plebiscites to establish its frontiers with Germany where nationalities were mixed. As to the growing pressure for the establishment of a corridor, they damned all proposals that aimed to take from Germany territory, forming part of the eastern and western provinces of Prussia and inhabited by Germans, in order to cede it to Poland as an avenue to the Baltic Sea. With Danzig as a free port under the League of Nations, the river Vistula was enough to afford Poland free and assured access to the sea.

Turning to western Europe, the conference opposed all attempts, open or veiled, to separate the Saar, the Palatinate, and the left bank of the Rhine from Germany. Such moves would do violence to the principle of self-determination and would lay the foundations of new wars. Agreeing that Germany must pay reparations, the International's Permanent Commission proposed a series of safeguards to ensure that "economic annexations" for reparation purposes should not be used to bring about political annexation. Elsewhere in western Europe, the conference's thoroughgoing support for self-determination led to the request that the Irish people be permitted to choose their own destiny, even if this should mean the political independence they had the right to claim.

Socialist dissatisfaction with the Paris version of the mandates system clearly showed in a resolution that again asked that all colonies and dependencies, not merely the German colonies, be placed as wards of the more advanced states capable of exercising the responsibility. Denouncing imperialist annexations, the resolution urged that mandates should not be assigned until the League of Nations was fully representative of the democratic nations, that is, until nations like Germany became members. Among the other resolutions was one that noted the character of the Jewish question, demanding full civil equality for Jews in every country and national autonomy where there was a compact and numerous Jewish population. The Labour and Socialist International furthermore recognized the right of the Jews to create a national center in Palestine under conditions to be determined by the League of Nations.

All of these proposals, in a sense, depended upon the League, which the International, like the British socialists, regarded as the linchpin of the future world. Approving the presentation of the plans for a League and for an International Labour Charter, the conference warned that the League could attain its objective, the methodical organization of a continuing regime of peace, only if certain conditions were met. It must be composed from the beginning of *all* the independent nations of the world willing to accept its obligations, having equal rights and duties and represented by delegations elected by their parliaments. A supernational authority must be empowered to secure the fulfillment of all obligations undertaken. Moreover, the supernational authority must establish regulations aimed at the gradual abolition of all legal hindrances to international commerce and the international organization of world production and distribution. The League of Nations must at once take measures to prohibit fresh armaments, bring about the progressive reduction of existing armaments, and control the manufacture of such weapons as might still be permitted. The ultimate goal should be total disarmament on land and sea. In order to forestall any danger to democracy, such armed forces the international situation might currently require should be placed under the control of the League. All League members must submit all disputes to decisions by the League through its court, binding themselves to accept these decisions and excluding recourse to war in any circumstances whatsoever. Finally, the governments must adopt the method of open diplomacy as the only technique guaranteeing that the claims of the different nations would be settled strictly on the basis of justice. These conditions, the resolution concluded, had not yet been realized by the Paris Conference. The Amsterdam Commission appealed, therefore, for "effective action" by the workers of all countries to raise their protest and demand that the League of Nations be organized on the solid basis of a durable peace.[52]

These detailed resolutions, drafted in large part by the British delegates, were the most comprehensive expression made by Labour of its demurrers while the Paris Conference was in session. There is little indication, however, that at this stage they had any appreciable impact on its deliberations. The Amsterdam Conference saw to it that a Committee of Action, which had been set up at Berne and included MacDonald, Henderson, and Stuart Bunning among its seven members, should remain in Paris in the hope of influencing the settlement, but whatever lobbying was attempted appears to have had little concrete result.[53] In part, of course, this reflected the fact that even the Paris negotiators were already faced with a series of accomplished facts, as in the establishment of Poland and Czechoslovakia or the seizure of large parts of the Turkish Empire and the German colonies. But whatever its reasons, the disregard of Labour's views ground in a lesson of weakness and impotence that contributed to a growing tone of frustration and bitterness in Labour's reactions to the emerging settlement.

That lesson was further emphasized little more than a week later. On May 8, a summary of the preliminaries of peace that had been presented to the German plenipotentiaries the day before was released. Immediately, British Labour began to develop its case against the treaty. Almost before the proposed terms had been circulated to the press, the Independent Labour party issued a manifesto whose tone reflected the disillusionment of its leaders. The National Administrative Council of the party proclaimed its strong denunciation of the terms of the document submitted to the German Republic. Those terms violated the conditions of the armistice and exposed the real aims of the Allies as the complete smashing of Germany, both politically and economically. But the proposed treaty would result in the consequent impoverishment and economic ruin of Europe as well. It would not bring an end to militarism, but would fasten the system more firmly on the peoples of the Allied countries. It contradicted everything for which people had been called upon to make stupendous sacrifices and was a complete negation and betrayal of democracy. It was a capitalist, militarist, and imperialist imposition, concluded the manifesto. "It aggravates every evil which existed in 1914. It does not give the world peace, but the certainty of other and more calamitous wars."[54]

On the same day the Labour party Executive issued its first manifesto, which, while not so unrestrained in vituperation as that of the ILP, clearly was designed to put its objections on record as quickly as possible. Recalling Labour's wartime struggle for a just settlement and its support for President Wilson's program, the Executive maintained that the published terms departed in certain essential particulars from Wilson's declarations and its own aims. Organized labor, which was not represented at Paris, could accept no responsibility for the violations of principle in the settlement. It called upon the working class to seek the eradication of the imperfections in the treaty and for its adaptation by the League of Nations to the needs of a changing European order.

Concretely, the Labour party document deplored the treaty's failure to provide equality of trade conditions for all its signatories, warned that any permanent denial of a League mandate to Germany must result in international strife, and predicted that the increase in colonial territories under Allied control would involve a corresponding increase in military and administrative burdens for the Allied peoples. Agreeing that Germany must make reparation for civilian damages, the Executive nevertheless demanded that she should have representation on the Reparations Commission and that her total payment should take into account her obligation to meet the needs of her own population. Moreover, the treaty, which imposed drastic disarmament upon Germany, included no provision for the progressive limitation of the armaments of other signatories, with the object of finally arriving at general total disarmament. Similarly, while admitting the temporary French claim upon Saar coal, the Labour Executive criticized the form of political and economic control envisaged in the treaty and protested against any attempt to separate the Saar from Germany permanently. Without attacking the arguments of France, the statement held that the inhabitants of Alsace-Lorraine should be consulted about their future, so as to remove a long-standing dispute from the common life of Europe. Plebiscites must be held in Malmedy and other contested areas between Belgium and Germany if the creation of another Alsace-Lorraine was to be prevented.

As for Germany's eastern territories, the Labour pronouncement welcomed the plebiscite promised for the southern and eastern districts of East Prussia, but deplored the treaty's failure to apply the principle in delimiting other boundaries on the Polish-German and Czechoslovak frontiers. Again, the people of German Austria ought to have free and unrestricted right to decide whether to join a federal Germany or remain independent. Any other solution would not only be an act of injustice, but might well imperil the peace of Europe. Noting that it was the workers who always suffered most in international conflicts, the declaration concluded with the hope that the treaty might even now be brought more into harmony with President Wilson's declaration that "all well-defined national aspirations shall be accorded the utmost statement that can be accorded them without introducing new or perpetuating old elements of discord and antagonism that would be likely in time to break the peace of Europe and consequently of the world."[55]

This manifesto, then, outlined the major areas in which British Labour found the peace proposals to be wanting. Even more detailed was the statement issued on May 12 by the International's Committee of Action. Since

MacDonald and Stuart Bunning had collaborated with Renaudel of France in its composition, it reflected the further thinking of the leaders of British Labour as they took the time to study the projected treaty. The Committee of Action recalled that at Berne and Amsterdam the International had laid down four great principles upon which a just and lasting peace could be built. Like the British Labour party, the International agreed that reparation must be made for the wanton destruction of Belgium, Northern France, and other invaded countries by the Central Powers. Second, it agreed that in redefining the national boundaries of Europe certain oppressed nationalities should be created into independent states, but held that in accordance with the principle of self-determination peoples should not be transferred from one state to another until they had been consulted. Next, militarism should be ended and a League of Nations representative of democratic influences should be established. Finally, the exploitation of native races by colonial imperialism should end.

Considering the peace proposals in the light of these principles, the committee found much to praise. But when the terms were judged in their full effect, they contained much that was menacing to the future peace of the world. The League of Nations in the first place retained all the defects identified at Berne and Amsterdam. It remained a League of governments and executives, not of peoples and parliaments. It did not compel its members fully to renounce war. It failed to include Germany and Russia, and seemed rather to be an instrument of the victorious coalition dominated by five great powers instead of an organ of international justice where all nations ought to find a place. The limitation of German arms was necessary, but the committee called upon the Allies themselves to indicate their intention immediately to reduce their own armaments on land and sea. It noted, parenthetically, that the settlement of frontiers for military reasons and the predominance of strategic considerations in certain provisions of the treaty would ensure the perpetuation of armaments. Polish borders were drawn in violation of the right of people to choose their political allegiance, while the division of Germany into two separate parts would remain a source of trouble and ill will. The Saar proposals were animated by a spirit of annexation and of capitalist exploitation. The creation of French economic interests in the district, the setting up of a special administrative authority, and the plebiscite in fifteen years justified suspicions that what was sought was not coal but territory, not compensation but dismemberment. Like the Labour party Executive in its manifesto, the Committee of Action protested against the disposal of the German colonies, interpreting the denial of a mandate to Germany as imperialism satisfying itself with the spoils of war. In a similar vein, the transfer to

Japan of economic control in the Shantung Peninsula could be considered as nothing less than a frank recognition of the right of conquest. The faults were serious, making it plain that "this is not our peace and that the nations are still menaced by the policy of victors sharing spoils without thought of inevitable consequences."[56]

Not until June 1 did the feeble parliamentary Labour party join officially in commenting on the peace proposals. On that date a second manifesto was issued by the Executive of the Labour party in conjunction with the parliamentary party. This brief statement rehearsed some of the major concrete objections already advanced in May but charged that the treaty was defective not so much because of "this or that detail of wrong done," but fundamentally because it accepted and indeed was based upon the very political principles that were the ultimate cause of war. In customary fashion, the manifesto called upon the organized workers of all countries to join in an effort to bring the treaty more into harmony with the working class conception of an enduring and democratic settlement. It offered no prescription, however, as to how this might immediately be done.[57]

In sum, aside from the territorial objections raised in its various manifestos, Labour was most exercised about the League of Nations. It placed great emphasis upon the introduction of a genuinely representative element into the machinery of the League, particularly on the representation of minority parties, contending that this would result in a true reflection of the main lines of political opinion in each country. And second, Labour insisted that the League must be something more than an instrument of conciliation to prevent war. It must be a true international body, coping with the gamut of world political, economic, and industrial problems, not only to prevent war, but to ensure progressive development by friendly cooperation among all nations.[58] In the circumstances of 1919 this was a millennial conception. It was a conception, however, held not alone by extremist groups on the fringe of the movement, but by virtually all elements including the dominant leadership of the political party and the major trade unions.

Further evidence of this point of view is to be found in an important memorandum drawn up for the Advisory Committee on International Questions by Norman Angell. As the postwar years passed, the former Liberal Angell was to exercise a moderating influence on Labour extremism and to help teach the movement that international authority required some sanction beyond the goodwill of sincere pacifists. But here, in a dispassionate analysis not designed for public consumption, he was a witness to the unanimity with which Labour's vision of international organization differed from the future outlined in the peace treaty. According to Angell, the treaty neither fulfilled the promises made by the Allied governments nor conformed to justice and right. It was imperative to create an international system under which security, fair treatment, and economic opportunity would be ensured to all peoples, yet neither the treaty nor the League took even the first indispensable step toward accomplishing this. While the repressive and prohibitive features of the treaty were exceedingly severe and while the League covenant provided elaborately for plans of coercion if its authority should be challenged, neither the one nor the other made provision for assuring the economic future or the political rights of the countries against which they were in fact directed.

The first task on the international scene, Angell suggested, was to establish a general organic law which should afford to all nations a minimum access to raw materials, to markets, to the resources of undeveloped countries, and across neighboring states to the sea. It was obvious that such an organic law would involve a limitation of national sovereignty. A society of nations whose members had complete sovereignty and independence was a contradiction in terms. The League must do the unprecedented things Wilson had once called upon it to do, regardless of whether great interests were challenged, national pride sacrificed, or some political factions in certain countries made hostile. The primary needs, then, were legislative in their nature, and for that reason emphasis must be placed on the legislative functions of the League. Logically, world legislation should not be the work of cabinets and executives whose legislative powers at home were limited. Yet in the proposed constitution of the League, cabinets and executives alone were to be represented. More than ever, Angell urged, Labour must insist upon the form of representation demanded by the Berne Conference. Only by some such representation of peoples as distinct from states and governments could the League become an instrument for ensuring continual and constitutional change of conditions which, if unchanged, would lead to conflict and war.

Finally, turning again to the economic side of the League, the memorandum warned that it would not suffice to establish an international regime of "equality," based upon laissez-faire and individual scramble. Wartime experience had shown the way to equitable control and distribution of the economic resources of the world. If such controls were placed in the hands of a completely democratic body, the workers of all nations would have some assurance of equality of treatment and would be in a position to exercise some check on the forces that had hitherto made for international conflict.[59]

While Angell concentrated on the spirit and structure of the League of Nations, another Advisory Committee memorandum argued against the injustice and the inadvisability of the repressive policy toward Germany. Such repres-

sion could only be maintained if Poland, Czechoslovakia, Rumania, Yugo-
slavia, Italy, Japan, America, and Russia all would remain as one in political
purpose with France and England. If in the future Germany should, for
instance, be able to detach Poland and Russia from the anti-German coalition,
the present disarmament of Germany would immediately become ineffective.
Since Poland was now to be armed as a measure *against* Germany, the greater
would be the military power accruing to Germany "if the political policy which
determines the direction in which the guns shall shoot is changed." The
German policy of the treaty only made sense if it was assumed that the states of
the alliance would remain united for about three decades. Unfortunately,
there was no precedent in history for such an extended unity.[60]

These Advisory Committee analyses were incorporated into a propaganda
pamphlet issued by the Labour party under the authorship of Arthur Henderson.[61] Henderson followed the main lines of the Advisory Committee arguments and appended to his discussion of the peace terms the texts of the
Labour manifestos of May 8 and May 11. Summing up Labour's general
reaction to the treaty, he declared that the treaty was based upon utterly
inconsistent principles. The principles of justice and the League of Nations
were, he acknowledged, included in the document, but only in the form of
generalizations, aspirations, and vague formulas. Most of the actualities created by the terms, down to the minutest details, were governed by the idea of
punishment, of strategy, or the snatching of some economic or territorial
advantage for one or another of the Allies. The result of such a settlement
could be predicted with certainty. No nation of sixty million people could be
expected to acquiesce in the violations of nationality and the economic servitude imposed by the treaty. The Allied governments and the new League of
Nations, therefore, would have to devote all their energies to the task of
"keeping Germany down," and the peoples of the world would live under the
shadow of a renewal of war at the first favorable occasion. Even if Germany
and Russia were not driven into an alliance, every international dispute
among the Allied powers—the question of Fiume already proved such a pre-
diction—would attain a dangerous and exaggerated importance as it opened
the opportunity to upset the unjust terms of the peace. "There can be no
security," Henderson warned, "no guarantee of peace, in the shadow of this
settlement."[62]

Henderson's criticisms were matched by similar views in the mainstream of
Labour politics. To be sure, Beatrice Webb noted in her diary that her husband Sidney felt that the peace terms were better than might have been
expected when each was examined in detail, but she herself had no doubt

about the treaty's failings. "A hard and brutal peace," she called it, "made more intolerable by the contumely of circumstances deliberately devised, in the method of its delivery to the representatives of the German people."[63]

Although Henderson was the epitome of the moderate, middle-of-the-road element in the Labour party, his strictures against the treaty were at this stage difficult to distinguish from those of the more extreme elements connected with Labour. A case in point is the Union of Democratic Control. As noted, the UDC was bitterly dissatisfied with the Draft Covenant of the League of Nations. It remained for the proposed German treaty, however, to bring the UDC to the pitch of passionate denunciation. On May 9, its Executive Committee issued a long statement which, like the official Labour manifestos, charged that the treaty violated the terms which had persuaded the German nation to lay down its arms. It constituted an indefensible breach of the very international morality that the Allied and Associated powers had claimed to be fighting to ensure. They had insisted that their quarrel was not with the German people but with its rulers. Now, in the form of the German Republic, they were dealing with the people. Yet the territorial arrangements that were concluded without consulting the peoples affected, particularly in eastern Germany, the Saar Valley, and Alsace-Lorraine, were marked by the same disregard for human rights that the German Government showed in 1871 and at Brest Litovsk. Poland, for example, which included large districts of a purely German population, must surely prove a center of bitter racial conflict in Europe. But individual instances merely typified the general purpose underlying every section of the treaty. That purpose was obvious. It was to reduce the new democratic Germany to the position of a vassal state, to make her commercial recovery impossible, to drive her out of international life, to crush the spirit of her people. Exclusion from the League of Nations, unilateral disarmament, the imposition of enormous and indefinite financial burdens, and the seizure of their colonies opened up for the Germans the prospect of becoming a "people of serfs working for their conquerors in arms." Perhaps the German people would have to accept the treaty rather than see their children starve under the blockade, but the terms would rouse every true democrat to work ceaselessly for their revision. For its part the UDC did not recognize the treaty as having any moral validity. It pledged itself to work for a peace that would correspond with President Wilson's Fourteen Points and with the aspirations and ideals of common people everywhere.[64]

Here were the major lines of attack that the Union of Democratic Control was to pursue during the coming years. Under the leadership of E. D. Morel, the group was to make the revision of the German settlement its particular cause, and it was to use every available technique to whip up emotions of sympathy for Germany and of contempt and anger toward her conquerors, above all toward France. And yet, as the May 9 statement demonstrates, the UDC, despite its overheated rhetoric, was at this stage quite close to the mainstream of Labour policy in its assessment of the postwar settlement.

For despair at the character of the proposed peace ran through almost every quarter of the labor movement. In the press, *Forward* featured an analysis by Ramsay MacDonald, who charged that the provisions outlined were an attempt literally to destroy Germany in the interests of capitalist imperialism.[65] The *Labour Leader*, another Independent Labour party organ, warned that it was a chimera to hope that the League of Nations might later alter the objectionable and impossible features of the treaty. The covenant was an instrument for the execution of the treaty and had been framed in every detail with that object in view. There could be no hope of amending the treaty so long as those who were responsible for it remained in power.[66] Even the *New Statesman*, which had welcomed the League of Nations with some warmth, was convinced that no treaty which embodied such terms as those published could lead to a permanent settlement. If the Germans felt obliged to sign it as it stood, then it would be upset and revised and revised again in the course of the next generation.[67] And the *Herald* published a comment that was to become, in its way, almost as well-known as J. M. Keynes's later *Economic Consequences of the Peace*. This was a cartoon drawn by Will Dyson after he heard that Clemenceau, leading his fellow delegates down the Hall of Mirrors at Versailles, had stopped and said, "Curious! I seem to hear a child weeping." Dyson sketched the picture in a powerful cartoon. The weeping child, with the peace treaty at its feet, wore a band above its head entitled "1940."[68]

Words like "mockery," "bare-faced swindle," and "sheer and unadulter-ated brigandage" were used almost constantly to characterize the treaty.[69] Only on the right of the labor movement could a good word be found for it in the press. Even here, as in the case of Robert Blatchford and Alexander Thompson in the *Clarion*, the implication generally seemed to be that the terms were about as good as one might have expected.[70] But this group on the right, though it may well have reflected the sentiments of many more of Labour's rank and file than party leaders would have ever cared to admit, nevertheless was clearly a minority opposed to the main currents of criticism that welled up increasingly in the labor movement, as disillusionment with the results of war grew day by day.

Labour's rejection of the Paris proposals continued through the days of the

German counterproposals, the slight modification of some terms, and the final capitulation of Germany.[71] Meanwhile, the Labour party was gathering at Southport for its annual conference. Here, for the moment at least, may be discerned some slight cracks in the monolith of denunciation that had developed since May 8. As the German delegates prepared to sign at Versailles, some of the Labour chieftains were torn between making the best of a bad situation in the hope of gradual improvement and a policy of complete and unadulterated rejection. The dilemma appears clearly in the major speeches on postwar economic policy delivered to the conference. No doubt conference oratory was frequently unrepresentative of the programs being pushed by the leaders of the party, but, particularly for a minority party struggling to be heard, the positions articulated by those leaders at the annual meeting were more than ordinarily revealing of where their movement stood.

In his address as chairman, J. M. McGurk of the Darwen Trades Council, while attacking the treaty's unhappy compromises and violations of principle, tended to look upon the League of Nations, unsatisfactory and weak though it was in certain details, as a substantial beginning in the direction of methodical organization to maintain peace. Similarly, Ramsay MacDonald, in introducing the conference's resolution on the peace treaty and the League of Nations, denounced the "peace of punishment," but then turned to the League as the one hope for the future. It was bad as it stood, but Labour must make it better. They must work up public opinion to change it from a League of National Executives to a League of Peoples inspired by "the peoples' mind."[72]

MacDonald's speech, as he no doubt intended, was essentially inspirational rhetoric. He was followed by J. R. Clynes, who was soon to succeed Will Adamson as leader of the parliamentary Labour party. Clynes brought the question back to earth, as he was often called upon to do in Parliament during the next couple of years. In detailing the flaws of the treaty, he summarized his argument by asserting that wrongs flagrantly committed and imposed upon a beaten foe were the real beginnings of the wars of the future. The treaty must be repaired and it could be repaired only through the machinery of the League of Nations. He did not conceive lightly of the League. It now had its defects, but those too could be mended. The beaten nations must be admitted, the work toward disarmament begun, the economic tasks of the League developed. As a labor movement, their responsibility now was to enlighten their people, to teach them to make the League a great cooperative agency to right the wrongs of the peace that had just been made. Once MacDonald and Clynes had spoken, the conference proceeded to adopt "with enthusiasm" the following resolution:

The Conference is of the opinion, now that Germany has decided to sign
the Treaty of Peace, thereby opening up the opportunity of cooperation
with the democracies of the world, that its speedy admission to the
League of Nations, and the immediate revision by the League of Nations
of the harsh provisions of the Treaty, which are inconsistent with the
statements made on behalf of the Allied Governments when the Armistice was made, are essential both on grounds of honour and expediency;
and it therefore calls upon the Labour Movement in conjunction with
the International to undertake a vigorous campaign for the winning of
popular support to this policy as a first step toward the reconstruction of
the peoples and the inauguration of a new era of international cooperation and goodwill.[73]

All the familiar elements of Labour's assessment of the treaty were embodied
in the resolution, yet the tone is curiously laconic. Aside from MacDonald's
and Clynes's speeches, there was no discussion of the resolution, although the
question of Allied intervention in Russia touched off considerable controversy. The report of the conference gives the impression that some of the
party's leaders were marking time, hesitating until the Versailles treaty was a
fact and, in the light of what followed, developing their attack more thoroughly.

That attack was certainly not exhibited in the House of Commons. Until the
signature of the Versailles treaty, the parliamentary Labour party had little to
contribute to the analysis of the emerging peace. Inadequately led, with most
of the important Labour figures defeated in the Coupon Election that had
given the Lloyd George coalition an overwhelming majority, the parliamentary delegation displayed little eagerness to cope with questions of international import. Most witnesses have emphasized the timidity of the parliamentary party, but it can be argued that in the matter of the Versailles treaty the
Labour M.P.'s—Clynes is a good example—had begun to realize that the treaty
was an accomplished fact, that their most responsible attitude would be to
accept it and work for its amendment rather than indulge in the luxurious
propaganda of complete rejection.[74] For despite the severe criticism to which
the parliamentary party was subjected in Labour circles, arguments such as
those of Clynes were eventually to become the orthodox position of the
Labour majority.[75]

Once the Versailles treaty was presented to Parliament, the Labour benches
had the opportunity to ventilate their party's case against it. Instead, William
Adamson, the nominal leader in the Commons, rather weakly expressed grat-
ification at its signature, only mildly criticizing certain features.[76] When the

debate was resumed on the second reading of the bill to approve the treaty, Clynes spoke for the Labour group in pointing out its blemishes. But, as his words at the annual conference had demonstrated, he still believed that the League of Nations might be used to remedy the defects of the treaty as a whole. And while he pleaded for the early admission of Germany, he revealed a substantially different viewpoint from most of the party leaders outside of Parliament. He had heard it said, he told the House of Commons, that the League of Nations was suspect because it had been set up by the victors. Actually, that fact would make it all the stronger, and he applauded the British Government for the role it had played in creating the League. This was hardly the usual diatribe against capitalist imperialism. Its author separated himself even more from those Labour stalwarts who insisted that the League must be a pacifist instrument when he warned that even an international body would require some physical strength and some form of physical force behind it to make its decrees effective.[77] Actually, the most exhaustive argument against the peace settlement was made by a Liberal who only later was to join the Labour party. Lt. Comdr. J. M. Kenworthy, one of the radicals in the Liberal party who had not yet come over to Labour, condemned the treaty, minimized the importance of the League of Nations, and damned the proposal for an Anglo-French alliance, which was also before the House. Improvement, he insisted, could come only if the treaty were rejected. But when the Commons divided on the issue, he was followed into the "No" lobby by only one Labour member.[78]

If the parliamentary party felt compelled to be temperate in its reception of the Versailles terms, the Labour press had no such inhibitions. Once the treaty was signed, a full-scale assault moved into high gear. The ILP's *Labour Leader*, for example, reacted violently to the caution of the parliamentary party. Noting that the Labour party might embark on a campaign for revision, the *Labour Leader* caustically predicted that if some of the same men were involved, "it will partake of the character of the debate in the House of Commons, and eulogies of Lloyd George and perfunctory references to Conscription and Armaments will be mixed up with energetic references to the admission of Germany to the League of Nations when she has cleaned herself sufficiently to be fit to associate with Mr. Lloyd George, Clemenceau, and Wilson."[79] Even the *New Statesman*, which had consistently been moderate in its approach, noted that with every passing week it was becoming clearer that frontiers drawn on the principle of recompensing friends and punishing enemies had no prospect of permanence. Unless, the *New Statesman* commented with uncharacteristic cynicism, the friends happened to be stronger than the enemies.[80]

The real press campaign, however, was the work of the big guns of the party: publicists like Brailsford, Lansbury, and Morel, politicians like Mac-Donald and Henderson. Lansbury's *Daily Herald*, in particular, kept up a running fire of vehement criticism. To Lansbury, the Versailles treaty was simply a "peace of hate" and June 28 a day of "militaristic attitudinising over the ruins of Europe." Lloyd George's parliamentary defense of the treaty was "one long scream of triumphant boasting over the fallen foe." Altogether, the *Herald* cried, what had happened was more than enough to make those who had hoped and worked for a clean peace despair of the future.[81]

In more concrete fashion, H. N. Brailsford spelled out the objections so emotionally defined by Lansbury. The historian of the future, he wrote, would see in Clemenceau the epic figure of the age. First he had reduced Germany to economic and military impotence from which it appeared she might never rise. Then he had created a network of satellites around her, each with its conscript army under French leaders—the Poles, the Czechs, and Rumanians. This alliance would of course be "defensive," as were all alliances of modern history, and it would be operated in the old way, with all the old evils of secret "conversations" between military staffs. France was now the dominant power on the Continent, seeking safety by imposing her will.[82]

Much like Brailsford in his point of view, yet sharing Lansbury's fervor, was E. D. Morel, the guiding genius of the Union of Democratic Control. With the first issue of *Foreign Affairs*, which he edited and which increasingly replaced the *UDC* as the vehicle for his views, Morel opened an attack upon the Versailles treaty and most of its works, together with an unrelenting presentation of the case for Germany.[83] His first editorial set the tone he was to follow consistently for the next five years. For the past five months, he cried, the statesmen and the diplomatists had been spinning new webs of war. They had set their seal to the rape of nations, the dismemberment of states, the disruption of communities. They had condemned a great people to a generation of economic servitude and to national disintegration. By starvation and by the promotion of civil war they sought to place another great people once again beneath the heel of ancient, or new, tyrannies. They had betrayed their peoples and the world. They had converted their promised league of free nations into a compact of a few dominant governments, and so ephemeral did they deem it that already they were creating sectional alliances within a bond that was to have been both singular and all-embracing. Morel had little patience with the view that the League might be used to modify the evils of the treaty. International machinery created to enforce such pacts of violence as the German treaty or its Austrian copy, he insisted, was machinery whose purpose was to guarantee stability to the institution of war. The project of a

League of Nations could only become realizable policy when present governments were swept from power.[84] Morel, then, left little room for compromise
or accommodation of Labour party policy to existing conditions in the world.

Even men like MacDonald and Henderson, shocked by the reality of the
treaty, rapidly dropped the temporary caution that had so recently colored
the debate at the Southport Conference. In Henderson's view the treaty was
neither a Wilson peace nor a Labour peace, but rather in certain respects
unreal, undemocratic, and unjust. It did violence to the principle of self-
determination. On territorial questions, on reparations, on armaments, the
provisions were more an emulation of the brutal demands made at Brest
Litovsk than an application of the principles for which the Allies and America
were said to have been fighting. What, then, should be Labour's attitude?
Henderson argued that the people must realize that deliverance could only
come if they themselves strengthened the League of Nations by rendering it
really democratic and properly representative.[85] He appeared to imply that
such a change was possible, but MacDonald, in one of his many public assessments, seemed to be carrying water on both shoulders. His comment was
characteristic. The wrong kind of League, he wrote, was worse than no
League at all. Of course there was a chance that if democracy came into power
in a sufficient number of states, the current "Executive of Executives" might
become a league of peoples. But while it would be a mistake to be un-
generous, Labour ought not to fall into the equally mischievous error of being
complacent and of accepting the League as something good in itself. It was
not that. "It may be the worst part of the Treaty; it may be a bulwark for all the
interests and methods with which we are at war—if they are to dominate
Europe I prefer that they should do so unallied in such a League—if democracy is to emerge it will be far easier for it to form its own League than to
amend this." That was why Germany, Austria, Hungary, and Russia should be
brought in from the very start. Without them the League would be weak "on
its democratic side."[86] Whatever may be the precise reading of MacDonald's
words, it is apparent that the bitter disappointment of a wide range of Labour
publicists was shared by the two men whom a majority in the labor movement
regarded as their leading spokesmen.[87]

The official position of the Labour party was summed up in a major pamphlet that epitomized its final reaction to the peace settlement. *Labour and
the Peace Treaty* was prepared as a handbook for Labour speakers. It contained the Labour declarations already noted and an analysis of the treaty
terms, German and Austrian, and other decisions of the Paris Conference in
relation to those declarations. An important section was devoted to the party's
major objections to the settlement. In the first place, the pamphlet com-

plained, the condition of "open covenants openly arrived at" had not been observed. Not only had conference proceedings and decisions been marked by the suppression of all opportunity for public discussion, but the bargains of the secret treaties had marked the peace terms themselves. In the decisions on the Russian Revolution and the socialist movement in Russia and Hungary, the democracies had been committed without their people's knowledge to the support of counterrevolutionary forces. Organized Labour and progressive and socialist movements had been completely without representation in the making of decisions that deeply concerned the general struggle for industrial democracy.

Second, the permanent causes of war—whether regarded as mainly nationalist rivalries or economic conflict—far from being removed had been rendered more acute and more numerous than ever. Nor did the constitution of the League of Nations afford adequate means for their removal. Entente statesmen had repeatedly pledged themselves to remove all cause for the enemies' militarism and to win them to a peaceful international cooperation by guaranteeing them political security and economic justice through an equal place in the League of Nations. These promises had been directly violated. Germany was not included in the League; she was not to enjoy the rights and privileges she was compelled to extend to others; and there was no provision giving her the opportunity to win those rights even by good behavior. The destruction of German militarism was offset by the intensified militarism imposed on those Allies whose duty it would be to hold Germany by the throat for a generation or more.

The Labour pamphlet went on to object that the Versailles treaty made no truly international arrangement for the equitable distribution of raw materials. Instead, Germany's economic life, both internal through the Reparations Commission and external through the Allied control of raw materials, was placed in the power of her former enemies and future competitors. They would be in a position to deny her population even the means of livelihood. Worse, the controls over Germany were given not to the League but to the "Big Four," who were free to act on their private interest and discretion. She was to be situated for years under an economic government in which she had no part, clearly a denial of democracy and self-government.

Finally, the League of Nations as devised by the Paris Conference, far from being mainly a democratic organ for the legislative modification of poor international conditions likely to cause war, was a machine by which coercive power was given primarily to the executive branches of a few great governments. To make matters worse the project for a Triple Alliance among France, America, and Britain was a violation of President Wilson's dictum that there could be no league or alliance or special covenants or undertakings within the general and common family of the League of Nations.[88] "If," cautioned the pamphlet, "we expect others—Poles, Ukrainians, Czechs, to say nothing of Germans and Austrians—to trust to the League for defence as well as justice, we must show that we ourselves believe in it, and have no special obligations which conflict with impartial justice for all its members."[89]

The analysis then proceeded to put flesh on the bones of these general objections in a point-by-point consideration of the various parts of the treaty. It exposed the League covenant, territorial provisions, colonies and mandates, and financial arrangements to detailed criticism. The pamphlet then drew up Labour's summary of points upon which revisionist efforts must concentrate. Aside from the territorial suggestions that followed lines already developed, the first and foremost was the immediate admission of Germany and Austria to the League of Nations. Along with this must go amendment of the peace treaties in their various aspects. On the economic side, arrangements for securing payment through the Reparations Commission should be made by the League of Nations, not merely by the Allies. German and Austrian access to raw materials and economic opportunities should be assured by definite provisions, guaranteed by the League and not left to the discretionary power of Germany's late enemies and present economic rivals. The control of credit, shipping, food, and raw materials should be entrusted definitely to bodies in which the late enemy states had representation under the League, instead of being in fact in the hands of bodies dominated by two or three of the chief Allies. The consideration governing the apportioning of the necessities of life should be the degree of vital need, not the degree of the capacity to pay.

The control of colonial areas was another major problem to which considerable attention was given. The Labour party demanded that equality of economic opportunity in all nonself-governing colonies be assured under the League of Nations. All such colonies and not merely the conquered German ones should be ceded to the League and Germany should be given the opportunity to become a mandatory state.

The most exhaustive provisions for revision centered about the League of Nations. The Labour party proposed constitutional changes involving the creation of a body, separate from the Assembly, representing the people, as distinct from states, "in the same sense in which the American House of Representatives, composed of Delegates from the people, is distinct from the Senate, which is composed of Delegates from the States." Whatever may be thought of this interpretation of the American system of representation, the Labour party expressed conviction that such a revision would fulfill the demand of the Berne International for a central organ representative of the peoples of the world. Next, the party wanted to see established under the League of Nations a permanent World Economic Council to investigate and supervise the distribution of foodstuffs and raw materials, with the object of preventing monopoly, unfair pressure upon the weak, and international profiteering. Finally, the pamphlet called upon the new League to discuss the solution of the more pressing of those problems that, apart from the changes made by the war, might affect the peace of the world. Such problems included the position of subject nations like Egypt, India, and Ireland and of old possessions like Cyprus, whose cession to Greece ought to be considered.[90]

By the time *Labour and the Peace Treaty* was published, the Labour party, still bitter in its reaction to the peace settlement, had begun to think in terms of how it might be modified. Labour's proposals at this time were so immoderate that they leave the impression of being designed to build a propaganda case rather than to achieve any real immediate success. Certainly there is little indication that leadership within the ranks of Labour, with the possible exception of a few M.P.'s in the weak parliamentary group, had as yet reconciled themselves to the major lineaments of the postwar decisions and settled down to work within the system devised at Paris for the achievement of their ultimate aims. What is striking about the Labour response is not so much its dissatisfaction with many of the specific terms of the Versailles treaty, but rather the air of hopelessness and rejection that permeated virtually all of the movement's pronouncements in the spring and summer of 1919. Even in the case of the League of Nations, which it did not repudiate entirely, Labour insisted that until it was sufficiently revised so as to be a different organization it had no real value and merited little support. Whether it could shake off its disillusionment and move toward a more realistic assessment of what was possible on the international scene was still unrevealed as the labor movement pondered its policy for the future.

CHAPTER 3

THE AFTERMATH OF WAR

In the wake of Labour's initial disillusionment with the Paris settlement, three issues dominated the movement's focus on foreign affairs: concern about the plight of Germany, concern about revolutionary Russia, and concern about the inadequacies of the fledgling League of Nations. For several years, these issues kept Labour from abandoning a blanket rejection of the new international order and moving toward a more realistic foreign policy. Yet even in these early years, at least occasionally, a small element within the movement gave hints of a less rigid posture in international affairs. This group sounded a different note, one more willing to accept the postwar arrangements, particularly the League of Nations, and to work for their reform rather than outright rejection. That note, quite faint for two or three years after the war, gradually became more prominent as the twenties progressed.

Meanwhile, bitter rejection of the Paris treaties continued to dominate almost every section of the labor movement well up to the time that the first Labour government took office in 1924. Late in 1919, for example, Norman Angell completed a little book he called *The Peace Treaty and the Economic Chaos of Europe*. By then he had become a member of the Labour party and his pamphlet faithfully mirrored the official position of the party as it began to sort out its foreign policy ideas in their relation to the postwar world. Published shortly after the appearance of John Maynard Keynes's *The Economic Consequences of the Peace*, Angell's independent critique might nevertheless well have been a popular version of Keynes's devastating attack, with the exception that Angell, echoing the attitudes of much of the labor movement, emphasized the failure of the Allies to create a powerful League of Nations and proposed amendments to make it a central pivot of a new internationalism. Like Keynes, Angell proposed to investigate the economic implications of the Versailles settlement, but also like Keynes, he proceeded to pen a moral indictment, the passion of which was scarcely concealed by a cool surface of economic analysis.

As he examined the condition of Europe on the eve of the second postwar winter, Angell saw large areas not only threatened but already engulfed by the horrible reality of actual famine. Malnutrition and disease, especially in Germany, were in part the aftermath of war itself, but at the same time were being aggravated by the terms of the peace treaty. Granting that the German people must be punished for their transgressions, Angell insisted that the indiscriminate starvation of a whole nation would enable the guilty to escape and victimize the innocent. Children, unborn at the time of the invasion of Belgium, were being condemned "for an offense for which they were not responsible and which they could not have prevented."[1] But even aside from the matter of justice, Angell questioned whether the settlement could in fact contribute to the future peace of Europe and to the economic restoration of the Allied nations themselves.

The dilemma faced by the victors, he argued, was that Germany's recovery was necessary for the recovery of her victims. Britain, for example, was dependent upon trade for her very existence, yet the treaty, if carried out, must inevitably cut her off from continental markets milked dry to meet its exactions. Not only did the prosperity of Europe as a whole hinge upon the German contribution; even the indemnity demanded could only be paid if her people were permitted to produce goods for export on a basis of equality with other states. The main fault of the treaty was that it sought to do two mutually exclusive things: "It has attempted to reduce the economic power of Germany *and* to provide funds for Reparation; to place the German population in a position of having a very restricted industry *and* to restore Europe in general to work and quietude; to turn the thoughts of this naturally active, laborious, disciplined people of 60 or 70 millions from projects of aggression *and* to give them no adequate reward for peaceful labour."[2]

What was to be done to wean the Germans away from dreams of revenge and to promote the peaceful recovery of all of Europe? Angell listed a series of treaty revisions as indispensable to both aims. To start with, the maximum sum in reparation should be fixed as quickly as possible, should be within Germany's obvious capacity to pay in five or ten years, and its payment should be encouraged by provision for complete evacuation of the occupied territories when the debt was discharged. Second, the arrangements for ensuring payment *and* for allocating the economic facilities upon which Germany's ability to pay depended ought to be in the hands of the Supreme Economic Council or another international body responsible to the League of Nations rather than in those of the Reparations Commission. Next, Germany should be given access to the ore of Alsace-Lorraine, restrictions upon her commercial intercourse with Russia and other neighbors should be abolished, and the commercial rights and privileges granted by her to the Allies should be reciprocated. In addition, the League of Nations must revise armistice and treaty provisions for the distribution of railway stock, agricultural machinery, and milch cows, to ensure such distribution in the order of the most pressing need. Finally, the exploitation of underdeveloped countries and the enforcement of the open door should be entrusted to bodies in which the ex-enemy states were represented, instead of being in control of groups dominated by two or three of the chief Allies. To achieve these aims, Angell contended, Germany would probably have to be admitted at once to the League of Nations. The League, in turn, must agree that equality of economic access to nonself-governing colonies should be guaranteed; that all such colonies, not merely those conquered from Germany, should come under the mandate principle; that the conquered colonies should be ceded to the League and mandates granted by the League, not the Allies; and that Germany should have the opportunity to become a mandatory.[3] Unless some such changes were made, Europe would look forward to a future of economic chaos and political danger. The treaty, Angell insisted as he brought his analysis to a Cassandra-like conclusion, was purely repressive, punitive, and negative. A settlement that insisted upon treating the whole German people as criminals and upon excluding them from the Society of Nations, he concluded, would not secure justice; it would enable the most guilty to escape punishment and punish those who were not guilty. It would not secure indemnification for the Belgian or French people, nor would it lift the burden of war from their shoulders. Instead of healing the wounds of the innocent victims in France and Belgium it would cause fresh pain. To the millions who had suffered it would add other millions who would be made to suffer in like fashion.[4]

Angell's positive suggestions were a virtual summary of similar proposals that had gained widespread acceptance in most Labour circles. They were also almost exactly the same as recommendations that were accepted by the Permanent Commission of the Labour and Socialist International when it met at Lucerne in August. Because British socialist leaders believed it important to maintain their collaboration with their continental brethren, they hoped at Lucerne to frame a common position on international questions. There the widening rift in the socialist movement did not prevent certain common decisions, most of which reflected the reasoning of the British delegates. The Lucerne conferees were able to agree on a joint resolution pertaining to territorial and national questions as well as to economic and colonial concerns. In essence, the International pleaded for much more lenient treatment of Germany in matters of reparation, economic recovery, and the administration of colonial areas. Denouncing the exploitation of colonies by the capitalism of the Great Powers, the resolution demanded that, since the colonial system continued to exist, the projected League of Nations take much more definite steps than appeared to be planned to protect the interests of native populations. Furthermore, in assuring equality of economic opportunity in the colonies, the League should give Germany the chance to become a mandatory power. In all of these proposals the International was quite faithfully mirroring demands that reflected the views of all sections of British Labour.

But whatever stamp of unity the International's general resolution might have implied, the deep-seated cleavage in European socialism precipitated by the Bolshevik revolution was apparent in Lucerne's other pronouncements. Here a majority of the delegates, among whom were the representatives of British Labour, showed themselves deeply concerned with the "forms of democracy and representative institutions, the place of revolutions in the transformation of Society, the relations between industrial and political organisation and mass action." Behind these formulas were a commitment to gradualism in the achievement of working class goals and a determination to work within the framework of democratic institutions, both political and industrial, in the struggle for socialism. The result was a bitter rejection of the newly created "Third International" sponsored by Moscow.

As the Labour and Socialist International met, however, formidable White Russian armies were striving to destroy the Bolshevik regime. A substantial minority of the delegates believed it necessary at almost any cost to preserve "working class" unity. They maneuvered to postpone for as long as possible any judgment upon Bolshevik tactics or even upon the central question of democracy versus dictatorship. Unable to agree upon a form of words that might conceal their differences, majority and minority took their stand behind alternative resolutions on the political situation. The international labor and socialist community was hopelessly divided on its relation to the new Bolshevik regime and that division was increasingly apparent on the left of the British labor movement as well. Despite the action of the British delegates at Lucerne, the Scottish ILP, for example, voted in December to affiliate with the Third International.

The split at Lucerne was evident not only on the issue of collaboration with the Bolsheviks but also in regard to the postwar settlement. The majority of the representatives, led in large part by the British delegation, was much less intransigent than the minority. Tentatively, they declared that the present League of Nations had "the appearance of being" an organization of capitalist and bourgeois states. They recognized, nevertheless, that it was the first effective international organ, the skeleton of a juridical structure destined to prevent the use of force in the solution of international disputes. How important it might become depended upon how thoroughly it was influenced by socialism, which in turn depended upon how far each member nation was itself permeated with the spirit of democracy and socialism. Meanwhile, certain profound modifications of the present League of Nations were imperative. The League must include all nations as they demonstrated by adopting democratic constitutions their ability to keep their engagements. The covenant must be amended in order to form a "World Parliament" in which the people would have a direct voice. It should also be revised to do away with the right to make war under any circumstances, providing rigorous sanctions against violators of such a provision. The international body should also prohibit the private manufacture of armaments and move rapidly toward total disarmament. Finally, the Supreme Economic Council of the Allies ought to be transformed into an Economic Council of the League of Nations, with responsibility to oversee the swift restoration of the world's economic life by eliminating protectionism and by organizing credit and the liquidation of war debts on a genuinely international basis. Altogether, while the majority was not enthusiastic about the League of Nations, it professed to see opportunities for its development in the direction desired by socialists everywhere.

For a time, such a point of view, which placed revision of the covenant and of the entire treaty structure in the forefront, was to be a characteristic element in the foreign policy pronouncements of the British Labour party. It was a position upon which all elements of the labor movement could agree in the first few years after the war. During this period, the Hendersons and MacDonalds, who were the leading advocates of a moderate stance in foreign affairs, nevertheless continued to make the case for fundamental change, even as they searched for positions more likely to promote cooperation with other European nations. Only gradually did the attempt to overthrow the peace settlement give way to an implied acceptance of the settlement and an emphasis on working constructively to improve the new institutions of international organization.

If the complex attitudes of Labour in this formative period are to be accurately portrayed, however, the position of the minority at Lucerne merits notice. That group insisted that the German peace treaty, no less than the policy of the Entente governments toward Russia and Hungary, exemplified the exploitation of victory by capitalist states determined to enlarge the sources of profit for their ruling classes. As a result, they had little use for the supposedly international institutions erected at Paris. Condemning the exclusion of Germany, Austria, and Russia from the League, they nevertheless insisted that, however necessary the revision of clauses most contrary to justice might be, the signal rebuff to President Wilson's proposals at Paris

proved that the capitalism of the Entente states was resolved to defend the
fruits of its victory. Their position was summarized in one long sentence:
"Whilst declaring itself resolved to pursue with all the strength at its command, a revision of the Treaty on the basis indicated and, with this object in
view, to employ all means afforded it by the increasing strength of organised
labor throughout the world, the Conference reminds all the oppressed—class,
race, or nationality—that nothing but the universal triumph of Socialism will
permit the reign of justice among nations as among individuals."[5]

During the next couple of years, the minority position expressed by the
International was championed by a considerable group, mostly on the Left,
within the Labour party. Its almost inflexible insistence that socialism was a
prerequisite for international peace and security ensured that its advocates
would give short shrift to pleas that socialists could only achieve their international goals by accommodating themselves to the realities of the world in
which they lived. What is important to note is that most supporters of the
majority position as expressed at Lucerne nevertheless shared an uncompromising insistence that the extraordinary penalties imposed upon Germany
and her Allies at Paris must be revised. This ambivalence was well illustrated
by the Labour press in the months after Versailles. The *Daily Herald*, briefly
enjoying a unique and peculiar position under the editorship of George Lansbury, continued to throb with righteous indignation at the settlement.[6] Crying
that President Wilson, in sacrificing everything to his League of Nations, had
succeeded only in obtaining a "Clique of Cabinets," the *Herald* watched its
reception in the United States with a kind of macabre satisfaction. When the
treaty was rejected, the *Herald* noted that at least Senator Lodge was putting
the League on ice, where it would remain, to be joined by all other similar
attempts to compromise with capitalism. "The only International that will
work is the Red International—the true union of peoples."[7] At the same time
the *Herald*, for all its disillusionment, continued to call for a "reformed"
League of Nations, which should include Germany and Russia and immediately do away with the punitive "guarantees" of the Versailles treaty. But
during this period the call for reform was a good deal more perfunctory than
the clear expectation that no good could possibly come from the League as it
was presently constituted.[8]

Both the Independent Labour party and the Union of Democratic Control,
many of whose leaders were by this time almost interchangeable, exhibited
much the same temper. The Executive Committee of the UDC, for example,
recalled in the pages of *Foreign Affairs* that the organization had been among
the first to advocate a League of Nations in 1914. The covenant of the League
that had actually been formed, however, was not in accord with any of the

principles the UDC had demanded. Point by point, the statement enumerated the objections. Yet it concluded that "the existence of any international instrument by which some months' delay must elapse between the commencement of a dispute and the possible outbreak of hostilities, will afford an opportunity for the cooling of passions and the informing of public opinion, and consequently conduce to the avoidance of war." That the governments of the world should have assented to such a procedure was to the UDC a hopeful sign.[9]

The UDC position reflected compromises that stemmed from the varied emphases of its signatories. However grudging its admission that there might be some good in the peace settlement, the UDC as an organization was trying officially to be constructive in assessing Versailles. But E. D. Morel, who was its very heart and soul, found himself increasingly unable to accept, even contingently, the world of 1919. Speaking in Glasgow in December, Morel declared that if the Versailles treaty stood, then the League of Nations, instead of being the salvation of the world, would be the most powerful engine of oppression it had ever seen. "It will be built upon a lie. It will be rooted in dishonour." It would inevitably promote war.[10] The only true League of Nations, he wrote at about the same time, would not be constructed by rulers whose own acts had already destroyed the ideal that that institution was intended to crystallize. It would be made by the peoples of the world, who, having torn the bandage of deception from their eyes, would unite in universal brotherhood.[11] Morel's rhetoric summed up a scathing indictment of Versailles and a repudiation of its international arrangements. It offered no constructive alternative to the emerging League of Nations.

Key leaders of Labour echoed some parts of Morel's attack. Ramsay MacDonald had recently attended the Geneva meeting of the Second International, where the ILP was of course not represented. Unsurprisingly, although he reluctantly agreed to serve as joint secretary of the International with headquarters in London, he found it a skeleton of its old self with no chance of survival as it was. As he confided to his diary, some of his most unpleasant experiences were with the "petty minded" members of the British Labour party delegation, who, along with the German right-wing socialists, dominated the ailing organization. At the same time he found himself more and more disenchanted with his ILP associates.[12] MacDonald's position was a difficult one. Not yet back in the House of Commons, he needed his affiliation with the ILP as a base for his political activity. Yet he was determined to use his secretaryship of the rump democratic International to isolate the Bolsheviks by driving a wedge between them and the rest of the international working class movement. MacDonald shared much of the ILP's general out-

look on international relations even though he differed increasingly on specific details of foreign policy no less than on issues of socialist organization. In
public, therefore, he continued to press the position favored by many of those
with whom he was increasingly becoming impatient. The League, for example, was for him "the latest topical costume in which Imperialism appears at a
fancy dress ball."[13] Similarly, Philip Snowden greeted the torpedoing of the
covenant by the American Senate with a frank confession that he had few
regrets. If the United States should stay out of the League, then sooner or later
revision of the peace treaties and the covenant would become essential. Without American support France and Britain simply could not enforce their
harsh and vindictive terms.[14] Altogether, the ILP position might be summed
up in the comment of its leading newspaper that it was utterly futile to talk
about a League of Nations so long as the present peace treaty remained.
Under existing circumstances, declared the *Labour Leader*, the League was
an instrument of aggression that would provoke future wars rather than
insure the peace.[15]

The balance of power within the labor movement after the war was both
uncertain and shifting, reflecting and exacerbating Labour's deep divisions
over foreign policy. The position of the ILP was central for a time, in part
because such leaders as Philip Snowden and Ramsay MacDonald depended
significantly upon its support to bolster their positions in the broader movement, but also because so many of the new recruits to Labour had chosen the
ILP as their gateway to participation in Labour politics. But the ILP's angry
and apparently unfruitful repudiation of the new international organization
obviously troubled the secretary of the Labour party, Arthur Henderson. As
one of the key leaders of the party, he was concerned that if Labour simply
rejected all the unsatisfactory international institutions created after the war,
it would miss the opportunity to use those institutions as instruments of
peaceful change. Because the war had thrown the leadership of the Labour
party into disarray, Henderson assumed a crucial role in holding the movement together. Already William Gillies of the International Department of the
Labour party, under his tutelage, was pushing the Trades Union Congress,
many of whose leaders shared Henderson's suspicions of the ILP, not only to
join in propaganda for the admission of Germany into the League of Nations,
but more fundamentally in issuing propaganda in support of the League
itself.[16]

As early as November 1919, Henderson asked the Advisory Committee on
International Questions to tackle the problem posed by possible American
rejection of the Versailles treaty. The Advisory Committee, in that event, saw
two courses open to Europe. The first was to relapse into a "more or less

avowed militarism on traditional lines"; the second, to make a resolute effort to rescue the plan for a League of Nations in spite of American hesitation. As the committee saw it, Europe was never more in need of a strong and benevolent international organization. The Allied Supreme Council had little authority left; Hungarian reaction seemed likely to spread; the lack of a coherent Russian policy threatened anarchy and ruin to all of its border states; the economic crisis was spreading throughout all of Europe. If Europe could not count on American collaboration, then it must learn "mutual aid." In short, the doubt about America was a challenge to Europe to make the League effective.

This advice was a far cry from the ILP position articulated by such prominent figures as Snowden and MacDonald, but on the issue of a possible alternative, the alliance with France, the Advisory Committee was as adamant as any group on the Labour Left. Such an alliance, the committee warned, was hardly compatible with the hope that the League of Nations would play an ever more important role in the affairs of Europe. France scarcely needed extraordinary protection against an exhausted Germany; the League would be weakened and perhaps destroyed by any special alliance formed among its members; any such system would set up armed camps leading, as in the past, to tension and conflict—these were some of the reasons cited. Accordingly, the Advisory Committee recommended an early declaration against revival of the old system of alliances within the new League and also against concluding a special alliance with any European power, that is, France. At the same time the Labour party should make it clear that it adhered firmly to the covenant of the League and demand that, once the League was formally constituted, the special ties between Britain and France should be dissolved. Europe, said the Advisory Committee, was a single society. It could be saved only by cooperation and the recognition of mutual rights.[17]

Within the next six weeks, Henderson began to make public use of the Advisory Committee recommendations. During the House of Commons debate on Russian policy that took place on November 17, he repeated almost verbatim the committee's words about the need for the League of Nations to begin its work, even though, as was inevitable in the light of official Labour pronouncements, he insisted on the parallel need to revise the peace treaty and expand the League's membership.[18] To a Reuters representative he denied that if America should abstain, the League would lose its practical value. If Europe must stand alone, he argued, it could only do so by "mutual aid." Asked whether he supported a French alliance, he again ran through the Advisory Committee's arguments, insisting, however, that French security must be guaranteed within a wider international system.[19] Already the role that Henderson was to play in taming and shaping the foreign policy views of Labour was beginning to emerge. Even when he repeated the arguments of the Labour extremists—as he was often to do during the next couple of years—his words and his tone consistently revealed the gulf that separated him from the more intransigent of his fellow Labourites.

The future of Germany and the fate of Russia competed with the inadequacies of the League of Nations as the major international issues of these early postwar years. Of the three, Labour's attention was more and more absorbed, during 1919 and 1920, by the Russian question, particularly by the government's intervention in Russia. The well-known story need not be repeated in detail, but it seems plausible to argue that the attention devoted to the Russian issue by all groups in the labor movement helped draw attention away not only from the German question but also from a careful consideration of how best to make use of the infant Society of Nations. The deeply rooted pacifism that swept through Labour's ranks after the war was certainly one element that impelled the Labour opposition in Parliament and the trade union leadership outside to demand that Britain not become involved in the Russo-Polish conflict. In addition, Labour as a whole was convinced that the handling of Russia was a test of the government's attitude toward a wide-ranging complex of international problems in the postwar world. As one observer put it, the hopes for an end to militarism, the reduction of armaments, open diplomacy, a more unified Europe, and a more secure peace all were tied up with the question. Labour looked upon better relations with Russia much as it viewed better relations with Germany. So long as either nation was resentful, suspicious, or goaded into intransigence by the wartime victors, most Labour spokesmen argued, the pacification of Europe would be blocked by the militaristic fruits of xenophobic fears.[20] Even for the leaders of Labour who had no illusions about the character of the Bolshevik regime, the right of the "people" of Russia to make their own decisions was taken as axiomatic. Given this frame of reference, it followed almost automatically, when the trade unions succeeded in preventing the shipment of munitions to the Poles, that the action should have given considerable impetus to a more activist policy in all matters concerned with foreign affairs. Equally, while the Council of Action set up in 1920 may have had less to do with forcing the withdrawal of troops from Russia than has often been assumed in Labour accounts, many within the Labour party drew the lesson, from these experiences of 1919 and 1920, that only an aggressive and uncompromising stand would effectively promote the peaceful, equalitarian society desired by its members.[21]

Not just Russia but the whole future of Europe appeared to some in the

Labour party to be jeopardized by the dangerous fires burning in eastern Europe. The Independent Labour party was little disposed toward an uncritical enthusiasm for the League of Nations. Having argued for an organization in which each member was prepared to subordinate its own interests to the "larger welfare of the world," the ILP now viewed the League as no more than the politicians' formal concession to a popular expectation.[22] Anticipating little, these Labour left-wingers were, for all that, not prevented from making use of the League whenever it might serve to illuminate the mistakes of those who had created it. As the Polish armies plunged deep into the Ukraine in the late spring of 1920, the ILP remembered that Poland had been admitted into the League of Nations and that the conditions of the covenant were supposed to be obligatory upon her. Since the covenant provided that no member state might make war without the League's consent, the Supreme Council, which the ILP press realistically equated with the leadership of the League, could not relieve itself from responsibility for the actions of Poland. That country, "bankrupt, and famine stricken and typhus ridden," could not continue the war for a single day without the material support of the Great Powers. And the new war, which those powers condoned, ensured that the popular hope for peaceful international relationships and the reconstruction of Europe's economic life would be indefinitely postponed despite the League of Nations.[23] Given such an assessment, it was hardly to be expected that the ILP—or indeed the Labour Left in general—would give much credence to those who argued the case for pursuing Labour's international aims through the new instruments created by "capitalist" governments.

While the Russian situation absorbed most of the ILP's passion during the larger part of 1920, attention was also directed toward Germany and France. The new Germany continued to be portrayed as the innocent victim of an impossible settlement. The Kapp Putsch of March 1920, a right-wing effort to overthrow the German government, was seen as the inevitable result of the maintenance of the blockade and of a treaty that left the German people without hope. Responsibility for its outbreak rested upon the Allied governments. Similarly, surveying preparations for the plebiscite in Upper Silesia, the ILP could see nothing beyond "wickedness" and "crime." The territory had been uninterruptedly German for six centuries. Its cultural, industrial, and economic life had been wholly developed by Germans. But now France, motivated by blind hatred and fear of Gemany, was using its influence, here as elsewhere, to prevent the economic restoration of her enemy. So long as France was permitted to wield her disproportionate influence in European politics, there was no likelihood that the Allies would adopt a sensible policy. Vindictiveness ensured that the League of Nations would persist as a "union

of conquerors" and that the "peace to end peace" would long remain un-
stable.[24]

The view that the League was in reality a committee of the Allies, a "League
of Pharisees," appeared in ILP propaganda as part of a systematic campaign
of denigration. Its most colorful proponent, as was perhaps to be expected,
was Ramsay MacDonald. Not yet reinstated in the leadership of the Labour
party nor even in the House of Commons, he continued to be closely associated for a few postwar years with the ILP position on foreign affairs. He found
it heart-breaking, in the face of the Polish invasion of Russia and the French
occupation of additional German territory, that the League of Nations should
confess to the world that it had "no independence, no power, no will, no self-
respect." The Supreme Council decided everything—mandates, wars, territories; and the "poor League of Nations has not even the mind of a chicken to
protest." If the "gentlemen now composing the League" would do their duty
and draw the reins on France and Poland, they would win the people's respect
and support. Until they did so, no one would take the least interest in them.
The League could be regarded as stillborn.[25] MacDonald's angry dismissal of
the League is revealing, coming as it did from one of the few Labour leaders
who, almost from the beginning of our period, saw the need to persuade
Labour to accommodate itself in some fashion to the postwar settlement. In
these early years, even he felt it necessary to denigrate the League, question
its possible efficacy, and consign it to the scrap heap of other lost causes.

Philip Snowden was as intense as MacDonald, if somewhat less heart-
broken. Addressing the ILP's annual conference from the chair, he found in
what had happened since the armistice a complete vindication of the party's
opposition to the war. It had understood that the whole propaganda of the
struggle was based upon lies. Now the peace treaties exposed the real aims for
which millions of men had been killed or maimed. Great hopes that had been
entertained for a League of Nations were doomed to disappointment. The
covenant was an instrument for the exaction of the terms of the treaties.
Those treaties had destroyed the economic unity of Central Europe. If peace
was to be secured and famine eliminated, two things were urgently needed, a
drastic revision of the treaties and international cooperation to set the wheels
of industry moving again. Neither was likely to be undertaken by the present
rulers of Europe. In their hands, predicted Snowden, "matters will go from
bad to worse until the whole of Europe is economically ruined, and universal
chaos and famine overwhelm civilisation."[26]

Neither MacDonald nor Snowden was hopeful about the revision of the
postwar settlement at this stage, but both were incurable optimists when
compared with H. N. Brailsford. To him, a Europe in shambles was the direct

creation of the economic system socialism hoped eventually to replace. Liberals, he wrote, believed that the League of Nations could begin to work or that the treaties could now be revised by general consent. Such people turned a blind eye to capitalist imperialism, the real force that governed the world. Its excesses might be pruned away by men of goodwill like Asquith or the Frenchman Caillaux, if they were ever returned to office, but they would be the last to give away the power that enabled economic gain to be extorted by naval and military mastery. The idealism of the League of Nations, the Christian internationalism of a Robert Cecil, the humanity of a part of the Liberal press testified to the genuineness of the English civilization. But in the light of the willful ruin of Europe, they seemed, nevertheless, a pathetic attempt to build upon an unsound foundation. While the profit motive ruled, while competition rather than social service was the law, in a word, while capitalism survived, it was vain to dream of a genuine internationalism.[27]

Within this conceptual framework, Brailsford found fault with virtually every element in the peace settlement. Mandates were no more than a disguise to cover the fact of annexation, millions of Germans were imprisoned in unwanted subjection to Czech rule, and Germany herself had quite simply been robbed of the means and the motive for production. The fragmentation of Europe under the purported fulfillment of national self-determination was in reality a scheme to impose British and French control more easily. "The Balkanisation of Central and Eastern Europe has meant not the reality of national independence for these peoples," he insisted, "but their subjection to Western Imperialism."[28] Western imperialism, in turn, meant the policy of contemporary France. Brailsford shared in full measure the ILP resentment that France should now dominate the continent, threatening to overshadow its neighbors as in the Napoleonic days a century past.[29]

Could anything be done to remedy the situation? Brailsford offered some characteristic suggestions. He proposed, not very optimistically, that if Labour ever came to power it should make an end to the "informal alliance of the Victors" and work for the cancellation of the war debts and a general reduction in German reparations. In addition, he returned to his wartime proposal for an "Economic League of Nations," to constitute a vast economic unit and so undo the mischief of Balkanization. He proposed to include the British Empire, Germany, Russia, Italy, all the former Hapsburg states, and any other state that cared to join. Contemporary observers may see in the proposal a prevision of the European Economic Community, but it is not hard to discern from this list that, at least obliquely, Brailsford's program was directed against France. He rather thought that France would not look with favor upon such a development: "In that case a rivalry would ensue in Europe between her military League and our own Economic League."[30] But he was not really sanguine of success. In this respect, his passionate vision was an accurate reflection of the underlying assumptions of the policy makers in the Independent Labour party. Rejecting capitalism and all its works, ILP spokesmen used positive proposals for change as tactical weapons in the constant battle against the existing economic and political system. They required no particular hope of success to serve that purpose.

Publicly, most leaders of the Union of Democratic Control continued to match the revisionist demands of the Independent Labour party. Arthur Ponsonby, for example, mirrored this official attitude at an international conference of the UDC in July. Describing the League of Nations as a caricature of the original idea, he nevertheless considered that it should not be swept away. Its defects were shocking, yet there were good points worth retaining. The UDC could do much to influence governments to amend the League's constitution and to build in its place a genuinely representative body. As usual, the conference passed a unanimous resolution calling for open diplomacy, popular control of foreign policy, and a "real" League of Nations consisting of representatives of all nations. These demands, along with the ubiquitous cry for an immediate revision of the peace treaties, continued as before to be the core of the UDC program in the tense summer of 1920.[31]

It is difficult to square such official pronouncements with the constant stream of hostile commentary that flowed through the pages of E. D. Morel's *Foreign Affairs*, the supposed organ of the UDC. Morel's editorial assertions might almost have been designed deliberately to undercut the purported purposes of UDC resolutions. Many people, he wrote, were now being induced to support the League of Nations, although they were by no means satisfied with its constitution or its conduct. But they argued that it would be "what the people choose to make it" and they must contribute to its improvement. If they faced the facts, they would realize that they were wasting their energies. The governments controlling the League acted daily to defeat the very end that body was created to achieve. "Wars are made possible by secret diplomacy, bad territorial arrangements, and blocking of nations from getting of raw materials needed for modern industry," he declared. "All these still exist. . . . The only possible chance of making any headway against the Institution of War is to expose the specific agencies which make wars inevitable, under a capitalistic form of society."[32]

Indeed, the League of Nations, whether reformed or not, was scarcely Morel's major concern. While *Foreign Affairs* continued to hammer away at the issues that troubled all of the Left during 1920—the invasion of Russia, the impotence of the League, the evils of secret diplomacy—Morel's own personal crusade increasingly centered on redress of the wrongs he felt had been inflicted upon Germany. More than Keynes or Angell, more even than Brailsford and various ILP stalwarts, Morel regarded the Versailles treaty as criminal and self-defeating. Writing to Dundee after he had agreed to become the constituency's Labour candidate, he charged that the treaty was framed with the deliberate intention of annihilating the German people both economically and—in a quite literal sense—physically. It was certainly succeeding in doing so. But apart from the wickedness of the policy, it was a suicidal one from the point of view of the interests of Britain's working class. Germany before the war was the economic pivot of Europe. In large measure the prosperity of the greater part of the continent of Europe depended upon German industry and prosperity. Hence, if Germany finally went to pieces, the economic reconstruction of Europe would be utterly impossible, with incalculable effects upon the British people.[33]

Reasoned economic analysis, however, was not Morel's chief stock in trade. Much more characteristic were his undoubtedly sincere but emotionally supercharged strictures against France for its "victimization" of the German people. Nowhere does this appear more clearly than in a sensational pamphlet, *The Horror on the Rhine*, which Morel issued in August 1920 under the UDC imprint. Passionately opposed to French policy, he drew a frightening but warped picture of the French occupation. Curiously enough, the man who had been the outstanding defender of the colored peoples in the Belgian Congo now was almost hysterical in denouncing the French authorities for their use of colored troops in the Rhineland. Tales of rape and rapine, officially supported brothels for colored soldiers, and the spread of venereal disease paraded through the pamphlet as Morel tried to demonstrate a "deliberate, calculated, purposeful" plot. France had introduced thousands of African troops, "men in the prime of life, separated from their women-kind," to terrorize German womanhood and break the will of all Germans. Britain, he concluded, must oppose the French lust for power in every way possible. The present militarist and imperialist France had no more use for a real League of Nations than did the militarist and imperialist influences in Great Britain. French policy was to forge a military alliance with Britain, America, and Belgium against the Germany of tomorrow, which French militarism was goading into a fury of revengeful emotion. America wanted no part of the alliance. If Belgium chose to rush to her ruin that was her concern. But the question for Britain was: "Are our infant sons to be doomed to a violent and senseless death in manhood because French militarism is sowing seeds of ineradicable hatred in Europe?"[34]

Even before *The Horror on the Rhine* appeared, the *Daily Herald* had been protesting the use of black troops in Germany, where the French were accused of permitting "sexual horrors that will not bear description."[35] Constantly, during 1920, the *Herald* hammered out a repetitive refrain of bitter criticism and loose accusations against the leaders of the ex-Allied nations. Most of George Lansbury's collaborators on the paper—W. N. Ewer, Francis Meynell, William Mellor—were at this stage supporters of the Russian Communists. But it was Lansbury himself, passionately sincere, but unsystematic, often ill-informed, and seeing the international scene through heavily pacifist glasses, who dominated the paper during these days of its major influence on the labor movement.[36] Throughout the year, as the inept handling of a subvention offered by the Bolshevik government added immeasurably to the *Herald*'s difficulties, Lansbury continued his defense of the Russian regime. His support of the Bolsheviks extended rather far beyond a mere sympathy for the victims of aggression. In Central Europe he saw the same forces at work. Here, his leader writer declared, Germany was confronted with the alternatives of two dictatorships. One possibility was a dictatorship of the military, leading inevitably to a revival of the monarchy, a reborn imperialism, and finally to further revolution—since no military dictatorship could be permanent any longer. The alternative was a dictatorship of the proletariat—"the supremacy of the organised workers"—leading to the final overthrow of capitalism and its creatures and the establishment of a "second great Communist Republic."[37]

Whatever may be thought of Lansbury's conception of the dictatorship of the proletariat, his conviction of Germany's wrongs did not prevent him from passionately criticizing the current leaders of that country, no less than the extreme groups trying to drive them out of office. Again and again, as at the time of the right-wing attempt to overthrow the Weimar Republic in the Kapp Putsch, he condemned not only the "militarism" of the conservatives, but also the "half-concealed and therefore more dangerous militarism of the pseudo-Socialists and 'moderate' parties."[38] Even the French occupation of Frankfurt was explained in part as the deliberate choice of the Muller government in Germany. The German leaders could not stand up to France because they were too busy fighting their own people at home. "They prefer to suffer invasion rather than to run the risk of revolution." In this view, Lansbury charged, they were supported by British politicians who, having destroyed German trade and appropriated German colonies, were now concerned to use the German government to smash Bolshevism. For no other reason had Britain opposed the French move in the Rhineland. The French still wanted "a little more vengeance"; the British had already attained their ends.[39]

Other than revolution, Lansbury had little to offer in the way of a constructive approach to Europe's problems. The League of Nations, he was
convinced, was dead. It had, in fact, never lived; from its inception it had been
a machine without a spirit. And when it continued to reject Russia and Germany, Lansbury declared that it had stultified all its pretension to international authority. Its past record had been black enough. The refusal to expand
the League was the end. Perhaps there was some hope in the birth of a new
International, but it must be definitely and uncompromisingly socialist, utterly free from any entanglement with capitalist parties or a capitalist policy.[40]

The posture of the Labour Left appears to be a reasonably accurate reflection of the main currents of Labour opinion throughout 1920. As we have
noted, support for Russia, sympathy for Germany, and suspicion of the
League of Nations were its major themes, whatever might have been particular differences in detail. Even the trade unions shared generally in this Left
interpretation of the outstanding foreign policy issues. Absorbed as they were
by the Russian question, trade union leaders, it is true, were less concerned
with German suffering or the future of international organization. Nonetheless, the impact of the struggle over Russia left its mark. All through 1919 and
1920, despite the caution of mainstream industrial leaders like J. H. Thomas
and J. R. Clynes, men like Robert Smillie and Frank Hodges of the Miners'
Federation and Bob Williams of the Transport Workers had been successful in
persuading the Trades Union Congress to support direct action to stop intervention in Russia.[41] So successful, indeed, that even the cautious Thomas,
who agreed so little with their motives for supporting Russia that he compared the Bolshevists unfavorably with the German Kaiser, felt compelled to
swim with the tide.[42] As late as September 1920, he found it expedient, in his
presidential address to the TUC, to contrast the weakness of the League of
Nations with the growing power and influence of the International. At a time
when Thomas, better than most, knew how nonsensical it was to attribute
such strength to the divided International, it revealed how little faith the
trade unions had in the new machinery for foreign relations for him to
declare, even rhetorically, that in the direction of the International lay the
power to enforce peace.[43] In similar fashion, W. H. Hutchinson of the Amalgamated Society of Engineers seized the occasion of his chairman's address to
the Labour party to attack the peace treaties, brand the Supreme Council a
continuing military alliance of the victorious powers, and insist that those
powers had quietly and deliberately strangled the League of Nations almost at
the moment of its birth.[44] Examples might be multiplied, but they hardly
seem necessary to make the point that most trade union chieftains, insofar as

they concerned themselves with questions of foreign policy other than Russia, shared fairly completely the angry and sometimes hopeless attitudes of the Labour Left.

These attitudes, then, were almost universal among Labour leaders and their supporters. They extended not only into the trade unions, but well beyond the quarters usually influenced by the views of left-wing spokesmen. The *New Statesman* is a good case in point. Reflecting an almost Asquithian liberalism under the editorship of Clifford Sharp, it searched for whatever favorable signs it could find in the terms of the peace settlement. Yet Sharp, too, revealed his sympathy with Labour's approach over and over again. When the San Remo Conference earmarked the Syrian mandate for France and those of Palestine and Mesopotamia for Great Britain, the *New Statesman* wondered suspiciously if the substance of Article XXII, the mandates article of the League covenant, was in fact being honored. If not, then the whole mandatory system was nothing but a worthless scrap of paper. Criticism of the Allied refusal to permit the union of Austria with Germany paralleled the outlook of the Left, as did the wry observation that French occupation of the Frankfurt area had less to do with the enforcement of the Versailles treaty than with the aim of keeping Germany in subjection. Indeed, although the *New Statesman* did not condemn France as wholeheartedly as did a Brailsford or a Morel, it did in 1920 stress the opinion, which they would have seconded, that it was impossible to maintain, in time of peace, an entente between two countries so profoundly different in temperament and outlook as Great Britain and France.[45]

Even in the *Clarion*, where Robert Blatchford and his staff almost made it a point of honor to differ with the rest of the labor movement, there was general acceptance of the feeling that things had turned out badly. A League of Nations without Russia and Germany, to say nothing of the United States, was a "spurious article," while France's unilateral move into the Ruhr basin simply made the whole concept a "delusion and a mockery."[46] And J. R. Clynes, using the pages of *Clarion* to plead for support of the League whatever its defects, nevertheless confessed that he considered it to be almost helpless in face of America's unwillingness to participate and France's intransigence toward Germany.[47]

Yet Clynes was almost literally the only Labour leader to insist, without an overwhelming list of qualifications, that the new League could be made to work. Throughout the year, he reiterated that war could be exorcised only by turning to the newly devised instrument. Some Labour spokesmen, he told the House of Commons, had been offering an alternative suggestion—the broad, general, ambitious alternative of cementing friendship amongst the nations of the world on the basis of a great worldwide and international understanding, so as to make wars impossible. Unlike MacDonald, whose constant point of reference was the gradual development of an "international spirit," Clynes maintained that even if the nations of the world should all become socialist, some instrument must still be provided to adjust differences between countries. At present, he commented tartly, there were sufficient differences among socialists to caution against too great confidence in the amity of nations merely because they shared certain economic and political arrangements. If it was true that capitalist governments could not be trusted to avoid war, this was all the more reason for a strong League of Nations. It would reduce their temptation to engage in warlike measures and so contribute to greater security. Frankly admitting that Labour had not done enough to create a public opinion in favor of the League, Clynes publicly and repeatedly pleaded with his party to change its tactics so as to encourage the government to support it wholeheartedly.[48]

The role played by Clynes in tempering Labour's millennialism during this period is easily underestimated. Aside from an occasional ex-Liberal, his was almost the only Labour voice to be raised in the House of Commons on the fundamental questions of international policy.[49] As leader of the parliamentary party after Will Adamson's unfortunate endeavors, he managed to create the impression that its responsible heads stood strongly behind the League.[50] This was hardly the case, but Clynes's activities, in and out of Parliament, did much to prepare the way for a shift in Labour's position when his point of view was later buttressed by the Advisory Committee on International Questions and publicly emphasized by colleagues such as Arthur Henderson.

For the moment, Clynes's enthusiasm was not shared among the groups making up the Labour party. By way of illustration, the resolutions and agenda circulated in advance of the annual conference showed little interest in the existing League.[51] This was perhaps natural, but the attitude was confirmed by the party leaders. The conference passed a composite resolution that they supported, in which the emphasis was on the need for a "league of Peoples" with broad economic functions (as urged by the Independent Labour party), along with castigation of secret diplomacy, condemnation of the Polish war with Russia, and a similar list of familiar grievances.[52] Not Clynes but the Left continued to place its stamp on Labour's "official" foreign policy positions.

In similar fashion, behind the scenes the memoranda of the Advisory Committee on International Questions sounded a note of almost constant dissatisfaction. Thus the draft treaty with Turkey was branded for its flagrant violations of self-determination in Egypt, Cyprus, the Dodecanese, Smyrna, and

Eastern and Western Thrace, while the assignment of mandates agreed upon at San Remo appeared to make a mockery of the whole mandate idea. Chaos in Central Europe, the continuation of the blockade, and alleged British support for the Polish attack on Russia all rendered any talk of the League of Nations a "bad joke."[53] The Advisory Committee, to be sure, did give some attention to a scheme for a European federation within the League as it did to other projects for its improvement, but committee members apparently took little cheer from these suggestions.[54]

For one thing, the Advisory Committee was unhappy about its role in formulating Labour policy. Writing to the Executive in July, the committee protested that its work was not being used effectively, particularly by the parliamentary party. Parliament should be the best platform from which to put Labour's views before the country, yet its representatives continued to neglect international questions there. The Advisory Committee was concerned because its members were deeply pessimistic about conditions in Europe. The League of Nations, upon which high hopes had been based, was condemned to a "shadowy and hypocritical futility," not merely because Germany or Russia or America remained outside, nor even because its constitution was undemocratic. Such faults could be amended. The fatal obstacle was that if the League should attempt to function it would have to administer the impossible peace treaties. Only force could impose them, and only a military alliance could exert sufficient force. The present military alliance, governing Europe through the Supreme Council, was utterly incompatible with any true League of Nations. Should the Labour party, then, continue to demand revision of the treaties along constructive lines? The Advisory Committee was not especially anxious to take such a line. The broad fact was that capitalism, in its more extreme phases of imperialism and militarism, was shattering the material bases of civilization. It was not producing the goods. By smashing the German industrial machine and barricading off the Russian grainfields, it was creating the dearth of goods from which all peoples were in some measure suffering—"scarcity here, famine elsewhere." Literal ruin was coming from capitalism's lack of any principle of fraternity or cooperation.

To the Advisory Committee it seemed useless at this point to go on talking as though some little efforts to prune away this or that error from a treaty would be of help. "We achieve nothing practical in this way," its revealing letter to the Executive insisted, "while by adopting this pose of mild criticism, we miss our broad effect on the masses. Our task is not to deflect the Foreign Office a little from its crazy path. Our task is to make the masses understand the ruin wrought in the world by Imperialist Capitalism."[55] As yet unreconciled to the more cautious approach illustrated by Clynes, the Advisory Committee suggested that the Labour party undertake a campaign along the lines outlined in the letter. At this stage, it was far from adjusting its program to the perhaps unpalatable facts of life in the postwar world.

This despondent letter may have served as a kind of catharsis for its authors, for the committee was shortly to change its tack. Meanwhile, its melancholy tones were echoed in many quarters throughout the labor movement. During 1921 and 1922, the wartime hope that somehow the end of hostilities would usher in a new era continued to be mocked by events. Reparation figures were finally set, but Germany's ability to pay remained a violently controversial question. The Russo-Polish war came to an end, yet famine and chaos in Russia raised problems of tremendous complexity. When a plebiscite was held to establish Germany's boundaries in Upper Silesia, its results were interpreted so as to make the plebiscite meaningless. And meanwhile, the dangerous sparks of the Greco-Turkish conflict threatened to make the Eastern Question once again the catalyst of another European-wide conflagration. Most Labour spokesmen responded to each crisis almost predictably, again and again seeing the issues of the postwar world through eyes heavily clouded by suspicion of all the major Allied governments and in particular by their lack of confidence in their own.

E. D. Morel, for example, undeterred by the heart condition that was later to kill him, kept up his constant propaganda against the "German plot." Convinced, like a number of his ex-Liberal colleagues, of his superiority to rank and file and leaders alike, Morel often found it difficult to be patient with the Labour party's hesitations and qualifications on the German question.[56] Fed by such German publicists as Count Max Montgelas, he continued to publicize details of German suffering and humiliation, of Allied cruelty and insensitivity.[57] When Upper Silesia was partitioned in a compromise that may have been wise but certainly flouted the results of the League of Nations' own plebiscite, Morel added spice to the Union of Democratic Control's denunciation by branding the area the "latest Alsace-Lorraine" of Europe.[58] Even when the poison of right-wing intransigence began to pollute German public life, Morel found reasons to explain it away. After the murder of Walter Rathenau, Germany's brilliant Jewish foreign minister, *Foreign Affairs* declared that exasperation, which could not be directed against the foreign oppressor, turned naturally in Germany upon men like Rathenau. They were doing their best under impossible circumstances but were regarded as too submissive to implacable pressure and ceaseless insult. It was lamentable, thought Morel, but hardly surprising.[59] As French pressure on Germany during the reparation crisis of 1922 came to a head, Morel led the UDC in demanding that Britain immediately abandon her share of the indemnity and cancel the French war debt on condition, among others, that the Rhineland be evacuated by all Allied troops.[60] Seen in retrospect, this latter proposal seems the very essence of common sense, but it could make little impression at a time when France was preparing the ground for the Ruhr invasion of early 1923.

While German recovery and the revision of the Versailles treaty were his main concern, Morel continued also to plead for disarmament, for an end to "secret diplomacy," for a genuine peace with Russia, and finally for some kind of equity in the distribution of the world's store of raw materials and finished commodities.[61] His reactions to specific issues reflected these views. The Greco-Turkish war, he held, could be promptly settled if Britain honored repeated pledges made to Turkey, particularly by showing a willingness to evacuate Constantinople as soon as peace was concluded. Seizing upon the proposed security treaty with France as proof of the British government's blundering, Morel dramatized UDC opposition in a frightening picture of the helplessness of a Britain tied to the juggernaut of French militarism.[62] In the circumstances, he could find little hope in a League of Nations to which some of his Labour associates were beginning to look for possible solutions. Events merely confirmed his earlier judgments that the League would be useless until the Treaty of Versailles was rewritten and a peace of conquest replaced by terms of conciliation. Only on the basis of such a peace could an all-inclusive, "democratic" League with wide powers be created.[63] Consistently Morel underestimated the difficulties in the way of achieving his purposes, largely because he was convinced that most of them stemmed from policies deliberately adopted by the governments of France and Britain. Under his constant prodding, the UDC remained a substantial element holding the labor movement to a line of sweeping rejection of the existing international system well beyond the months of disappointment that followed the signing of the peace treaties.[64]

Morel's strictures took little account of the conciliatory spirit that marked most of Lloyd George's policy during 1921 and 1922. Despite the occupation of Duisburg, Ruhrort, and Dusseldorf in March, this policy had a promising success when Germany's total liability for reparations was finally negotiated by the spring of 1921. In Washington, Foreign Secretary Arthur Balfour represented Great Britain at the conference that, for the time at least, gave hope of heading off a costly naval race and guaranteeing the status quo in the Pacific. And at Cannes, early in 1922, the prime minister appeared to reach a virtual meeting of minds with Aristide Briand on the crucial issue of Anglo-French security against Germany.

Cannes was the turning point. Partly because the French press exploited public suspicion of Lloyd George's wiles, Briand, who seemed ready to move cautiously toward reconciliation with Germany, was driven from office. He was succeeded by the more rigid and uncompromising Raymond Poincaré. When, therefore, Lloyd George promoted his ambitious economic conference of the European powers at Genoa, Poincaré pointedly boycotted the meetings. In the event little was achieved except the defiant Russo-German treaty of Rapallo. Meanwhile, the Greco-Turkish conflict boiled to a climax. Here Lloyd George departed from his role as the pacificator of Europe and obstinately challenged Turkish belligerence. Ironically, it was largely on this issue, which brought his opposition from the Left to fever pitch, that he was forced to resign by his Tory coalitionists.

Throughout this period of controversial personal diplomacy, the weak and scattered Labour press more or less echoed Morel's recriminations. Left-wing newspaper critics followed the reparations negotiations with a characteristically jaundiced eye. Essentially, they charged that the Allies were making demands they knew to be economically impossible in order to make sure that Germany could not pay. When the agreement of May 1921 was reached, they insisted that the Germans would never be able to fulfill their promises. Sooner or later, Germany must default. And then sanctions, leaving aside their immorality, would hardly improve the situation. The only way to make Germany pay was by trade—yet Allied policy was deliberately killing off trade and thus creating unemployment at home while strangling Germany.[65] Even the *New Statesman*, a more or less unenthusiastic supporter of reparations, commented wryly that French public opinion still seemed to hope against hope that Germany would pay France's debts. While it reluctantly approved the March 8 sanctions at the outset, it soon came to regard the move as a "ridiculous" political and economic blunder.[66] Similarly, after applauding the reference of the Upper Silesian question to the League of Nations, the *New Statesman*, shocked by the award actually made, joined less sanguine Labour observers in regarding the decision as an enormous blunder, founded neither on justice nor common sense.[67] It is true that the *New Statesman* differed from other press supporters of Labour in applauding the proceedings of the Washington Conference. It even professed to see certain signs that the League of Nations was beginning to establish itself as a viable international organization.[68] Yet in a sense these differences tended to make all the more revealing the more frequent instances of its agreement with the more left-wing Labour press.

As Lloyd George made his pilgrimages from London and Cannes to Paris and Genoa, the possibility of an Anglo-French pact roused the Labour papers to a continued chorus of denunciation. While they put varying assessments on the validity of France's fears, they were at one in rejecting the project for an alliance as the road to safety. To Lansbury's *Herald*, France was the "mad dog" and President Alexandre Millerand the "bad man" of Europe. The Entente itself was the "curse of Europe and the padlock on the gate to a new world." These cliches were the emotional incantations of an evaluation that took it for granted that the "world imperialism" of Britain and the "European imperialism" of France must diverge and eventually break apart.[69] Accordingly, the *Herald*, along with such ILP organs as the *Labour Leader* and *Bradford Pioneer*, accepted the breakdown of Lloyd George's policy, particularly at Genoa, with scarcely disguised satisfaction.[70] And as usual, the *New Statesman*, while regretful over the failures of Cannes and Genoa and sympathetically aware of the reasons for French insecurity, nevertheless repudiated French proposals for a hard-and-fast alliance as utterly alien to British traditions, interests, and ideals.[71]

These reactions were the day-to-day evidence that most Labour attitudes were not shifting during 1921 and 1922. They reflected in particular how strong an influence the thinking of the ILP ideologues still exerted in all quarters of the labor movement. In the ILP old-line Socialists joined with newer recruits, usually pacifist ex-radicals, to continue an interpretation of the postwar world that left little room for adjustment as the conflict receded into the background. Characteristic of the ILP position were two long resolutions passed unanimously at its annual conference in March 1921. In brief, these resolutions reiterated the earlier refrain of the party. They called among other things for the democratic conduct of foreign policy, the establishment of a real League of Nations, general disarmament, and equal access to the resources and markets of the world for all nations. Above all, the ILP was concerned with the immediate revision of the peace treaties on lines that would admit that the "past vicious imperialism" and foreign policy of the Great Powers were responsible for the war.[72] These general positions were related, during the course of the year, to specific developments that elicited an unbroken chorus of denunciation. One of the major themes was the failure of the League of Nations. It was blamed for not preventing Polish aggression in Upper Silesia and Vilna, for acquiescence in British imperialist designs in Mesopotamia, for impotence on the question of German reparations, for the lack of any significant move toward disarmament, and for the militaristic posture of France. At East Woolwich, where he stood for Parliament and was defeated by 683 votes, Ramsay MacDonald repeated this theme in his election address and other ILP spokesmen followed suit. No League of Nations, ran the unchanging argument, could be of value so long as it was controlled by imperialist and capitalist governments and so long as it held to the notion not of peace but of revenge.[73]

In the circumstances of the time such a posture implied that the ILP proposals for revision of the covenant were really proposals that it be revised out of existence. Equally negative were the reactions to other specific issues as 1921 gave way to 1922. Lloyd George's secrecy at Genoa and Russia's virtual isolation there shared the ILP's wrath with the mishandling of German reparations, the mistakes of the Washington Conference, and the proposed military pact with France.[74] Above all, however, 1922 saw the ILP bring to a focus the underlying pacifism that increasingly informed its analysis of the international scene. Openly opposed to any war, defensive or aggressive, ILP members argued that the banning or limitation of particular weapons was meaningless. Only total disarmament could ensure lasting peace.[75] This theme was officially accepted in the first of the "no more war" resolutions that in the next few years were to become a common feature of the propaganda of the ILP, and from time to time of the Labour party as well. At the 1922 conference a majority of the delegates, despite their verbal commitment to a species of class-war doctrine, voted down an amendment to interpret the party's antiwar stand as a rejection only of "capitalist" wars. They then proceeded to adopt without further discussion a resolution expressing the conference's opinion that socialists everywhere should refuse to support every war entered into by any government, even if such a war was nominally a defensive one. Meanwhile, the conference "recommended" a general strike as a means of combatting the threat of war and pledged to use every propaganda effort to promote such a strike if war became a likelihood. Declaring that mutual confidence and goodwill between nations could only be shown effectively by the abandonment of all material preparations for war, the resolution urged the abolition of armaments, the disbanding of all military, naval, and air forces, and the prohibition of the manufacture and import or export of munitions of war.[76] The conference resolution, it almost goes without saying, patently ignored the experience of the socialist parties at the outbreak of war in 1914, indicating perhaps that its intent was more rhetorical than a firm proposal for action.

While the ILP was developing its inflexible position, the trade unions gave little attention to international events. In 1921 they were deeply involved in the bitter coal strike that led to the collapse of the Triple Alliance and the disillusioning shock of "Black Friday." The following year the growing slump and the serious spread of unemployment absorbed the greater part of union attention. At the annual meetings of the Trades Union Congress, for example, delegates spent little time and appeared to have less concern with questions of foreign policy. It is true that various resolutions were properly adopted, calling for, among other things, the use of the League of Nations wherever possible, but even these resolutions emphasized refrains familiar in left-wing Labour circles.

In 1921 and again in 1922, such moderate leaders as J. R. Clynes and J. H. Thomas still considered it necessary to apologize for their defection from the spirit of all-out militancy. In so doing, they were responding to the temper of their TUC cohorts. Clynes, as noted, was one of the few leaders of Labour enthusiastically to urge that the League of Nations be supported in its various day-to-day activities. Nevertheless, he too felt compelled to admit the absence of "that representative and truly democratic machinery" without which a real League of Nations could not work. Noting that peace could ultimately be assured only by universal working class solidarity, he repudiated "a League of Diplomats—a League of secret diplomats." And a year later, Thomas, when he introduced a resolution on Corfu, was also moved to preface it by an apology for the inadequacy of the League as then constituted. Finally, while the various resolutions were approved, they were automatically adopted with relatively little discussion and, so far as can be judged, made little impact upon the conference.[77]

Many of the delegates, far from being enthusiastic for a League of Nations to keep the peace, clearly agreed with one V. Beacham of the Operative House and Ship Painters, who mirrored ILP sentiment in demanding a firm statement that workers would engage in a general strike in case of war.[78] A common theme was suspicion of the capitalist governments and of the international instruments they had devised. A typical, not unique, example of this standpoint was the presidential address of R. B. Walker in 1922. He argued that the League of Nations was not a real League—there was evidence enough of that already. "When we have . . . Workers' Governments in the different countries of the world," he told the congress, "the hope of a genuine agreement between them will be nearer its fulfillment. Then, and only then, will international understandings be fully possible. . . . We know that capitalism cannot build a new world, and we believe that we can."[79]

Since the weak parliamentary delegation of the Labour party was made up largely of trade unionists, it is not surprising that Labour's position on foreign affairs received little ventilation in the House of Commons. Indeed, aside from an occasional suggestion that the League of Nations might be used to settle the reparations problem or an occasional caveat against French policy, the parliamentary party contributed virtually nothing to the public definition of foreign policy stances in 1921 and 1922.[80] The failure of Labour M.P.'s to state their case in Parliament, like the perfunctory discussion of international issues at the TUC conferences, should not be described without one qualification. The parliamentary Labour party and the General Council of the TUC did join the National Executive of the Labour party on several occasions in 1921 and 1922 to issue formal manifestos condemning the exorbitant reparations bill and the rapaciousness of France and opposing the proposed Anglo-French security pact.[81] But the fact still remains that, aside from these almost routine gestures, the parliamentarians and trade unionists alike were scarcely disposed to do more than criticize. Certainly they contributed little, for the moment, to the shaping of a constructive foreign policy for Labour.

Probably more effective than parliamentary spokesmen, at least within the labor movement, were the pamphlets issued during this period by the Labour party. Prepared under the general supervision of the Advisory Committee on International Questions, such brief policy statements were more important for Labour than for the Conservatives or Liberals, if only because the Labour press was so weak and inadequate. Characteristic of these publications during 1921 was one entitled *Unemployment, the Peace and the Indemnity*. Authored by H. N. Brailsford, its fundamental theme was the familiar attack on the peace treaties and a demand for their revision. In some ways even more revealing were two pamphlets dealing with the reorganization of the Foreign Office and the control of foreign policy. Published under the party's imprint, they attacked secrecy and the lack of parliamentary control of diplomacy and proposed a far-reaching reform of the diplomatic and consular corps. Both pamphlets charged that the Foreign Office was the refuge of special privilege and outlined schemes to assure that merit should govern selection and promotion within the Foreign Service.[82] What stands out is the continued indication of Labour party support for proposals that had long been the stock-in-trade of the UDC and of many of the ex-Liberal recruits to the labor movement. As yet, then, the aims of these groups remained a real influence on the propaganda of the Labour party.

Ideas similar to those of the UDC and the ex-Liberals were prominent at the annual conferences of the Labour party. At Brighton in 1921, for example, a long resolution on the peace treaties and reparations was introduced by J. H. Hudson of the ILP and seconded by the fiery James Kirkwood. Condemning militarism and imperialism, the motion likewise indicted the peace treaties for flouting the terms of the Armistice. After demanding revision of the treaties, it then went on to call for the equitable exploitation of the world's resources and the protection of native interests in "non-adult" colonial areas. Finally, tacked on to this composite resolution was an appeal for "the communication to the House of Commons and the public of full and prompt information upon all Foreign and Colonial negotiations, it being, in particular, expressly laid down that no Treaty or Convention of any kind shall be binding on this country, or will be adhered to by any future Labour Government, unless it has been ratified and confirmed by Parliament." This demand for parliamentary ratification of all treaties stemmed directly from Labour's characteristic suspicion of secret "capitalistic" diplomacy, a suspicion not confined to the Labour left wing during this period. A further indication of the ubiquitousness of this frame of mind may be gleaned from the fact that the only discussion of the resolution came in a wholehearted endorsement by Norman Angell, after which it was carried unanimously.[83]

At the same conference, trade union speakers stood as one with the Labour Left in their condemnation of what was transpiring in Europe. John Bromley of the Amalgamated Society of Locomotive Engineers, for example, proposed the resolution warning against the project for an Anglo-French alliance. Such an alliance, argued Bromley, was intended to give a free hand to British and French imperialists. Imperialism in turn led to conflict. So long as the capitalist system lasted there was bound to be war. An alliance would merely encourage the truculent military party in France to precipitate the next war more quickly. Labour's opposition to the alliance may well have been a reasonable position, but the manner of the opposition is enlightening. Bromley's speech hardly reflected the temperate and pragmatic caution about international issues so often associated with the trade union leaders or for that matter with most of the leaders of the Labour party. Yet the resolution, like its ILP companion, was carried unanimously, this time without any debate.[84] Too much, perhaps, should not be made of the contents of these 1921 resolutions, but their tone and the spirit in which they were proposed add to the evidence of Labour's disenchantment with the shape of the postwar world and of the essentially negative character of its criticism.

Attacks upon the military party in France were not merely rhetoric touched off by the emotional atmosphere of a party conference. Over the course of the next year persistent opposition to French policy was a constant theme in Labour publications and meetings. The Advisory Committee on International Questions was particularly alert to the threat of a French alliance. It capped its consideration, early in 1922, with the drafting of a resolution for submission to the National Executive of the party. The Advisory Committee opposed the pact, first, because such a treaty might involve Britain in a war owing to the actions of an ally over whom it had no control and, second, because the Labour party favored a real and inclusive League of Nations with which military alliances were fundamentally inconsistent.[85] Presented to the National Joint Council of the Labour party, the parliamentary party, and the

Trades Union Congress in almost exactly the words used by the Advisory Committee, the resolution was published as a manifesto on February 1, 1922. Subsequent meetings were followed by conferences with the French Socialist party and the General Confederation of Trade Unions to ensure a common stand in opposition to the project. The interchange of opinion was still going on when the question of an alliance was swallowed up in the broader issues of Franco-British relations that surfaced at the Genoa Conference. Again British Labour chieftains communicated with their French and Belgian counterparts, this time in the face of a threat that the military pressure on Germany might be intensified. The result was a resolution, adopted unanimously, condemning the threatened military occupation of the Ruhr and calling upon the League of Nations to appoint an impartial court to deal with the various difficulties arising from the execution of the postwar treaties.[86]

The Edinburgh Conference of the Labour party substantially followed the lines laid down in these various manifestos. In presenting a long, complex resolution for the Executive Committee, Tom Shaw summarized it as advocating a fixed sum and fixed methods of payment for German reparations, hands off Russia, and opposition to individual pacts and the balance of power. As usual, the resolution called for the revision of the Versailles treaty including the familiar plea for a "real" League of Nations. More revealing than any of its terms was Ramsay MacDonald's seconding speech. While he did not speak for the ILP, his support for the international resolution reflected, if somewhat imprecisely, the posture of that party within Labour. In the general context of a rather ill-defined pacifism, MacDonald noted that the resolution contained nothing new. It was like a confession of faith made by the Labour party year after year until one day that confession would be carried out in world policy. It turned to the French and said, "Why do you go back to your military ideas of pacts and force and so on? Have they ever defended you? It is perfectly true that you are afraid trouble may come. It is perfectly true that you see a cloud beyond the Rhine. It is perfectly true that you want security; but will you tell us when an army ever made you secure?" Clearly enough, the answer was never. In characteristic fashion, passionately, movingly, and quite vaguely, he brought his speech to its peroration: "The League of Nations,—a society of nations, a community of nations, united not merely in common interest and common sentiment, united not merely to produce comfort, happiness, human values, human wealth, human riches: that was their idea and that was the only idea that would save Europe from further wars, and that was embodied in this programme."

Much more concrete than MacDonald's rousing words were two amendments proposed from the floor. One was moved by E. D. Rowlinson of the

Sheffield Federated Trades and Labour Council and seconded by Josiah Wedgwood, another of the ex-Liberals in the Labour party. It asked the party to repudiate in advance all responsibility for any military alliance or pact entered into by the British government. The second amendment was proposed by an ILP delegate. Taking issue with the original resolution because it called merely for limitation of armaments, it requested that the British government take the initiative in making a definite proposal for immediate universal disarmament by mutual agreement. Both amendments were accepted with little difficulty from the Executive of the party and incorporated in the statement finally endorsed by unanimous vote of the conference. From the point of view of public rhetoric, the resolution reflected substantial agreement within the labor movement. Its demand that the government use the machinery of an extended League of Nations wherever possible might have appeared unnecessary to the militant cohort in the Labour party, but for the most part its thrust was very similar to the position articulated by the Independent Labour party earlier in the year.[87]

This parallelism is made strikingly evident by the fate of a second resolution that came before the conference. It will be recalled that 1922 witnessed the first of the ILP's "no more war" resolutions. Here at Edinburgh that same policy was urged upon the Labour party as a whole. Calling upon socialists and organized workers to declare that they would support no war whatever, R. C. Wallhead of the ILP introduced the proposal in a short speech heavily laden with bitter memories of 1914. As at the ILP conference, an amendment was quickly tabled. Tom Kennedy of the parliamentary party insisted that the working classes should be free to support any nation forced by armed aggression to defend its independence or its democratic institutions. Pointing out that the resolution was simply a pious statement of pacific intentions, he insisted that Labour must realistically face the probability that force would be necessary and sometimes justified in dealing, for example, with aggression. Using the words so popular with all segments of the labor movement, Kennedy declared that he too looked forward to the time when the League of Nations would not be a League of Governments, but a League of Peoples organized to maintain the world's peace. But, and this was the point of his amendment, the League of Nations, however organized, would be futile if it did not have the means to enforce its decisions.

This first faint glimmer of acceptance of the contemporary character of international politics was, ironically, the position of the moribund Social Democratic Federation, of which Kennedy and the seconder of his amendment were members. It was accepted, however, by only a small segment of the conference delegates. The reasons for its rejection were perhaps best summarized by Robert Smillie of the Miners' Federation. Kennedy, he noted, had said that even it they passed the resolution they would still have to have means to assist any nation that was wrongly invaded; "but if they succeeded in the theory that was laid down in the resolution it would really convert humanity to their way of thinking and there would be no nation in a position to be aggressive to another nation." This millennial outcome was to be achieved by propaganda, by endeavoring to get the labor movements in other nations to set their face against war.

When the vote on the amendment was taken, it was overwhelmingly defeated. The numbers, 3,231,000 to 194,000, reflected the enormous weight of the big battalions in the trade union delegations. Subsequently, the following resolution was passed by a show of hands: "That this Conference is of opinion that the Socialist and Labour Parties of all nations should agree to oppose any War entered into by any Government, whatever the ostensible object of the war, and asks the Labour Party delegates to bring forward this policy at the next International Socialist Congress."[88] Thus the Labour party joined the ILP in what appeared to be an almost root-and-branch pacifism. Later developments were to indicate that few members of the labor movement had really thought through the implications of "no more war"—nor indeed had really meant what they seemed to be voting for. Nevertheless, the Edinburgh Conference demonstrates clearly enough how much the sentiments of the left wing and especially of the ILP dominated the Labour party's view of international questions well into 1922.

, At the same time, while Labour was publicly still vehement in its denunciations of the evil machinations of all the Great Powers, a perceptible change in emphasis began to take place in the private deliberations of the Labour party's advisors. The majority of the Advisory Committee on International Questions began to shift ground. The committee's July 1920 letter, rejecting the League of Nations out of hand, seems, for example, to have marked the nadir of postwar pessimism among them.[89] By early 1922, the advisory body was prepared to consider the League as a "real beginning" in international cooperation and to suggest that with different governments in power it would be capable of improvement both in form and in spirit. Even at this time, however, the Advisory Committee centered its support for the League mainly in pacifist arguments. "The League for which British Labour stands," declared one of its draft reports, "is an instrument of internationalism and of pacifism, a new method which will in actual fact substitute pacific settlement for war, impartial international decisions for violence and threats of violence with which at present independent states seek to impose their will or gain their ends in international disputes and cooperation for hostility and competition."[90] Accordingly, the Advisory Committee looked upon the progress of disarmament as the real test of the League's genuineness, good faith, and efficiency.

This point of view was shared, indeed overtaken, by Arthur Henderson as he worked out the pattern of his own approach to foreign policy. It would be misleading to assert that from the beginning he had a clear vision of the direction in which he was moving. His ideas, like those of members of the Advisory Committee, gradually developed as the shape of the postwar world began to be revealed. As we have seen, in his 1919 pamphlet, *The Peace Terms*, Henderson reflected most of the attitudes then prevalent in Labour circles. But by 1922 he and his advisors apparently felt that the time was ripe to modify the orientation of Labour policy. His new outlook was given clear expression when he published an important policy statement on *Labour and Foreign Affairs*. Depending heavily upon the proposals of the Advisory Committee on International Questions, it nevertheless demonstrated as well how much Henderson had changed his views since 1919.

Labour and Foreign Affairs was a full-dress survey of international policy. In most cases it mirrored the attitudes already described in this chapter. Thus, to cite an example, Henderson had a good deal to say about the substitution of open diplomacy for the methods traditionally employed. He paraded the arguments for the periodic revision of treaties, for parliamentary ratification of all foreign agreements, and for a parliamentary Foreign Affairs Committee to check executive intrigue and secret commitments. Similarly, he attacked the handling of the reparations question, the extended Allied occupation of the Rhineland, and Lloyd George's Near Eastern policy. In all of this he was clearly on familiar territory. But significantly, when Henderson outlined his arguments for supporting the League of Nations, however ineffective it might be, he broke fresh ground. Like the Advisory Committee, he looked to the League as the only means by which disarmament could be realized. But at the same time—and in this he was almost alone in the labor movement—he flatly insisted that Labour must work to strengthen, rather than to abandon, the sanctions features of the covenant. At present, he wrote, the League did not guarantee its members against aggression. Some such guarantee was an essential preliminary to universal disarmament. The League, he insisted, "ought clearly to undertake that if any member . . . is subjected to an act of aggression by another state which refuses to submit a dispute to pacific settlement, all the other members of the League will come to the assistance of the member against which a warlike act has been committed."[91]

In 1922, Henderson's advocacy of League support for the victim of aggression was essentially an unorthodox doctrine in the labor movement. It was his most important and most characteristic contribution to the molding of a workable foreign policy for Labour. As yet, quite obviously, he had not raised the issue of how the League was to render its assistance. The years that followed were to see him develop the implications of his position still further.

Whatever Henderson's attitude, the great majority of the labor movement continued to look backwards in the years between the peace conference and the General Election of 1922. Incensed by the settlement, embittered by the subsequent policies of the French and British governments, frightened by the specter of another war, Labour found it difficult to adjust to the postwar world. Heavily influenced by the anticapitalist, anti-imperialist, "no more war" appeals made by leaders of the Independent Labour party, the Union of Democratic Control, and (often the same people) the ex-Liberal recruits, virtually the entire labor movement, including trade unionists, continued to despair of a viable international order. Certainly they rejected all hope that it might be achieved within the framework of existing institutions. Doctrinaire pacifism and theoretical class war dominated the Labour press, its propaganda, and, to a large extent, its program.

By the middle of 1922 the first indications of a change in outlook were dimly apparent. But it would be inaccurate to assert that the new position of the Advisory Committee and especially of Arthur Henderson signalized a new policy for Labour. The altered tone toward the League of Nations and the support for some form of sanctions were merely hints of the pattern into which the outlook of some of Labour's most important leaders was eventually to be stamped. As yet, most spokesmen for Labour were neither willing to accept those hints nor prepared to urge upon the rank and file the need for a change in their basic assumptions.

CHAPTER 4

THE BEGINNINGS OF CHANGE

By 1922 and even more in the following year, some of the leaders of British Labour were beginning to explore a more positive and constructive approach to the international arena. They ventured slowly to go beyond simply denouncing Versailles, denigrating the League of Nations, and demanding wholesale reforms that were hardly likely to materialize in the conditions of the 1920s. As they began to see the possibility that their party could take responsibility in the direction of British affairs, they searched for a more realistic policy. In particular, they sought a formula to substitute some universal sanction against aggression for the bilateral and even multilateral alliances and agreements of the past. Increasingly, a handful of them began to envision the use of international instruments to adjudicate controversies as a constructive alternative to the posture of almost total rejection of the new international machinery that had characterized almost all quarters of the labor movement after the war.

The most conspicuous part in this reformulation was played by Ramsay MacDonald and Arthur Henderson. When he resumed the leadership of the party, MacDonald's skills in dealing with complex international issues were demonstrated as he shepherded the Labour party toward a clarification of its positions. But Arthur Henderson also performed a major role in keeping before the labor movement the need to approach each issue within a broader framework that acknowledged the limitations of Britain's position in European politics. He was concerned with realistic solutions and not merely points to be made on the platform or in the press.

Both MacDonald and Henderson would no doubt have agreed with an article that Leonard Woolf published in 1933, in which he reflected on the fundamentals of Labour's policy. Although he was trying to explain the attitudes of a somewhat later period, his comments illuminate the issues that were increasingly to characterize the debate about foreign policy among the constituent groups in the labor movement during the 1920s. As Woolf saw it, Europe had reached a point at the end of the nineteenth century where it

needed to take one or two steps forward to promote a stable form of civilization. First, it had to make an orderly transition from the individualist capitalist economic system to some form of communal or socialist economic system.
Second, it had to establish an ordered international structure regulating the
relations between states and preventing war. The two steps, he noted, were
not really dissociated; they were intimately connected. The logical evolution
of nineteenth-century civilization into a pacific equalitarian society was frustrated by the refusal of the capitalist and middle classes peacefully to allow
the transition to economic equality. War and the breakdown of the current
economic order went hand in hand.[1] Woolf's coupling of economic prosperity
and peace with support for the international institutions designed to promote
them summarized views that a few key representatives of Labour were coming to adopt in the early twenties.

For leaders such as MacDonald and Philip Snowden, the shift in foreign
policy attitudes was gradual, marking their separation from their base in the
Independent Labour party. Various scholars have exhaustively analyzed their
alienation from the ILP on the character and pace of domestic change. It was
paralleled by a similar alienation on matters of international policy. There the
rhetoric of their comments on the League of Nations provided the clue to the
beginnings of a shift in position. Snowden's defection came before that of
MacDonald. By April 1922 he had resigned from the ILP's National Administrative Council and, by October, he was warning that even so great an idea as
that of the League of Nations required a long and difficult process to translate
it into practical form. "I would not suggest that Labour should give its support
to a scheme or an idea merely because it is popular," he wrote, "but I believe
that encouragement of the League of Nations offers the only means of escape
from the tragedy of the international situation." Although Snowden loyally
supported Labour's declaration in favor of superseding the Supreme Council,
the Reparations Commission, and the various special conferences that characterized Lloyd George's style in international relations, he now believed that
Labour had no alternative to championing the international body.[2] Snowden's split with the ILP was basically over matters of domestic policy, but
clearly he was increasingly drawing away from the ILP position on foreign
policy as well.

MacDonald, David Marquand has suggested, was less impatient with the
young men in a hurry who were taking over the leadership of the ILP, as he
attempted to bridge the gap between the prewar and postwar generations.[3]
Perhaps too he felt the need to hold on to his one solid political base until the
election of November 1922 transformed his position in the Labour party.
Even before that election, he had begun to hedge in his all-out opposition to

the League. Writing his regular column in the *Socialist Review* of October, 1922, he noted that the League "has the makings of a really powerful body, and there are always at [its] meetings signs that it knows its own value, if it were only free to do its work." But the dominant powers preferred not to use the League. They chose to go their own way and for their own interests. While that was so, the League had no chance. "The scraps of European problems are thrown to it for food," he complained, "and it is allowed to do little more than debate." He went on to outline all the areas in which the League was defi-cient, from its failure to explain the farce of mandates in Mesopotamia to the absence of any notice of the secret agreements between France and Poland. "Robustness"—presumably a synonym for courage or forthrightness—and a jealous guarding of its own status as an impartial international body would alone save the League from decay while yet in its cradle. And even debate, he reminded his readers, was not useless.[4] This was hardly a ringing endorse-ment of the new international body, but its tone reflected a modest adjust-ment to the realities of the emerging world order.

By the end of 1922, then, the first faint signs of a break in Labour's almost universal rejection of the postwar settlement had begun to appear. It was no accident that Arthur Henderson, the secretary of the party, should have been one of the leaders promoting the change. Unlike MacDonald or Snowden, he had never been a member of the ILP and thus was not faced with the ticklish problem of separating himself from the extremism of the left, whether on domestic or foreign issues. In December he was warning, in a speech at the World Peace Congress, that peace could not be guaranteed by armaments and secret treaties. It could not even be guaranteed by parliamentary control of foreign policy, if the policy itself was based on wrong principles. "Peace can only be secured," he insisted, "by encouraging every nation to find its guaran-tees of security and freedom in the League of Nations." To be sure, he argued, the League needed to be expanded and modified. At present it was largely the instrument of Allied policy. It must become all-inclusive and its Assembly, representing all of the nations in the organization, must become its sovereign authority in place of the Council dominated by the Great Powers. The rule of unanimity, which rendered all discussion a mere academic exercise, must be abandoned and the League must take an ever-greater role in administering the day-to-day activities of the world community.[5] In his plea for changes in the League covenant, Henderson, like MacDonald and Snowden, clearly still shared many of the criteria of the Labour Left, but, equally clearly, his tone, no less than his proposals, revealed a significant movement toward accom-modation and compromise in thinking about international affairs.

As various Labour spokesmen sorted out their principles and positions, the shaky Lloyd George coalition was coming to a somewhat abrupt end. To the government's attempt to unravel the tangled threads of Turko-Greek conflict, Labour pronounced a plague on both the unrealistic pro-Greek policy of Lloyd George and on Lord Curzon's unbending posture in negotiations with the Turks. But Conservative backbenchers and a substantial cohort of their leadership had concluded that it was time to take over control from a prime minister whom they had followed at best reluctantly. The confrontation with the Turks at Chanak, which threatened to involve Britain in a meaningless conflict, was perhaps the reason, perhaps the excuse, for the decision to dump Lloyd George, but the Conservative revolt at the Carlton Club in October forced a General Election in November that transformed the position of Labour.

At the election, many of the leaders of Labour who had been out of Parliament since the war were returned. A number of them, such as E. D. Morel, Arthur Ponsonby, Charles Trevelyan, H. B. Lees Smith, Charles and Noel Buxton, and Josiah Wedgwood, were former Liberals, almost all of whom had affiliated with the Independent Labour party rather than make their way in the new constituency parties. Philip Snowden likewise was successful, but Arthur Henderson, handicapped by his responsibilities as secretary in organizing the election campaign and never a very effective campaigner in his own interest, was defeated and came into Parliament a little later in a by-election. Above all, Ramsay MacDonald, ostracized from Parliament since the postwar election of 1918, joined his fellow Labour M.P.'s on the Opposition benches. Although the choice of MacDonald over Clynes as leader of the parliamentary party was not as automatic as it has appeared in retrospect, the support of Henderson and the votes of the ILP and the radical Clydesiders ensured his victory.

While the election confirmed the growing strength of Labour in the country, the victory of many aggressive former Liberals was also a signal that the Labour party's leaders would have no easy task in persuading their associates to temper their rhetoric and seek constructive ways to make the new international institutions work. A number of the former Liberals were among the most extreme critics of virtually all that had taken place on the international scene since the end of the war. In particular, when Franco-German tensions came to a head, they denounced French policy as proof that they had been right all along.

There is a certain irony in the fact that the government of Andrew Bonar Law, brought into existence partly by the threat of a war with Turkey, was compelled to devote the greater part of its attention to the threat of war or of chaos in the heart of Europe. Soon after the British election of 1922, Germany was declared by the Reparations Commission to have defaulted on its deliveries of timber. Bonar Law's attempts to find a way out of the dilemma were rejected and, after the commission also found Germany in arrears in coal deliveries, French and Belgian troops marched into the heavily industrialized Ruhr. While the French and their ally asserted that they had occupied the Ruhr in order to ensure implementation of the German treaty, both the Germans and virtually all of the British labor movement took it for granted that the French were really seeking to annex the Ruhr for strategic and economic reasons.[6]

British Labour unanimously regarded the Ruhr occupation as a trial of the new international system. Some of the major mainstream leaders approached the issue with caution, hoping that it might demonstrate the need to revise the Versailles settlement and to turn to the League of Nations for genuinely international solutions to admittedly difficult problems. On the other hand, the League's apparent passivity as French and Belgian troops marched further into Germany came as no surprise to the Labour Left. Its spokesmen had no faith in the international body and took it for granted that it would simply do the bidding of the former Allies. Accordingly, they demanded that Labour urge the British government to compel the French to moderate their pressure against Germany. For months, indeed in most cases for years, left-wing spokesmen had been predicting that reparation demands would lead to further French victimization of Germany. Now they could point to the French action as dramatic confirmation that their warnings had been well founded. Several articles by Charles Roden Buxton summed up the analysis of the left. Why, he asked, did the devastated areas of France remain devastated still? The average Frenchman would answer, "no money" and "the Boche won't pay" and leave it at that. But in fact, the reparation clauses of the treaty had yielded nothing because practically the whole of the receipts had been eaten up in the costs of the army of occupation. The remedy was for Britain to have some vision and a little generosity. The British should remit the debt owed them by France, whether America remitted British war debts or not. They should organize a reconstruction loan, to be raised and administered internationally, as proposed by the Labour and Socialist Conferences at Amsterdam and Frankfurt. And all this should be conditional, of course, upon the French government accepting the revision of reparation payments and the withdrawal of the armies of occupation from Germany.[7]

While condemnation of French policy found ready acceptance in the labor movement, some leaders sought to find common ground upon which to build a united policy. As early as June 10, 1922, Ramsay MacDonald presided at a conference sponsored by the Union of Democratic Control at which some 320 representatives from Labour parties, trades councils, ILP branches, and Women's Co-operative Guilds were present. The very presence of MacDonald in the chair at the UDC's conference suggests that that organization was seeking ways to collaborate with the mainstream leaders of Labour. The conference passed a long resolution protesting any further invasion of German territory. It called upon the British government to cancel the French debt to Britain and to renounce its share of reparations. Tying in the unrealistic exaction of reparations with the economic health of the British people, the resolution blamed the "unjust and unworkable" Treaty of Versailles for the decline in British industry and the consequent unemployment that bore so heavily upon the country's working-class population. Along with its specific indictment of the reparation policy, the resolution paraded the critics' usual bundle of demands—the revision of the treaty, the inclusion of all powers in the new international assemblage, the end of secret diplomacy, and an attack upon the problem of armaments.[8]

For several years, E. D. Morel was the heart and soul of the struggle to overthrow the Versailles "diktat" lock, stock, and barrel. Unlike some of his UDC fellows, he had little use for compromise. Nevertheless, although he differed from various elements of the Labour Left on many issues, he provided them, week after week and month after month, with data and arguments to carry on their campaign against France and the other former Allies as well as for a radical transformation of the existing League of Nations. His attacks upon French policy in the Ruhr, no less than upon the British reaction, were part and parcel of his passionate and persistent effort to head off those spokesmen in the labor movement who were moving toward a pragmatic if incomplete acceptance of the existing international order. His sudden death in 1924 deprived the most intransigent elements of Labour of a constant goad and spur as well as their most eloquent spokesman.

In his journal *Foreign Affairs*, Morel spelled out his own prescription for a "surgical operation" to be followed by a new and constructive policy. Along with a series of measures to help Germany get back on her feet, he proposed that Britain abandon all reparation payments along with the war debts owed by France in return for a complete evacuation of the Rhineland. At the same time, he pleaded for the termination of the Supreme Council and the reform of the covenant of the League of Nations to abolish the rule of unanimity and to welcome both Germany and Russia on terms of full equality. Britain should invite the reformed League to draw up a disarmament scheme and intimate her willingness under certain conditions to abandon the weapon of the blockade. Finally, as a basis upon which his other suggestions rested, Morel called upon Britain to facilitate an investigation into the causes of the war before which Germany could make her defense.[9] Morel took it for granted that all he proposed could be accomplished if only Britain took the lead.

As the tension between France and Germany mounted, so did the stridency of Morel's castigations of France. He insisted that its policies were designed to achieve the political disruption and the economic death of Germany. As if that were not enough, Morel went on to argue again that French policy was making for the economic paralysis of the European continent and thus driving hundreds of thousands of British working men upon the streets. It was costing the British taxpayers something like 500,000 pounds a day. Altogether, blind support of France, he insisted, was a strategy of industrial suicide for Britain.[10] Morel's economic argument was clearly an attempt to use the self-interest of the working class to demonstrate how directly they were affected by the inadequacies of current international arrangements. Similarly, when he denounced the British government's failure to press for serious revision of the League of Nations covenant and its reluctance to use the League to deal with the Franco-German problem, his reproaches were as much directed against his fellow Labourites, who naively trusted in the League and other capitalist instruments, as they were against their enemies.

French aggressiveness in the Ruhr drew the various elements of the Labour Left closer together in a common chorus of denunciation. Disapproval not only of the French and British governments, but of the League of Nations that they dominated, was most fervently duplicated in the official *Daily Herald* and in the *New Leader*, which had almost overnight become the most interesting, and perhaps the most influential, of the organs of opinion of the Left. The very different editors of the two papers, George Lansbury and H. N. Brailsford, were both important in the formation of Labour opinions, particularly in those circles that found much to criticize in the strategy of Labour's official leaders. Ramsay MacDonald, for one, although he was infuriated by their criticism, nevertheless paid attention to their papers and took them seriously.[11]

Morel's strictures in *Foreign Affairs* and through the UDC were paralleled by Brailsford's constant barrage of criticism of the French in the pages of the *New Leader*, where he had all along stressed the most corrosive disapproval of the postwar settlement. Condemning what he regarded as the numerous violations of the peace treaty by the occupying authorities, Brailsford, as late as the beginning of December, was speculating on whether France really wanted to take the Ruhr and absorb it with the rest of the Rhineland or whether its threat was partly to frighten the British, partly to make German big business more pliable. Several months later, before the French made their move, he no longer had any doubts. French capital, he declared, aimed primarily at uniting the iron ore of Lorraine, which it already possessed, with the coal of the Ruhr. With a guard of a few battalions in the goods yard of the Essen station, on the quays of the Rhine ports and the lock-gates of the canals, the French would control the lifeblood of German industry. That control would give them a power such as Napoleon never realized, and it would open up for them, and for the whole investing class of France, dreams of untold wealth.[12]

Predictably, Lansbury, in the last months of his editorship of the *Daily Herald*, mirrored the views of Morel and Brailsford. He observed that the British people would not long support the intolerable French efforts to present the German people as the only villains in the world, and as such to be continually punished by futile and cruel attempts to exact from them pounds of flesh they were unable to provide. Giving his own particular twist to the issue, Lansbury reiterated the standard proposal that America and Europe abandon all war debts, but only, he warned, if they also abandoned their armies and fleets and the imperialist policies of which weapons were the costly apparatus.[13]

Trade union leaders used economic concerns to persuade their rank and file that changes in the international settlement were directly related to their personal well-being. They found ready attention within the ranks of the trade union movement, where there was more than passing sympathy for the arguments paraded. For R. B. Walker of the National Union of Agricultural Workers, as he made his presidential address to the annual meeting of the Trades Union Congress, the issue was even broader than the simple matter of French policy. The Versailles treaty, he cautioned, was working itself out in unemployment and slow starvation for the workers in all the countries affected by the treaty. It must not be preserved intact and, since it was clear that capitalist governments could not discover the way to remedy it, it was up to the working populations to exchange opinions and experience and to work to impress their views on their home governments. It was all very well to blame France, conceded Walker. Indeed, no one could reasonably support any plan seeking to reduce Germany to a position of economic slavery or to assist France in becoming the dictator of the European continent. But it was not much use condemning French politicians, who had to struggle with unbalanced budgets, who hungered to become the lords of Europe, and who served big capitalist interests, while at the same time refraining from pointing an accusing finger at so-called statesmen in Britain itself. To settle the outstanding European issues was a matter of bread and butter for the workers of Britain, but such settlement was highly unlikely until there were workers' governments in the various countries.[14]

Significantly, it was J. H. Thomas, hardly on the left of the trade union movement, who supported Walker's argument that a sensible solution of international tension was essential for the economic welfare of the British worker. Thomas proposed the resolution designed to bring Walker's rhetoric down to the level of action. In so doing, he pointed out that the question of unemployment was a crucial issue for the organized labor movement. And there was no resolution so important, and with so close a relationship to the unemployment problem, as that which concerned the international diffi-culties. Thus Germany had already paid to the French and British govern-ments money that could have been used to meet reparation payments, but instead had been spent to keep the army of occupation on the Rhine—with disastrous results to the trade union and labor movements. Until very re-cently, an English sergeant on the Rhine had been paid more than a German cabinet minister. The result was that the German government was faced with threats from the left and from the right. The success of either would be equally disastrous to the peace of Europe.

Despite his passionate rhetoric, Thomas proposed that the TUC support a constructive attempt to bring about international change. His resolution called for the abandonment of the Rhineland occupation, the acceptance of Germany and Russia into the League of Nations, and the arbitration of Ger-many's obligations before a court set up by the League. Other speakers agreed with the assessment of the leaders of the TUC. Those who did not demurred because they wanted more radical action than envisaged by the resolution. The young Emanuel Shinwell, representing the Amalgamated Marine Work-ers, argued, for example, that there should be a complete international can-cellation of debts. Precisely because payment had been made by Germany the shipbuilding and engineering industries in Britain had been wrecked. Ger-many could pay only if she could sell her products. Were the shipbuilding trades prepared to receive one single ship from Germany? Were the coal miners prepared to receive one ton of coal from her? Labour had made blundering and stupid statements in the past about these issues. The time had come to cut their losses and to say with simple sanity, "No reparations, no indemnities, cancellation of war debts." The TUC accepted the rather limited resolution presented by its leadership, however much a minority of delegates regretted its compromises. Nevertheless, the language of the supposedly more prudent leaders of the Congress was difficult to differentiate from the words of those who chafed at limitations, nor indeed from the bombast of a fire-brand like E. D. Morel.[15]

Differing from most Labour spokesmen, Will Arnold-Forster pleaded for a realistic understanding of France's position along with a program to make effective use of existing international institutions in dealing with the Franco-German problem. His UDC pamphlet, to which reference has already been made, takes on even added significance when considered in the light of the vehement rejection of the implications of French policy by Labour publicists and trade union leaders alike. That such a pamphlet should have been published in the spring of 1922, and even more that it should have been published under the imprint of the Union of Democratic Control, borders on the remarkable.

With the passing of time, the triumvirate of Will Arnold-Forster, Philip Noel-Baker, and Hugh Dalton was to become more important in framing the arguments, not only for the faithful acceptance of the existing League of Nations, but also for strengthening it by the provision of some kind of international constraint to enforce its rulings. As early as 1920, Arnold-Forster had insisted that Labour must take a sensible view of sanctions, urging that the blockade be abandoned as an instrument of "private war" and its use restricted to the League of Nations.[16] Now, in this publication of the UDC, the majority of whose leadership surely did not agree with him, he pleaded for an equally realistic posture toward the claims of France against Germany. In some twenty carefully reasoned pages, he set the problem squarely in the context of the embryo system of international organization and decision making. He attempted to answer the questions, "How far should this country go in the effort to work with France: should the Entente still be mended if possible, or should it frankly be ended?" Arnold-Forster, whose role in the deliberations of Labour's Advisory Committee on International Questions was steadily growing, had no illusions about how serious the antagonism was between British and French policy, an antagonism heightened by the advent of Raymond Poincaré to power. Considering the case for abandoning the attempt to work with France, he admitted that collaboration to date had not persuaded the French to adhere to the Treaty of Versailles, let alone agree to revise it. Certainly there appeared to be little hope of any liberal transformation of French policy in the near future. Whatever might be the inclination of the French people, the present Chamber of Deputies, elected at a moment when hatred of Germany and of Bolshevism were especially intense, still had two years of life before it.

And yet, Arnold-Forster argued, it was surely worth making a very great effort to avoid any further widening of the breach with France. Without Anglo-French cooperation, the two greatest international tasks (quite aside from the relief of famine in Russia) facing the world—the restoration of the economic life of Europe and the development of a real League of Nations—would be made immeasurably more difficult. Did anyone suppose, for example, that the reparation clauses of the Treaty of Versailles could be revised without French concurrence?

Although Britain should in no way accede to Poincaré's obvious desire for a military alliance, Arnold-Forster advised, she needed to realize the validity of French concerns about security. Nevertheless, any guarantee that Britain might give must fulfill three conditions. It must conform with the idea of the League of Nations, not with that of the balance of power. It must leave Britain free to judge for herself whether an attack was direct and unprovoked. And lastly, it must give so much reassurance to the parties guaranteed as to increase the prospects for a lasting peace. If France could meet those conditions there was a very good case for giving her the official reassurance she sought.

In Arnold-Forster's estimation there were three possible approaches to the matter of guarantees. One was a pledge of support by Britain to France (and perhaps vice versa) against unprovoked aggression by Germany. Next was a treaty or reciprocal guarantee between France, Britain, and Germany, perhaps including others. And third was a more extended international guarantee, for example by all the nations of Europe. Rejecting the first as disastrous and the third as highly unlikely in the present state of international affairs, he concluded that a reciprocal guarantee that would reassure both France and Germany would be an invaluable achievement. Any such guarantee, he warned, must be made public and must be submitted to the free judgment of Parliament. In a real sense, Arnold-Forster's conception of a mutual guarantee prefigured the central idea of the Locarno agreements sponsored by the Baldwin government a few years later.[17]

Arnold-Forster was an active member of the Advisory Committee on International Questions, but as yet his was only one voice among several. Differences of viewpoint, if not outright conflict, characterized the process of analysis that went on behind the scenes among the counselors to the leaders of the Labour party. The Advisory Committee, which, as has been noted, was now formally reporting to the Executives of both the Trades Union Congress and the Labour party, was in reality mainly an instrument of the latter. Even before the French march into the Ruhr, members of the committee resolved to draft a memorandum recommending a policy to be adopted by the Labour party. If France moved, the British government should clearly state to France that it considered the Entente broken. As soon as France entered the Ruhr, Great Britain should call upon her to pay interest on her debt. On the other hand, if France agreed to a moratorium of two years as a minimum, a reduction of the total German debt, and a withdrawal from the occupied territory within a short time, then Britain should forego her share of reparations and cancel France's debt to herself.[18]

Once the French had made their move, the Advisory Committee noted that the question any British government—or critic of its policy—must answer was this: "Are we prepared to accept a new European settlement based on a Rhine frontier for France, the dismemberment of Germany, the control of Germany's main resources and industrial organisation by the French, and the domination of the Continent by French military power?" The French had never really accepted that reparations depended upon the economic restoration of Germany. Since they no longer bothered to disguise their political aims and had committed an act of war, it should have been the duty of the British government to invoke the League of Nations and to urge upon France recourse to the League before acting alone.

Already such a policy, it should be stressed, was far removed from the Labour Left's lock, stock, and barrel repudiation of all existing international machinery. But the Advisory Committee went further. A Labour government, it argued, would undoubtedly have made every effort to secure resort to the League, not only to determine what action France and her allies were entitled to take under the Treaty of Versailles, but as a way to arrive at some settlement of the whole reparations problem. If despite these efforts, France had used force and had refused reference to the League, then a Labour government would have denounced the reparations and punitive clauses of the treaty, would have withdrawn its army of occupation and by that action would have compelled French public opinion to take cognizance of the isolation of the French government and of the danger inherent in a policy that could only depend upon overwhelming force. Having outlined what a Labour government might have done, the Advisory Committee's memorandum then proceeded to appraise the arguments for and against the withdrawal of British troops from the Rhineland, concluding, apparently against its own advice, that the consensus in the Labour party was not in favor of withdrawing troops. Nevertheless, the committee was certain that the British government must refuse any settlement of the reparations question so long as a French army remained in the Ruhr valley.[19]

Another memorandum, sent to the press and the prime minister after sanction had been obtained from the National Joint Committee of the Labour party and the TUC, outlined the steps that the British government should be called upon to take. It should refrain from all measures of support or cooperation with the French troops, for example by not allowing them to pass through British occupied territory, and should formally dissociate itself from all complicity with the present French government. It should refuse to share in cash payments, coal, or deliveries in kind that might be obtained as a result of the French action. It must take all possible steps to secure the withdrawal of all armies of occupation and support the United States in urging the submission of the Franco-German dispute to an impartial body, while at the same time formally proposing that the whole reparation problem be referred to the League of Nations.[20]

The Advisory Committee's recommendations were considerably more cautious than the demands that appeared in the various manifestos of the Labour Left. It proposed no specific plan for dealing with the delivery of payments in cash or in kind, but instead called for international consideration of the issue. Nor did it demand the removal of British troops from areas in the Rhineland as a means of bringing pressure to bear upon the French. To a certain extent, the restraint of the committee reflected the gradual tempering of attitudes as Labour approached more closely to the prospect of having to take office and to act upon the implications of its slogans and sweeping pronouncements. It also needs to be remembered how assorted a group were the Labour party's sympathizers who took part in the deliberations of the Advisory Committee. Although Leonard Woolf functioned as secretary and served as an element of consistency for the committee, at different times so disparate a collection of participants as MacDonald and Brailsford, Norman Angell and Morel, G. Lowes Dickinson and the Buxtons, R. Palme Dutt and Arnold Toynbee came to the meetings. Almost inevitably, the committee's advice revealed diverse emphases. It frequently found itself on the fence as issues unfolded.

As the Ruhr difficulty came to a head, other advice offered to Labour's leaders reflected a similar caution about specific and concrete international approaches to the crisis. An example was the counsel of a delegation that visited the Ruhr in March. Its membership included C. R. Buxton along with Will Adamson, Tom Shaw, and Brigadier General C. B. Thomson. The report of this heterogeneous group, published by the Labour party as *Labour and the Ruhr*, gave the appearance of solid agreement among its members, but the agreement was mainly over condemnation of the French rather than on any detailed prescription for effective action. France, the report contended, was "using a whale to catch a sprat" and the result was likely to be disastrous. Even if the continuation of the present state of war in the Ruhr were possible without bloodshed, its effect on world trade, and especially British trade, would be profound. But other consequences might well be more disquieting. If the occupation was legal, then might was right. In any case, the situation could not be dealt with by existing machinery provided under the Treaty of Versailles, but required a new instrument, international in character, in the framing of which the German people should have a part. Since British interests were more directly involved than those of any other state besides France, Belgium, and Germany, the initiative to bring such a new body into existence ought to be taken by the British government. No effort must be spared to keep in touch with both sides and to try to narrow the gap between their conflicting claims.[21] The report, which was signed by Buxton, Adamson, and Thomson, was perhaps more significant for what it did not say than for its specific recommendations. Given the composition of the delegation, complete agreement was hardly to be expected and its rather minimal proposals presumably reflected all that the groups represented might be willing to agree upon.

The initial response of the Executive Committee of the Labour party and the General Council of the Trades Union Congress to these various assessments of the Ruhr issue concentrated upon denunciation rather than on specific proposals. The combined committee called upon all sections of the labor movement to condemn in the strongest possible terms the Ruhr invasion, as well as methods of force and violence as a means of solving the problem of reparations. Enclosing a draft resolution for the guidance of local Labour parties and trades councils, the secretaries of the two bodies requested the constituent organizations to send such resolutions to the prime minister and to endeavor to have them published in the local press and trade journals.[22]

Once French and Belgian troops had marched into the Ruhr, the sober advice of Arnold-Forster and the Advisory Committee was substantially paralleled in the approach taken by Ramsay MacDonald as leader of the parliamentary Labour party. Writing in the *New Leader*, he argued that the calamity threatened by the Ruhr invasion could only be avoided by going back to the treaties and reconsidering everything that had been done since the armistice. The Ruhr venture was a breakdown of Versailles and signaled the failure of the League of Nations. Labour knew that nothing could be achieved by an appeal to the League of Nations, nor by anything that merely dealt with the Ruhr occupation as an isolated problem. Only within "comprehensive views of the European problem" could the Ruhr issue be successfully approached.[23]

Writing confidentially to the prime minister on January 29, MacDonald noted that the Labour members considered French policy in the Ruhr to be one of the greatest danger. It was destroying what limited beginnings had been made toward a settlement and reconstruction in Central Europe. At the same time, it was intensifying the dislocation of world trade and would result in serious damage and deepened industrial distress in Britain. Taken in conjunction with what was happening at Lausanne in discussions with the Turkish government, it threatened a renewed outbreak of war of the most devastating kind. MacDonald acknowledged the delicacy of the situation, but asked for a discussion under conditions that "whilst imposing responsibility" nevertheless would allow a frank statement of the opinion of a great and powerful mass in the country. Such a discussion would permit the making of various well-considered proposals about how Great Britain could become an active agent for peace and sanity and could challenge Europe to face the plain facts of real politics. He urged Bonar Law to summon Parliament immediately in order to consult on the international outlook.[24]

Bonar Law did not respond as promptly as the parliamentary Labour party might have hoped, but MacDonald's caution was more or less echoed in governmental circles. Although the prime minister's colleagues deplored the occupation, they neither wished to undertake mediation nor to break with France. Throughout 1923, even as they were repeatedly embarrassed by French measures taken in Allied-occupied territories, the cabinet held firm to the view that Britain should maintain its forces in the Rhineland and avoid incidents that might impel the British public to demand withdrawal.[25]

Similar caution was evident as the parliamentary Labour party staked out its positions in the House of Commons. During the debate on the address in February, J. R. Clynes was chosen to move an amendment to the traditional vote of thanks, which branded the dangerous condition of affairs in Europe as the certain source of future wars as well as a serious aggravation of unemployment and reduced wages in Britain. The amendment went on to criticize the government for its failures in all of the international areas of concern to Labour—on war debts, the use of conciliation and arbitration on such critical matters as the occupation of the Ruhr, and on the reconsideration of the clauses of the peace treaties that interfered with the proper reconstruction of Europe. Labour's view, Clynes pointed out, was that the main remedy for Europe's turmoil was to be found in a fearless revision of the peace treaty. That revision could not take place without a world conference, but in turn a conference could not occur without the intervention of the League of Nations. Taking into account that critics—"indeed, some of them associated with Labour"—regarded the League as a sham, Clynes warned that it made more sense to try to improve the League than to fail completely in the effort to start a new or even a rival organization.[26]

That key figures in Labour's parliamentary delegation differed significantly was evident in the debate. Neither Philip Snowden nor E. D. Morel, for example, saw the issue quite like Clynes. Both were caustic in the denunciation of France and each urged the steps outlined in Labour's amendment. But despite some limited lip service to the League that each had publicly given earlier, neither was enthusiastic for its use as a trigger of international action. Morel read the Labour party's proposal to mean that the matter of the Ruhr should be referred *not* to the League but directly to a world conference.

Otherwise, the United States, so essential for an economic settlement, would not participate. For Snowden, the world conference should be used not only to revise the peace treaties, but to reconstruct, "or rather to construct," a real and efficient League.

Even Ramsay MacDonald, however far his alienation from the Labour Left may have proceeded, was more concerned, in arguing the case against France, with cataloguing the failures of Bonar Law's government than with employing existing mechanisms of international organization to address the crisis. Neither France nor Britain, he declared, had accepted the League, neither had put the League in a position of independence and authority, neither had taken any other attitude but that the League should confirm everything they had already decided. The governments of both nations demanded that the League must support their approach to European settlement, whatever it might be.[27]

It remained for Arthur Henderson, summing up for Labour, to reiterate J. R. Clynes's insistence upon the use of the machinery of the existing League of Nations. Trying to square the circle of the somewhat conflicting interpretations placed upon their own amendment by his colleagues, he asserted that neither the recovery of reparations nor the future peace of Europe could be achieved by the policies of the French and British governments. Instead, he insisted, it was urgent to seek effective security against aggression through international guarantees. Placing his emphasis rather differently from Snowden or Morel, or even MacDonald, he told the House that he could not understand why the Ruhr issue had not been referred to the League of Nations. The Labour party, he contended with perhaps more certainty than was warranted, was strongly in favor of submitting the controversy to that body, provided its Council could act speedily and constructively. Henderson admitted that the League fell far short of what it ought to be in its membership, its constitution, and its procedures. It was too much an Allied instrument instead of being a free and impartial body. It should be reformed, above all to include Germany and Russia. Despite all that, reference of the reparation issue to the League, even as constituted, would be far more acceptable than dealing with the problem in accordance with the policy of the French government. Precisely because she was an ally, Britain could take the initiative under the charter of the League to tackle the situation that was endangering the peace of Europe.

By now the role that Henderson was to play in the evolution of Labour's international policy was emerging. More than most of the leaders of the Labour party, more perhaps even than MacDonald, who clearly was Labour's most prominent spokesman on international questions, Henderson urged that his colleagues understand the very real limits within which any policy initiatives had to operate. Unlike the Morels and the Maxtons, no less than the Ponsonbys and the Lansburys, he recognized that a viable policy required compromise and a sensitivity to the concerns and the fears of other nations. In the case of France, for example, he agreed that if she were "influenced by fears that are well-founded, of future suspected dangers of attack, she is entitled to security; but that security should be secured through an all-inclusive and more powerful League of Nations." British Labour, he was increasingly convinced, could not impose its views unilaterally on the rest of the world. The rhetoric that suggested otherwise served neither the Labour party nor the British people in a responsible way.[28]

In their dealings with socialists from other countries, MacDonald, Henderson, and their fellows likewise kept in the forefront of their consideration of French policy toward Germany the broader issue of international security. While they wrestled with the implications of the occupation, the leaders of the labor movement continued to meet with comrades from other countries in order to try to influence policy by demonstrating a common international front of Labour and Socialist organizations. Early on, a heterogeneous group of labor movement and trade union representatives had met at Amsterdam with their fellows of the Labour and Socialist International, the Vienna Union, and the International Federation of Trade Unions. Here Thomas represented the British section of the IFTU and Cramp, Williams, and Gillies the British Labour and Socialist International. A two-day discussion resulted in agreement on a resolution calling for a campaign of propaganda against the occupation and for submission of the question in dispute to the League of Nations, to which Germany must be admitted with the same rights as all other nations.[29]

A few weeks later, Henderson, MacDonald, Shaw, Thomas, and Gillies met at Paris in an interparliamentary conference with French, Belgian, and Italian socialists where common understanding was reached on a series of propositions. The conferees acknowledged that the loyal execution of legitimate reparations was an essential part of the peace of Europe. But they insisted that real peace, the renunciation of acts of violence and the occupation of territory, the reestablishment of economic life and a "complete and final" arrangement between Germany and her creditors were conditions indispensable to that execution. France and Belgium must be freed of the burden that actually weighed on them at present, but on the other hand Germany must be enabled to make reparation without having to suffer consequences that had a crushing effect on her exchanges and would result in increasing distress. Current annual payments were arbitrary, taking into account neither Germany's ability to pay nor the need for financial restoration of Germany in order to make payment possible. Instead, the Allied socialists proposed payments in cash, which would have to depend upon loans directly guaranteed and rapidly issued. Insisting that the peace of Europe and the security of France would be most surely protected by a strengthening of the Weimar Republic and democracy in Germany, the groups spelled out in considerable detail a number of steps, including much fuller use of international instruments, that should be taken to implement the proposed new approach. It was agreed that each national delegation would begin to act in its parliament along the general lines of the conference consensus.[30]

The torrent of criticism that continued throughout most of the French occupation of the Ruhr confirmed that the cautious internationalism of the leadership had not yet been accepted by a significant sector of the labor movement. To be sure, only a few publications bore the brunt of disseminating the movement's opinions and those few were disproportionately representative of the Left. Nevertheless, the criticism reflected a wide spectrum of reactions, from the view that the struggle in the Ruhr represented the "worldwide warfare of capital against the workers" with capital pressing its advance over the dead bodies of innumerable humble victims to the assumption that morally and physically a new war had begun.[31] Proposals in ILP publications such as *Forward*, the *Bradford Pioneer*, or the *New Leader* ranged from the obvious step of protest through the formal scrapping of the postwar treaties to a total withdrawal of British troops from the Rhine.[32] To the *Herald* the occupation signaled "the next war in all but name," a sentiment echoed in the *Nation*, where Leonard Woolf prepared a leader entitled "The Next Great War Begins" that accused the French of seeking a definite assimilation of a new western province into their country. Marshal Foch and the military men were once more in the saddle and were presently trying to gain precisely what they had failed to achieve in the Versailles treaty.[33] Even the *New Statesman*, by now inclined to support the right wing of the labor movement, agreed that the French were attempting to realize the claims frustrated in 1919 during the peace negotiations.[34]

The almost total rejection of the moderation adopted by the leaders of the labor movement was of course reflected again and again in the pages of *Foreign Affairs*.[35] There E. D. Morel continued his campaign for vindication of a Germany that had suffered "the most fearful injuries ever inflicted upon any nation in modern history," a suffering legalized by a so-called League of Nations. That League in turn could be nothing but a committee of the victors so long as it remained closed to Germany and Russia. Possibly signaling a slight nod to the realities of the international order, Morel conceded that there was no use pretending that international working class solidarity for opposing war and the nationalistic and imperialistic policies making for war existed at the present time. Accordingly, some kind of League, but a *real* League, was the only hope for some time to come. The concession was hardly a significant gesture, for Morel was clearly convinced that the changes that would create such a real League were unlikely to materialize.[36]

Whatever the differences of approach revealed in the various Labour publications, the intensity of the reaction was palpable. Beatrice Webb summed it up strikingly in the pages of her diary. "There is today," she wrote, "owing to the French action in Germany, exactly the same nightmare feeling as there was during the War. The world is again at war, and at war in a peculiarly horrible way. The trampling of Germany by France is a disgusting vision—making the whole of our sacrifices during and since the War a detestable combination of suicide and murder."[37]

All of the public commentary was the obbligato that accompanied the more formal actions of the various branches of the labor movement. The immediate response of the Union of Democratic Control, which as we have seen was overwhelmingly an organization of labor supporters, paralleled that of the Independent Labour party. Early in February, the UDC's Executive Committee issued a manifesto denouncing the Ruhr adventure and disputing that reparations were the crucial object of French policy. The chief aim was "security," by which Poincaré meant the dismemberment of Germany and the establishment of a Rhine frontier. Beyond that, the manifesto held, a further objective aimed at the creation of a vast coal, iron, and steel trust under the control of the French government to be used as an instrument of French politico-economic domination of Europe. If France were to succeed in controlling the Rhineland and the Ruhr, she would become, along with her Polish ally, the mistress of perhaps two-thirds of the European raw materials required for industry and war. The UDC's prescriptions were familiar ones: dissociation from the French idea of security, the revision of the peace treaties, a general scheme of disarmament based on an all-inclusive League of Nations, withdrawal of all foreign troops from German soil, the cancellation of all foreign war debts by Britain, and an international loan to finance the reconstruction of devastated areas, to which Germany should be required to contribute in material and labor. Only by promoting some such policy, the document suggested, could the British give proof of their intentions and avert the peril, so much more imminent in the past few weeks, of a new world war leading to anarchy and chaos.[38]

The UDC position was reiterated in a resolution passed at the eighth annual General Council meeting held at Caxton Hall on March 9, 1923. The resolution reflected once again that the General Council was slowly distancing itself from the most extravagant pronouncements of Morel when it proposed a generous offer to France in the matter of the French debt, a pledge to participate in an international loan to cover the expenses for actual damage in the devastated areas, and that Britain participate in a guarantee of mutual security through an all-inclusive League of Nations, conditionally upon France agreeing to withdraw her troops from German soil east of the Rhine and joining in a world conference to reconsider the political settlement of 1919.[39] As secretary of the UDC, Morel loyally supported its resolutions, but his public comments made it abundantly clear that he was much less willing than were some of his fellows to work with the French to seek solutions.

Throughout 1923, the UDC as a group, even as it called for international intervention, remained skeptical of the likelihood of League of Nations action to resolve the Ruhr dilemma. For the most part, the organization concentrated upon its campaign to depict German suffering and denounce French iniquity. If Morel sometimes went beyond its formal positions, other collaborators were almost equally incensed by developments on the continent. Arthur Ponsonby wrote bitterly that the failure of passive resistance against armed force was a world disaster. The collapse of the unarmed gave further encouragement to the upholders of the doctrine of violence and justified them in their reliance on bombs, armored cars, airplanes, and all the diabolical machinery of destruction.[40] Not all the members of the UDC—and certainly not E. D. Morel—shared Ponsonby's pacifism, but what they did share was a profound and continuing disillusionment with the ability of existing international institutions to deal with the problems of the postwar world.

The Independent Labour party also had little use for the League of Nations in its assessment of the current emergency. By 1923 the gulf between the ILP and the parliamentary party had begun to widen. The latter, in the words of Robert Dowse, the historian of the ILP, "had lost much of its 'revolutionary' fervour and was settling down to the compromises and retreats from principle which the parliamentary system of government necessitates." The former, attempting a "democratic-revolutionary" synthesis between the Communist party to its left and the mainstream of the Labour party to the right, was increasingly isolated.[41] Just as many of its leaders were unwilling to face the implications of "responsible" opposition or government on matters of domestic tactics, so they were impatient with the emerging "realism" of Labour party spokesmen, some of whom continued to be nominal members of the ILP, on matters of international policy. Early in the year, the ILP's National

Administrative Council (NAC) issued a manifesto that denounced the Ruhr occupation as a breach of international law and called upon the British government to demand that all Allied occupation of Germany be brought to an end. After repeating the familiar litany—that Britain waive all claims for reparations, that she work toward a cancellation of allied war debts, and that French reconstruction be aided by an international loan—the NAC went on to assert that Britain must give practical proof of her desire to assist in the settlement of the general European problem. This could be shown by a series of actions that ranged from a recognition of the Russian government to the replacement of the Versailles treaty by a new pact and the promotion of a world conference to ensure that the League of Nations be provided with a revised and democratic constitution so that it might cease to be a cloak for the decisions of the victorious powers. Matching the demands of the UDC, the ILP leadership argued that only by some such comprehensive plan could Europe avoid the catastrophe that now threatened to engulf it.[42]

The ILP's continuing emphasis upon the construction of a new world organization rather than reliance on the League of Nations widened its breach with the parliamentary Labour party. Despite the ambivalence of some of the Labour party's leaders, they were gradually coming to realize that they would have to work within existing institutions to promote their international policies. Increasingly, they accepted that in order to do so they would have to learn how to negotiate and how to compromise. For most of the ILP stalwarts such a notion was anathema.

As the ILP denounced the actions of governments and League of Nations alike, it also took steps to indicate its solidarity with its continental comrades who were opposed to the Ruhr occupation. Letters were sent to the Socialist and Labor parties of Germany, France, and Belgium expressing support for those whose resistance required so much more courage than that of the ILP. Charles Buxton visited the Ruhr, as has already been noted, on behalf of the party to convey its sympathy to the German workers and to consult with the Executives of the German Social Democratic party in Berlin and the Belgian Labour party in Brussels. Subsequently Buxton reported to the National Administrative Council and ILP members of Parliament and addressed a large public meeting in the Memorial Hall.[43]

When the actions of the ILP leadership came before the organization's annual conference in April, substantial differences in the approach to the Ruhr crisis were revealed. The National Administrative Council proposed a resolution based upon collaboration of the workers of various countries to protest against the invasion and to demand the complete withdrawal of all armies of occupation from Germany. Going one step further, delegates from Norwich offered an amendment calling in any case for the withdrawal of British troops in order to dissociate the country from the French and Belgian outrage.

The ILP, however, was torn by the question of the use of force or even the threat of its use. The implication that Britain should be urged to use the withdrawal of troops to put pressure on the French and Belgians troubled several of the more insistent pacifists in the party, who took issue with both the NAC proposal and with the amendment. John Wheatley, the future minister of health in the first Labour government, argued against the position that "because they disagreed with the moral right of France to occupy the Ruhr they were prepared to use all the power of Britain to see that France got out of the Ruhr." Bluntly posing the question that was so often evaded in ILP rhetoric, he asked the conference: when they had lectured France and denounced the immorality of her policy and action, if France still refused to leave the Ruhr, were they prepared to abandon neutrality and use force? Harking back to 1914, Wheatley asked if the delegates did not think it would have been better, much as they detested the invasion of Belgium, if Britain had remained out of the war and saved the world one of the most tragic chapters in its history. France was in the Ruhr because the economic resources of that area combined with those of Lorraine would place her in the forefront of industrial nations. What Labour had to fear was not a policy of benevolent neutrality, but an aggressive military policy to get France out, not for any moral purpose, but to serve the economic interests of British capitalists who were diametrically opposed to the French occupation.

The fiery James Maxton predictably supported Wheatley, asserting that the condition of any nation in Europe was not so much worse than that of the British people as to justify adopting a policy that would imperil the lives of British working men. Maxton and Wheatley represented the more root-and-branch pacifists in ILP ranks, but they were in a small minority when compared with the delegates who, in a sense, attempted to carry water on both shoulders.

Advocates of the Norwich amendment like left-wing publicist Seymour Cocks, while commending the efforts of Ramsay MacDonald and others to construct a "golden bridge" by which French and Germans could approach each other without loss of dignity, nevertheless argued that no such action could influence the dominant group in France. Accordingly they urged the adoption of the Norwich amendment, since the withdrawal of British troops would demonstrate clearly that the terms of the peace treaties were no longer valid and needed to be revised. Although the NAC disapproved, the amendment was passed unanimously and, along with the more general affirmations of the NAC, was presented to the labor movement as ILP policy.[44]

Despite the misgivings in wide sectors of the labor movement about any form of international commitment, the Advisory Committee on International Questions worked constantly to focus attention on what might be practicable in the world as it existed. At the same time as it responded to contemporary crises, the committee attempted to address the issue of disarmament that occupied such importance in Labour circles. Looking forward to a time when a Labour government would have to deal directly with disarmament, the committee noted that however much the party might have taken the lead in the question, it had in fact done little more than adopt the prewar postulates upon which Conservative and Coalition governments had been acting. Recommending that the principles of a Labour disarmament policy be framed and published, it submitted a statement to serve as the basis for such a policy. In the first place, the Advisory Committee's memorandum insisted that the disarmament problem could not be addressed simply by voting against armament credits. "We may assume that, if and when the Labour Party came to power, it would not forthwith abolish the Army and Navy." Next, the document pointed out what it deemed the obvious fact, so often disregarded in some Labour circles, that disarmament could not be considered apart from policy. To demand disarmament on the assumption that the recent international situation would continue simply crystallized injustice. Parallel with any scheme of disarmament must proceed the development of some instrument for making the changes or for guaranteeing the security that had so far been part of the motives impelling resort to arms.

Disarmament could not be accomplished through a League of Nations that was merely a committee of victorious and highly armed powers. "In the absence of political justice," the advisory paper contended, "the same reasons which condemn unilateral disarmament make great caution necessary in respect of the restriction of armaments by ratio, alterations of military systems, or even attempts to mitigate the barbarities of war, or regulate it. These might well in certain circumstances mask an attempt to render permanent the military preponderance of one party." The key to the problem lay in the assumption of control over policy by the people. A supreme international body was needed to deal with the inevitable disputes that arose between nations and to exercise certain powers of supervision and control. Unlike many of their colleagues, the authors of the Advisory Committee's long analysis refused to paper over the fissures in the labor movement on matters of disarmament.

The main issue likely to divide the Labour party was whether it should ever, in any circumstances, be in favor of armed action, whether, for example, a League of Nations, however reformed, could rightly employ force. Assessing the choices available, the memorandum concluded that some sort of joint guarantee system based on compulsion was the lesser of evils open to the international community, but only if certain conditions were met. One was a clear definition of aggression that went beyond the unsatisfactory over-simplification of an actual invasion of territory. For when the point of invasion was reached, "war is there and cannot be stopped, and there is no possibility of impartial inquiry as to who the invader is." Looking forward to a test that was later to find its way into the abortive Geneva Protocol, the Advisory Committee suggested that aggression could be defined as any act of war, including mobilization, made before resort to the provisions of the League covenant for peaceable settlement of issues in controversy. The system must include most states; otherwise such a League scheme might be converted into an Anglo-French alliance against Germany and Russia. And the Labour party, if it favored such an approach, should endeavor to secure the maximum of disarmament to begin with, and its quickest possible development.

The remainder of this substantial memorandum on the principles of a disarmament policy spelled out in some detail a number of concrete questions that would have to be addressed. And an appendix even came close to tackling the less than simple question of a just war. A practical disarmament policy for a party coming into office under present conditions, the document argued, must face the fact that social or national wrongs too long unaddressed would indeed be righted by war. But such a war, though it could not be prohibited by authority or prevented by arbitration, could nevertheless be limited and localized. Thus a definition of the stages from peace to war was indispensable if an international authority was to be able to ascertain what constituted aggression in order to try to limit war.

The road to disarmament, concluded the Advisory Committee with perhaps unconscious understatement, would necessarily be long and need not be a single one. Disarmament could be furthered by developing the international authority that controlled disputes. It could also be facilitated by making war more difficult. Restrictions of the area of war and the penalization of its more barbarous weapons were both practical and had been practiced, though not without occasional failure. What was now required was the proclamation of clear principles based upon previous practice and providing for recent developments in warfare.[45]

Equally important among the acute explorations undertaken by the Advisory Committee in the summer of 1923 was one that dealt with the stance the party had assumed toward the League of Nations. After suggesting the usual remodeling of the League that was an article of faith in Labour circles, the committee significantly argued that such revision was not the important issue. It admonished that Labour, in concentrating almost exclusively on demands for reconstruction, was adopting a one-sided attitude that had definite disadvantages. Pointing out that the British government was only one of fifty-two members of the League, it conceded that the Labour party must indeed press for constitutional reform, but maintained that at the same time it must work away at current problems and develop a responsible opposition policy. Labour could not reconstruct the League until kindred governments came into power in many countries, but it could influence British policy in the League even while it was still in opposition. Then when it came into power, it could determine *British* policy. Meanwhile, various branches of the current League were doing all kinds of international work. The Labour party should press the British government to conduct its part of that international work more efficiently in order to increase the power and prestige of the League and all that it stood for.

The Advisory Committee outlined its conception of the machinery necessary to foster and to conduct a League policy. An intriguing proposal was for an international consultative parliament, perhaps by cultivating the Inter-Parliamentary Union, since governments would accept no more at present. Even more suggestive was the notion of redefining Article X of the covenant, which undertook to protect the territorial integrity and political independence of League members against aggression. Its scope might be reduced to satisfy the United States and others, while Lord Cecil's recent proposals for guarantees against aggression could be modified. They could stipulate that such guarantees could only be requested by a state whose dispute was before the League or that had accepted the League's final word in the matter at issue. The treaties should offer absolute security in exchange for an absolute obligation to settle disputes peacefully. Not only was the document a plea for realism in thinking about security issues, but in some ways it continued to surface the new connections between arbitration, disarmament, and security that were soon to find their way into the League Assembly's Geneva Protocol.[46]

While the Advisory Committee was hammering out materials for the consideration of the leaders of the movement, those leaders in turn were faced with the necessity of staking out positions in the day-to-day world of active politics. In doing so, they had to deal with a variety of points of view among the organizations affiliated with the Labour party. The ferment of differences that lay under the relatively smooth surface of resolutions and manifestos was evident when delegates from the various sections of the party met in conference in June. Some spokesmen did indeed demonstrate their understanding that American participation was essential if the reparations question was to be adequately managed, but various divisional parties and trades councils that presented resolutions for the conference demurred. From Barrow came the demand that the party condemn the mishandling of the Ruhr invasion by the Trades Union Congress and especially its plea that the "arch-capitalists" of America and the League of Nations should come to the assistance of Europe in order once again to "save democracy." The local Rushcliffe party called for resistance to the use of the League, as in the Saar valley, to mask dictation by the victor and to give an air of justice to military seizure and imperialism. From Hampstead came reiteration of the contention that the League was only an instrument in the hands of self-serving capitalist governments and insistence that the aims of working people could only be advanced by united actions through their own national and international organizations. These and a number of similar resolutions, instead of being rolled together in one composite resolution tailored to reflect the views of the party leadership, were for the most part printed without amendment for the perusal if not the consideration of conference delegates.[47]

Equal uncertainty was evident when the Trades Union Congress gathered in September. Harry Pollitt, who was of course on the extreme left of the labor movement, berated the General Council for not persuading the International Federation of Trade Unions to call a general strike in opposition to the French occupation of the Ruhr. He was answered by J. H. Thomas, who not only addressed Pollitt's argument, but also replied to a demand that the TUC support a unilateral withdrawal of British troops from their area of occupation in the Rhineland. Thomas contended that not only would a general strike be impossible, but that the German trade unions themselves did not want a British withdrawal. Such an action would only give the French a free hand in the area. Further discussion merely accentuated the compromise nature of a resolution, introduced by Margaret Bondfield and carried by the conference, which appealed to French and Belgian workers to recognize that the policy of violence nullified the purpose for which twenty million casualties were suffered in the war. It called upon them to try to change the national policy of their governments in order to promote peace among the nations.[48]

Throughout the summer of 1923, then, both the Labour party and the Trades Union Congress were still struggling, with considerable lack of clarity, to sharpen their response to French policy. That lack of clarity was underscored by the International Advisory Committee in a document which complained that a recent official statement featuring Labour's sympathy for the

French people inadequately expressed its opposition to the actions of the French government. It would be wise, the committee urged, to reiterate the policy, already declared, of renouncing Britain's share in reparations and its support for a generous settlement of inter-Allied war debts as part of the way to address the legitimate interests of the French.[49]

Some of the Advisory Committee's advice on how to shape Labour's posture on international organization and disarmament was reflected, and indeed even anticipated, in the proposals put forward in May by the TUC and the Labour party for consideration at the historic Hamburg International Socialist Conference, where the Vienna "Two-and-a-Half International" was finally united with the reactivated Second International. Although questions of international labor and socialist unity in the face of the rise of the Communist Third International held the center of attention at Hamburg, the British leadership prepared for the conference by exploring its own position on the related questions of disarmament and the League of Nations.[50] The resulting materials revealed how much they shared the rhetoric, if not the concrete proposals, of the more intransigent elements in the labor movement.

British Labour denounced the opinion that the existing League was so defective and so perverted by imperialistic policy that nothing could be done with it. It made its case in a private and confidential set of suggestions for draft resolutions to be presented to fellow socialists from other countries at the Hamburg Conference. The "suggestions" held that if the governments that composed the League genuinely renounced imperialistic, capitalistic, nationalist, and belligerent policy, the existing League could provide a framework that, if certain important defects were remedied, might become a powerful instrument of pacifist internationalism. Accordingly, the document summarized the defects that, in the opinion of the British Section of the International, were the most important, indicating ways in which British Labour believed those defects might be remedied.

In the first place, the draft resolutions inevitably noted, the League was only a partial one. It not only deliberately excluded some countries, but its constitution was framed to give power to a few nations to maintain that exclusion indefinitely. Every independent state should have the right to join simply by signifying its desire to do so and by accepting the obligations the League covenant imposed upon its members. Second, the League was being used as an instrument of the policies of the victorious Allies. One needed only to refer to the Vilna question, the Russo-Polish dispute, the Silesian issue, the Saar administration, and the Ruhr. The fault, to be sure, was not that of the League but of the governments that controlled it. The remedy? Admission of Germany, Russia, and Turkey to the League and of Germany and Russia to its

Council; elevation of the Assembly—representative of all the members—to the position of really sovereign organ of the international body; and abolition of the unanimity rule that enabled any state or group of two or three states to use the League to promote their own self-concerned policies.

Continuing the analysis, the Labour party and TUC document complained that the League did not prevent war. In actual fact, the covenant provided no binding obligation to use its machinery for pacific settlement and impartial decision, or indeed for delay before recourse to war. Therefore, in the future, every dispute, whatever its nature, must be submitted for inquiry and decision, whether to the Council, the Assembly, or the Court of International Justice, before any warlike steps were taken. An act of mobilization should be considered an act of aggression, while any party to a dispute must have the right to insist upon its submission to one of the instruments of settlement for decision.

Finally, the League was criticized because it did not guarantee its members against aggression, defined as any warlike act undertaken before a dispute was submitted to pacific settlement and impartial judgment. How could such a guarantee be strengthened? The proposal offered for presentation by the British Section of the International was that the League should pledge that all its members would come to the assistance of any of their number subjected to an act of aggression as defined. Only if it made some such definition of aggression and undertook to protect against it could the League proceed to a large and universal measure of disarmament. The recent Washington Conference agreements, which had set naval quotas for the major maritime powers, might serve as a guide to the fixing of ratios for the land and naval forces of the various nations.

As the draftsmen of the suggestions searched for a definition of aggression and attempted to outline ways to deal with such aggression, they proposed a number of steps that might be taken to make more effective use of the League of Nations. As yet the notions were tentative and still were far from characterizing the thinking of large sections of Labour. Nevertheless, they suggested that a substantial evolution was taking place, at least among certain leaders of the Labour party and the Trades Union Congress, as they in turn moved more fully into the mainstream of postwar political life. The discussion of the League and disarmament was by far the most revealing section of these "Suggestions for Draft Resolutions." By way of contrast, proposals for other revisions of the Versailles treaty and for parliamentary control of foreign policy advertised often-repeated positions that seemed to change very little no matter how much the world into which they had originally been born had been transformed.[51]

When the Hamburg Conference came together, the British Section's attempt at a positive approach to the keeping of the peace was largely lost in the more general aura of accusation and criticism that informed all that the sharply disparate delegations with widely differing agenda managed to consider. To be sure, a parcel of resolutions castigated the imperialist peace and demanded various conciliatory steps to solve the reparations dilemma. The delegates urged the cancellation of all inter-Allied war debts, called for general disarmament, and exhorted Labour in every country to exert continuous pressure upon its government to propose disarmament to other countries and to repudiate all alliances and secret treaties "which dispose of the life and liberty of the people for unknown aims." Harking back to the earlier, and somewhat vaguer, formulations of so much of the British propaganda, the international body called upon the working classes to resist the forces that were threatening to make the League of Nations a thing of no importance or an instrument of reaction and imperialism. It was their duty to exercise active control over their delegates to the League so as to make it an effective instrument for peace and for the revision of the existing peace treaties.[52] How this was to be accomplished was presumably left to the respective national delegations. Unfortunately, few of those delegations were fully agreed upon either policies or tactics.

Whatever the compromises they felt it necessary to make, the leaders of Labour were seeking a pragmatic and feasible position as their party's potential role in the direction of British affairs began to materialize. Their clearest statement of that position, at least with regard to the concrete question of the Ruhr, was published by the Executives of the party and the TUC on October 6, 1923. It called upon the British government to declare that it would never consent to any changes in the Treaty of Versailles that did not recognize that the administration and control of the Ruhr and Rhineland by the German people were essential to the fulfillment of any reparations agreement by the German government. It then proposed that the British government appeal to the United States to take its part in securing the peace and economic reconstruction of the world. To do so, the government should move to summon an immediate conference of the United States and the other powers concerned, looking toward an agreement on inter-Allied debts. If the French refused to join Britain in negotiations with Germany and to reconsider Poincaré's policy of continuous violation of the Treaty of Versailles, then Britain ought to convoke a conference of the signatories of that treaty to deal with the new situation.[53] The key element in the statement was its implied agreement with the Baldwin government that the United States must be brought in if there were to be any hope of a viable economic settlement.

By the end of 1923 the tone and indeed the substance of Labour's positions on international affairs had begun to change substantially. As the ranks of those who understood the limitations of real-world international politics expanded, publicists and counselors like Norman Angell, Will Arnold-Forster, and Leonard Woolf increasingly, if somewhat tentatively, bolstered the hitherto rather lonely position of a J. R. Clynes and urged the rejection of the all-or-nothing approach that had characterized so much of Labour's thinking and its pronouncements in the immediate aftermath of the war. Their advice, offered publicly and through participation in the deliberations of the Advisory Committee on International Questions, fitted in well with the temperamental predilections of some of Labour's key leaders, above all with the emerging views of Arthur Henderson and Ramsay MacDonald.

It would be patently unfair not to recognize how much MacDonald's perception of what might be achieved in foreign affairs had developed in a few short years. Indeed, as has been noted and as Kenneth Miller for one has pointed out, MacDonald at no time accepted the simple pacifism of a George Lansbury or many others in the labor movement. Such pacifism, however, reached close to the very top of the movement. To Arthur Ponsonby, one of the founders of the Union of Democratic Control, a Liberal who had become one of the leaders of the Labour party on matters of foreign affairs, and a politician who was soon to be MacDonald's undersecretary for foreign affairs in the first Labour government, the use of force in international intercourse was like trying to repair a watch with a sledge hammer.[54]

MacDonald, while he was asserting as early as 1920 that the only way to remove the necessity for an organization of force was to do away with the causes of war, nevertheless continued to use rhetoric similar to that of the ILP and the UDC, particularly in his regular column in *Socialist Review*. Yet by 1923, even though he could write of the occupation of the Ruhr as creating a position like that in 1905, "when Lord Grey failed to read the European situation and allowed himself to be used as a pawn in the war game that was opening," he clearly had moved further from the position of Labour's more militant groups. As the Ruhr impasse continued, MacDonald warned that Britain either had to back out altogether or return to the council boards where, unfortunately, British policy had contributed to the mischief. "The Socialist who values his International cannot look with any favour upon insular isolation. . . . Socialism finds no more guidance in the Cobdenite unconcern for the world—no more than it gets from the clap-trap Imperialism of Benjamin Disraeli." Not the least danger, MacDonald counseled, was that British Labour might drift from disagreement over policy into hostility to France, an outcome that must be avoided at all hazards.[55]

In other publications addressed to the labor movement, MacDonald insisted that in the long run nations would have to abandon every vestige of trust in military equipment. But in the meantime, ways must be devised to get through a transition period when they would have to maintain purely defensive forces that were "relatively adequate." While Britain must find in the League of Nations the focus for its contacts with Europe, it must have no sectional alliances and give no special guarantees. At the same time, until the League obtained the confidence of all important nations, Britain must not become the catspaw of the League's devotees and do nothing except through the League. But MacDonald's use of the language of Labour propaganda was quickly followed by a warning: "I am quite sure that no responsible statesman will ever persuade the people of this country to disarm in a world armed to the teeth. Their capacity to be afraid will prevent that. So long as the world is armed, the simple traditional determining purposes will remain active. We cannot feel safe if any one power should be able to dominate the Continent, and we shall therefore continue to be interested in a Balance of Power policy."[56]

Henderson, as has been noted, sometimes shared the postwar despair of his more intemperate colleagues. But from very early on he used his position as secretary of the party, where of necessity he was closely in touch with the various advisory committees, to push for a recognition that Labour's international theories could only be viable if they were designed for implementation in the world of existing national states. Even his argument for revision of the peace treaties, an argument that paralleled the position of most of the Labour Left, was based on the thesis that revision was part of Labour's program for the organization of world peace. An immediate political task, as he saw it, was the continued need to drive home the fact that the treaties had not ensured European peace. To him, they were a tissue of elaborate and contradictory provisions, the natural handiwork of capitalist governments that did not understand the economic interdependence of the nations.

He maintained that the present misfortunes of Europe were the consequences of the arrogant stupidity of the statesmen who served capitalist imperialism. To make his argument, he pointed to a weakened and impoverished Germany, the difficulties of an Austria or a Turkey or Bulgaria, "the policy of barbed wire fences round Russia, the policy of denying to other countries access to open water, the policy of oil and key industries and economic concessions." If from time to time he employed the imagery of anticapitalist, anti-imperialist, "working class" internationalism, he constantly warned his fellows in the labor movement that exposure of the defects of the existing order was not enough. Along with it, he insisted, must go a steady propaganda in support of a policy of international cooperation. "I regard it as essential," he once wrote, "that in all our criticism of the foreign policy of capitalist Governments, in Parliament and outside, we should pivot upon the League of Nations, as the guardian of world peace and the instrument of international co-operation."

Henderson's substantive recognition of the need for effective sanctions in any system of security was his most important contribution to the tutelage of Labour's rank and file. Even as he hammered away at the need for the League to be all-inclusive, for the rule of unanimity to be abandoned, or for the more representative Assembly to become its sovereign authority, he did not lose sight of the harsh realities of sheer power behind such organizational arrangements. The League of Nations, he told his somewhat unwilling fellow Labourites, "must be made the supreme independent international authority, and vested with power to enforce its decisions against recalcitrant Powers."[57]

MacDonald and Henderson in their very different ways were manifestly trying to shape the rhetoric as well as the expectations of their followers to conform to the actualities of the contemporary world. Their task was a formidable one, as the conflicting and often passionately held views described in this chapter may suggest. The inconsistencies and often self-delusions of the various positions staked out are apparent, yet by 1923 a number of the leaders of the Labour party and the TUC were beginning to face up to the political realities within which they had to operate. They did so hesitatingly and often inconsistently, but their approach helped ensure that when Labour came into office it would be as a responsible actor upon the international scene. The character of that approach, and the strength of the forces that were opposed to it, have been obscured in part because of the attention that inevitably had to be centered on the drama of the Ruhr and the immediate issues of reparations and debts, French security and the British economy. Shortly, the experience of a minority Labour government, as it endeavored to address both the short-term issues of France and the Ruhr and the interrelated longer-term questions of the organization of the international community, was to make much more evident the nature of Labour's emerging foreign policy—or, more accurately, foreign policies.

CHAPTER 5

LABOUR'S UNEASY SUCCESS

The formation of the first Labour government in British history came at a time when some of the leaders of the party, in particular both Ramsay Mac-Donald and Arthur Henderson, were beginning to escalate their calls for working within the imperfect international system in order to achieve at least some of their aims. As his own foreign secretary, the new prime minister was strikingly successful in the negotiations that culminated in the acceptance of the Dawes Plan for dealing with reparations and the Franco-Belgian occupation of the Ruhr. Henderson, for his part, continued to use the suggestions of the Advisory Committee on International Questions to frame his arguments in support of a strong international organization and, more than any of his fellow members of the government, to champion a policy that was later to be dubbed collective security backed by international force.

Most elements of the labor movement were as startled by the results of the election of 1923 as were the members of the two older parties. Although the parliamentary Labour party had been especially critical of Stanley Baldwin's handling of foreign affairs, the election itself stemmed from Baldwin's controversial decision to seek a mandate on the issue of protective tariffs. Labour clearly expected a Tory majority or at best a Tory-Liberal coalition. But the election not only appeared to reinforce the antiprotectionist cause; it fortified Labour's emerging role as an alternative to the Tories in place of the disintegrating Liberals.

The makeup the parliamentary party in the new House of Commons reflected the differences that characterized the labor movement as a whole, no less than disagreements about foreign policy. Of its 191 M.P.'s, the trade union contingent grew from eighty-four to ninety-eight, while candidates nominated by Divisional Labour parties increased even more. This indicated a strengthening of the middle class and intellectual elements in the legislative delegation as well as a tangible shift to the left.[1] The change ensured that there would be resistance, within the parliamentary Labour party as well as on the outside, to a policy that required more than token collaboration with the governments of the major powers.

The construction of the first Labour government after MacDonald had been summoned by George V has been exhaustively dissected. Much attention has been given to the new prime minister's supposedly cavalier treatment of Henderson, but MacDonald's biographer has been persuasive in explaining the reasons behind MacDonald's proposals to downgrade Henderson's participation in the government. He also makes clear that MacDonald consulted with Henderson openly and frankly on the issue. However that may be, the perceived affront to Henderson caused a great deal of ill feeling in the ranks of a party not particularly conspicuous for the smooth cooperation of its various constituent elements.[2] In some ways, the more telling point is the fact that E. D. Morel and some of his associates evidently believed that Morel was a viable candidate for the foreign secretaryship.[3] Both policy disagreements and personal friction made such a candidacy inconceivable. Yet the appointment of Arthur Ponsonby, a former Liberal, a pacifist, and a close collaborator with Morel, as undersecretary for foreign affairs illustrates the wide breadth of differences that still had to be accommodated in the Labour party. Ponsonby regarded it as part of his duty to make sure that MacDonald differentiated Labour's attitude toward the whole international situation from that of "the more woolly-headed Tories." While in office he kept in confidential touch with influential members, some of whom regarded the new prime minister as no more than a Victorian Liberal in foreign affairs. On occasion, Ponsonby even pleaded with one or another of them to communicate with MacDonald, calling attention to omissions in his policy and to what was being felt, for example, in ILP circles.[4]

At the same time, as MacDonald undertook a conciliatory approach to France, Ponsonby concluded that the strategy was correct. Clearly taking issue with his UDC collaborator, Morel, who relied on hammer blows rather than finesse, Ponsonby wrote to the latter that he was no longer a believer in big gestures. "If you want things *done*," he observed, "it must be by vigilance sympathy & help in small steps—spectacular demonstration is fatal as it is misunderstood or deliberately misinterpreted by the various scoundrels."[5]

The task here, in delineating the continuing evolution of Labour's stance on international questions, is to comprehend the various expressions of Labour opinion as elements within the movement attempted to evaluate the actual policy initiatives of their own Labour government. As is invariably the case, Labour's publicists, no less than the rank and file of the movement, had limited knowledge of the stratagems behind the public tactics of the government. There was the usual political tendency to read the best into the actions of their own leaders and sometimes to put the most plausible face on initiatives—or inactions—that were not easy for some sectors to accept. Nevertheless, the fissures that divided the movement on foreign policy multiplied. As the principal leaders of the party steered it into the mainstream of the existing international system, Labour's left wing became more and more disillusioned with an emphasis on what was merely realistic and practicable.

As MacDonald was putting together his government and for some time thereafter, the Labour press was singularly restrained in its comments on European relations, particularly with reference to the occupation of the Ruhr. Over the years since the end of the war, most of Labour's public discussion of contemporary events had been permeated with the insistence that both peace and a viable economic order could only be achieved by the substitution of a "genuine" and all-inclusive international organization for existing institutions. Ideal long-run objectives often took precedence over the day-to-day concerns with which all governments had to deal. From time to time, particular issues such as the recognition of the Soviet regime or the condemnation of French policy on the continent became the focal point of attention. Much more often than not they were used as object lessons to demonstrate the importance of adopting the thoroughgoing changes desired by various branches of the labor movement. Occasionally, however, when an emergency arose that appeared to demand prompt solution, even those Labour publicists who mistrusted any suggestion of compromise tended to check their millennialism in favor of calls for some kind of pragmatic action.

The continuing occupation of the Ruhr was a case in point. By the end of the year, German passive resistance had been abandoned, partly as a result of the exhaustion of the population, partly, it was thought, as a result of British influence behind the scenes. While the Tory government had not accepted the Labour view that League of Nations action was necessary in the dispute, it had evidently proceeded in other ways along lines advocated in Labour circles. As the new government took over and as Ramsay MacDonald moved pragmatically to try to influence the French government toward compromise, Labour's organs of opinion appeared to be waiting to see what the next steps might be. In *Foreign Affairs*, as might have been predicted, Morel gave his own particular twist to the interpretation of Labour policy, while the *Daily Herald* continued to criticize the French government even as it professed to have confidence in the policies of the new Labour administration.[6] Perhaps a reason for the initial moderation of the Labour press is to be found in the counsel of the *New Statesman* that it would be unwise for the new government to press British views upon the French leaders too strongly during the

next few months. Such pressure might result in checking the present tendency of French public opinion to move to the left, and furthermore secure
for Poincaré a fresh lease of power after the elections to be held in May. But
even the *New Statesman* commented that while peace was the greatest of
British interests, the British people were not disposed to purchase peace at an
extortionate and inequitable price. "We want a fair deal," it insisted, "and
there is no doubt that we can get it if the British Government has the brains
and courage to insist upon a just settlement. Fundamentally, there are no
divisions of opinion on these questions on this side of the Channel."[7]

Although Robert Dowse has shown how conditional was the ILP backing
for the new government, in matters of foreign affairs the initial tendency was
to be supportive.[8] In the *New Leader*, especially, H. N. Brailsford reached out
for a time to put a positive gloss on the activities of MacDonald and his
associates. Labour, he wrote in the early days of the new administration,
hoped that by methods of persuasion and broad constructive adjustments it
might bring the dangerous quarrel with France to an end. Somewhat later, he
praised the prime minister for opening a new chapter not only with France,
but also with Russia. Partly due to MacDonald's tact, partly from financial
necessity, the Franco-German question had entered a new phase. Almost
incredibly, even Poincaré appeared to be contemplating an evacuation of the
Ruhr—on terms, of course. As for the issue of disarmament, which loomed so
large in ILP propaganda, the *New Leader* now pointed out that reductions in
military expenditures could only be carried out at the expense of those items
that were least essential to defense. The really fruitful line of policy was to
begin by diminishing the causes of friction and abandoning commitments
that involved unnecessary armaments.[9] Brailsford's rather indulgent posture
was not to last, but for the moment his criticism of Labour's parliamentary
leadership was muted.

Even Morel, who complained in private of Henderson's stupidity and Mac-
Donald's secrecy, publicly emphasized the constructive steps that Labour
should take—the usual all-inclusive international body, co-operation with the
United States, disarmament and the end of military alliances, above all the
resolve to lift the whole European controversy "out of the reek and murk of
artificiality and make-believe," and on to the moral plane on which it be-
longed. Somehow, America in particular must be convinced that it now had to
deal not with an imperialistic British government, but with one willing to
approach international problems in a nonimperialist and generous spirit. But
like Brailsford, Morel was soon to resume his more derogatory judgments.[10]

From another point of view, on the Ruhr and the issue of security that lay
behind it, the more-or-less official *Herald*, which had consistently been no

more than indifferently supportive of Labour's leadership, maintained that the coming to power of a Labour government had altered the psychology of European diplomacy. The world was free from the mischievous provocations of Lloyd George and equally free from the pomposities of Lord Curzon. It knew that the present British government was genuinely seeking peace. Noting that if the French people would give power to men of goodwill, the "British people" would not hesitate to release them from their debt obligations, the *Herald* made clear that it had little sympathy for the existing German government, which in Thuringia was using much the same methods as those of the French in the Rhine provinces. Even now, however, the paper expressed hesitancy about making concessions to the French. Its concern was for the German workers. To offer debt cancellation—a symbol of British compromise—to those who at present held power in France would both outrage the German comrades and materially injure them.[11]

On disarmament, the *Herald* purported to see agreement with its radically pacifist position in the posture of Labour's chieftains. It heaped praises on the parliamentary statements of both MacDonald and William Leach, one of Labour's spokesmen on the issue. It was common sense, as they put it, that security lay, not in preparing for war, but in determining to be at peace. The *Herald* quoted "militarists and navalists" as saying: "Oh, yes, we are determined to be at peace with France—war with France is unthinkable; but France has more aeroplanes than we have. We are resolved not to quarrel with America, such a thing is out of the question; but America's navy must not be stronger than ours." That way, warned the *Herald*, lay madness—the madness of another war more hideous and destructive than the last.[12]

Few of the commentators in the Labour press were as yet prepared to tackle the delicate question of the sanctions against any hostile international action. An exception was Norman Angell, who differed from his fellow journalists in gradually coming to acknowledge that some measure of force could not be avoided. He insisted, both in the press and in private talks with MacDonald, that the effective collective defense of Europe depended in the first instance upon agreement between France and Britain as the nucleus of the police power of the League of Nations. As he had consistently argued since the end of the war, he emphasized the need to reduce arms, but made clear his belief that force would also be necessary in the process of gradually moving toward disarmament. His quite accurate judgment was that the new prime minister found the championing of arms reduction more palatable than support for military sanctions behind the international organization of the states.[13]

The new government, then, was not lacking in public advice from its followers and allies. Most of that friendly advice appeared in Labour-connected papers and journals, but from time to time it surfaced elsewhere. For example, George Young, an ex-diplomat whose paper on the reform of the foreign services had been one of the first considered by the Advisory Committee on International Questions, assessed in the *Contemporary Review* the chances of Ramsay MacDonald's success in "pacifying" Europe. Labour, as Young saw it, had a cleaner record in the eyes of foreign peoples and a closer relationship with them. Using colorful rhetoric, both figurative and literal, he declared that "Europe sees Liberalism with a grimy watermark round its neck of half washed-out secret entanglements and treaties. It sees the Conservatives with a bad brown aura of bloody interventions and oily intrigues. It sees Labour in a beautiful pink halo of moral appeals. The road to Versailles is paved with the good intentions of Labour Congresses." In short, Europe distrusted Lord Grey and Lord Curzon, Lloyd George and Asquith, while MacDonald had caught its eye and captured its ear. But, warned Young, it would trust him only for a time and up to a certain point. It was up to him to "bring his ship to port before the turn of the tide will leave him poking about in the ebbs and shallows of the 'diplomatic channels.'" The language was as cloudy as some of MacDonald's own pronouncements, yet its import was clear. Good intentions were not enough. The time had come for Labour to show its skill in guiding Europe toward a peaceful future.[14]

As for the Advisory Committee that Young had served, its role was to be somewhat diminished once a Labour government assumed office and had at its disposal the resources of the Foreign Office and other bureaucracies. Nevertheless, as that government moved into place, the committee continued to explore the tangled relationships of reparations, the Ruhr, and war debts. In a memorandum for the information of MacDonald, the advisory body pointed out that Germany must have some financial support, perhaps by way of a "food loan," and that there must be a moratorium on reparation payments. Then a conference of the principal governments concerned, including the United States and Germany on equal terms, should be called, whether or not France or any other nation participated, to discuss the interrelated issues of the financial settlement and of continental security. The British government should put before the conference proposals for the renunciation of all further reparation claims and, if other countries would confine their claims to bare restoration of devastated areas, it should be generous on debts owed to Britain. The conference, in turn, should lead toward a broader gathering for the reconstitution of the League of Nations, in order that such a renewed organization might deal effectively with other outstanding problems. In other words, there was a persistent sentiment within the Advisory Committee to insist on fundamental changes in international organization of a character not yet acceptable to many of the states with which the British government had to deal.

On the Ruhr, the Advisory Committee urged MacDonald to continue to emphasize that the occupation was contrary to the Versailles treaty, that Britain would not recognize any annexation, and that she demanded prompt restoration of normal civil life in the area. It suggested that "world opinion" should be mobilized to support a reasonable policy, using the British military position at Cologne as a bargaining counter with France. If France should remain recalcitrant, Britain should declare herself no longer bound by the treaty. In conclusion, the committee proposed that the Labour party issue a "Manifesto to the Peoples of the World" as a way of helping to influence the forthcoming elections in France. The purpose would be to show dramatically that Labour's methods of diplomacy were more democratic than those of other parties and other governments.[15]

As the weeks passed, Advisory Committee members became increasingly sensitive to the realities of international politics, which required a substantial measure of compromise if the British government was to work effectively with those of the other nations. Perhaps their most cogent piece of analysis appeared in February as MacDonald was already embarking on his policy of qualified conciliation, keeping up the pressure on France while at the same time urging her to accept a compromise. A long document prepared by the Advisory Committee under the title "Labour, the League and Reparations" emphasized that in the League of Nations, as in every other phase of foreign affairs, the success of any particular policy framed by any one government depended upon the extent to which it approached some middle ground. The committee urged Labour to understand how the international system actually worked. "Neither the Labour Government nor the Government of any other country," it declared, "can by merely having a League policy, make that the policy of the League any more than, by having a policy on reparations, it can make that the policy of its Allies." Warning that it might be unwise to look for dramatic and immediate results, the committee counseled that the air needed clearing to do away with the conception, so easily accepted in Labour circles, that Britain's part in the reparations controversy had been guided by selfish financial and trade interests. How might that be done? The committee suggested several initiatives. One might be to sign the Optional Clause of the League covenant, accepting compulsory jurisdiction of the Permanent Court of International Justice in legal disputes between governments. If the British government declared its willingness to accept such jurisdiction it would be an act of moral leadership and of wise national statesmanship. Or Britain might work toward getting Germany into the League and recognize Russia as a first step toward persuading others to do so. All such steps, however, presupposed a settlement of reparations. "The time for the League in this matter is not yet ripe," the committee warned, "and any endeavour to use the League as a weapon to force a settlement is more likely to be an obstacle than a help." At the proper time, once reparations had been dealt with, the prime minister should go to Geneva, where his presence would have great moral effect, raise the prestige of the League, and give Britain again a position of leadership.[16]

Some of the Advisory Committee proposals, notably the support for the Optional Clause, reflected ideas that had become common currency in some Labour circles. For example, Philip Noel-Baker, professor of International Relations at the University of London, who was becoming increasingly active in party politics, argued that the political institutions of the League of Nations now constituted a true parliament of man, so that the British government could rightly cooperate with other governments in giving obligatory jurisdiction to the Permanent Court without bringing injustice either upon itself or upon other members of the community of nations.[17]

MacDonald, as a practicing politician now in office, approached proposals for changes in the international system with great caution. While he acquiesced in some of the ultimate aims expressed in the Advisory Committee's memoranda, he had a quite different conception of the tactics to be employed in pursuing them. Because he was the leader of a party that had never before controlled the reins of government, it was almost inevitable that he should rely heavily upon the professionals who were responsible for continuity in the conduct of affairs. Never fully persuaded of the present strength of international institutions, he found his caution bolstered by the advice he was receiving from the permanent officials of the Foreign Office. Their views, along with those of the service departments, diverged considerably from the proposals of the informal Labour party "think tank." The Foreign Office bombarded him with reasons for rejecting the Optional Clause. In particular, it stressed the fear that Britain might not be able to avoid incurring a judgment of the court interpreting the laws of naval warfare in a manner that might cripple the British navy. Although Sir Cedric Hurst, the Foreign Office's legal advisor, concluded that by signing Britain had little to gain in peacetime and ran no serious risk in time of war, the weight of opinion in the Foreign Office was negative. Numerous memoranda referred back to the experience of the last war, noting that every point that neutral or enemy states had raised against Britain at the time would certainly have been brought before the court. The United States would undoubtedly have taken a leading part in obtaining decisions adverse to British interests, and Britain would have had to choose between losing the war or defying the International Court. When the Lord

Chancellor advised against signature, MacDonald commented that it was necessary to go beyond the "legal correctness" of Haldane's memorandum. If his "valuable" note should be published as the government's complete view it would be regarded as a serious slap in the face to arbitration. MacDonald asked that the dominions be informed that the government was considering the matter and that it wished to do so sympathetically.[18] In the event, Labour waited until its second term of office after 1929 before signaling its adherence, with significant reservations, to the notion of compulsory jurisdiction for the court in legal disputes.

Similarly, MacDonald was fully aware of War Office views that regarded French security as closely connected to British security. In the course of time, the Army leaders believed, Germany would again clash with France. France and Britain were military necessities to one another, France as a buffer between Germany and Britain, Britain as a cover for France on all fronts except the German one. A Foreign Office survey pointed out that the military strategists saw the danger time as 1935, when Germany would be "reconditioned and redisciplined" and thirsting for revenge. By then the manpower situation would be at its worst from France's point of view. Accordingly, the analysis advised, Britain had just ten years in which to prepare. From the War Office's point of view, the best security would be a definite military agreement, but that being impossible, the British government should concentrate on strengthening the power and prestige of the League of Nations, and, as a first step, try to get Germany and the United States to become members of that body.[19] To be sure, the professional soldiers' notions of strengthening the League had little in common with the proposals of many in the labor movement, and they may indeed have been a painless concession to the strange new Labour masters. But even the contingent endorsement of the international organization represented a giant step in the circumstances of the time.

MacDonald understood that behind the issue of reparations lay the much more complex problems of security and the Franco-German balance of power. Still, his views on the latter differed considerably from those of the French or the Germans or even of his own military advisors. He shared the standard Labour mistrust of reliance upon military equipment, rejected sectional alliances and special guarantees, and, in general terms, supported increased use of the League of Nations as the focus of diplomatic policy. He was no more ready than any other British politician to give the French a solid military guarantee against Germany. Nor was he willing to discuss security until reparations had been dealt with. On the other hand, he believed that a cordial but firm approach to Poincaré might hasten the movement toward a Ruhr accommodation that had begun under Baldwin.[20]

The sensitivity of the new government's position is perhaps best revealed in the curious incident of Arthur Henderson and the Burnley by-election. Shortly after his defeat in the General Election, Henderson found a relatively safe constituency from which to stand for the House of Commons. In the course of one of his campaign speeches he affirmed his support for the view that revision of both territorial and economic aspects of the Treaty of Versailles was very much overdue. Lloyd George immediately put down a private member's question, asking whether the statement represented the policy of MacDonald's government. The latter, fearful that the remarks of his own home secretary might jeopardize his negotiations with the French, was evasive and seemed indeed to repudiate his colleague.[21] Henderson's comments, in fact, represented the position that had been steadily taken by virtually every section of the labor movement from the time of its postwar disillusionment with the peace settlement. Indeed, a few days before Henderson's speech, MacDonald himself had spoken in Parliament of the need to enlarge the League if it were to be effective. But now, as foreign secretary, he was in effect changing the long-standing policy of his party. Like Henderson himself, he had been trying gradually to move Labour away from the crusading slogans of a sometimes irresponsible opposition toward positions that recognized the realities of the world in which foreign policy was executed. Henderson, no doubt, slipped in his judgment by not recognizing that a cabinet member could hardly have the same freedom of propaganda as an ordinary Opposition candidate. Yet MacDonald's embarrassment in the Commons possibly revealed more about his own secretiveness and suspicion of Henderson than about any fundamental differences in their posture toward foreign policy.[22]

The *contretemps* with Henderson aside, MacDonald's unconventional but friendly exchange of letters with Poincaré hardly concealed the resoluteness behind his words. The prime minister's purpose, according to his biographer, David Marquand, was to isolate the French by creating a united front of the other allies, to frighten them with rather vague warnings about the effect of their intransigence on Britain, and to reassure them that face could be saved only if they did what the British wanted. The policy, Marquand points out, was not very different from that of Curzon and closely in line with Foreign Office thinking.[23] It was made somewhat easier when the French elections of May substituted the more flexible Edouard Herriot for an unyielding Poincaré in the conduct of French policy. Already, in mid-1923, MacDonald as leader of the Opposition had met with French representatives and offered "enormous resistance" to the notion of an autonomous Rhineland state with international railroad control and a League of Nations gendarmerie. In addition, when Herriot came into office he was seriously handicapped in bargaining by the weakness of French finances.[24]

During their conversations at Chequers and especially during the inter-Allied conference that met in London between July 16 and August 16, MacDonald was at his best. By that time, the Dawes committee had issued its report establishing a financial framework within which Germany might reasonably be able to handle its reparations burden. The report had been accepted in principle, but matters of implementation and especially of the protections demanded by the French remained to be settled. At the conference, MacDonald made his way skillfully through the tangle of reparations and German economic viability. Reminding the French and Belgian governments that they had entered the Ruhr solely in order to secure economic results, he pushed for a progressive end to the Ruhr occupation. When the French insisted on a two-year delay, he managed to achieve a compromise limiting the occupation to one year. He was even able to finesse the issue of disarmament and mutual security, which he had fought to keep separated from the economic recommendations of the Dawes Report, by committing himself to join Herriot at the meeting of the League Assembly in the fall. That summer witnessed the peak of his political career.[25]

Labour publications did their best to commend the Dawes Plan to their readers. Not surprisingly, whatever may have been the suspicions of its editors, Labour's "official" organ exerted itself during the negotiations to urge that the experts' plan deserved discussion and then to affirm that it was workable so long as there was goodwill on both sides. The plan's great merit, claimed the *Daily Herald*, was that it placed the whole problem on a business basis.[26] Similarly, the more-or-less moderate *New Statesman* greeted the results of the London Conference as a practical agreement that would not be very pleasant for anyone, but had the great advantage of seeming likely to lead to peace.[27] And even the ILP's *New Leader* at first conceded that the agreement reached between the Allies registered progress.[28]

MacDonald's skills, however, were not enough to change the thinking of substantial sections of the labor movement. A case in point was George Lansbury, who regarded MacDonald as more adept "at intrigue and word twisting and word spinning than ever Lloyd George himself," and who confided to Beatrice Webb that he felt a bit of a criminal for keeping his doubts mainly to himself.[29] More seriously, from within the cabinet, Philip Snowden, whom Edouard Herriot in any case regarded as his own enemy and the enemy of his country, published a criticism of the London pact, suggesting that British trade interests had been betrayed by the acceptance of French views on reparations, no less than by their freedom to remain in the Ruhr for another year. As Beatrice Webb saw it, the criticism was designed to "take the gilt off the ginger-bread" of MacDonald's reputation as a European peacemaker.[30]

Major misgivings soon appeared on the Left of the movement, where the ILP and its various associates in and out of Parliament shortly resumed their suspicion of MacDonald's maneuvers. Particularly prickly was the *New Leader*, where H. N. Brailsford's early willingness to suspend judgment gave way to an increasingly critical stance. To talk about a "new era of peace," as the headlines in the daily papers were doing, was a kindly exaggeration. The Labour party, he was soon warning, had watched the negotiations with much that was in its mind unsaid. It had accepted the Dawes Report for the sake of the broad interests of peace but with many mental reservations. The agreement was a typical bankers' scheme. It threatened the impoverished German workers with heavy indirect taxes, it handed the national railways of Germany over to private enterprise, and even added to the difficulties of German Labour in reconquering the eight-hour day. Still, with a united party and with loyal backing from his colleagues it might yet be possible for the prime minister to turn a half-won peace into a settlement worthy of himself and of his supporters.[31]

MacDonald was disheartened by what he regarded as unwarranted criticism. He was aggravated by Brailsford's attacks and by the forum that the editor of the *New Leader* frequently offered challengers such as Morel. Although the ILP journal that had previously been his chief public platform later praised him as one of the great prime ministers in British history, he confided to his diary his view that no political party had been so badly served by its press. The *Daily Herald* did far more harm than good to the labor movement, both internally and externally. And he was particularly frustrated by the failure of his backbenchers to respond to new conditions.[32]

Whatever MacDonald's views about his back-bench colleagues, some of them were indeed less than enthusiastic about his pragmatic approach. Morel soon abandoned his early inclination to give the new government the benefit of the doubt. Caustic in his parliamentary condemnation of "this last attempt to square the circle and to make economic truths compatible with the violation of economic truths," he complained that "the realities came from the back benches and the unrealities from the front benches." Many on those back benches, he alleged, regarded the Dawes Report with a most profound apprehension, and that apprehension was not lessened by what they had heard from the prime minister. Not a few of the parliamentary Labour party shared Morel's concerns, both at what they saw as an abandonment of Labour's commitment to "no annexations and no indemnities" and because they feared the effects of the reparation proposals on the British economy—

and especially the British workers. As bits and pieces were revealed about the reparations negotiations, some critics feared that the lowering of German wages, which the Dawes proposals would require, might result in similar pressure for reductions in the pay of British workers. Others were concerned that proposed reparation payments in coal would undermine the market for British coal and seriously injure the livelihood of British miners.[33]

Morel in particular remained unreconciled. Even though he went along with the UDC Executive in May in hoping that the French and German governments would accept the Dawes Report, he insisted that the reparations policy be labeled morally wrong and politically unwise, and that the Executive urge its liquidation. His intransigence worried his collaborators within the government. Arthur Ponsonby, caught between his role in the Foreign Ministry and his long-standing position of leadership in the UDC, wrote to Morel expressing fear that "your manifesto" was going to cause trouble. The *Daily Telegraph*, he predicted, was going to make the most of it. There was great fear that the German nationalists would exploit the UDC position, and in France, too, suspicion would be aroused. A statement had been issued that the UDC was a private body in no way connected with the government, but of course the former connection of government members with that body made the situation extremely awkward.[34]

Morel was not to be deterred. Already he had castigated the Committee of Experts' judgment of Germany's capacity to pay. The whole scheme, he had written in a long article in *Foreign Affairs*, would bring ultimate disaster to all concerned. It could not work. Instead, he reiterated his customary proposals—a genuinely negotiated reparations settlement in which Germany was treated as an equal, the evacuation of alien troops from German soil, the cancellations of French and Italian debts to Britain, the expansion of the League of Nations to include Germany and Russia, and finally a world conference on disarmament. Above all, every effort should be made to convince the American people of Britain's willingness to go as far as self-respect permitted for the purpose of world peace. Calling for a "declaration which would live in history," Morel argued that if it fell because of such a policy, the British Labour government would have won the moral leadership of the world.[35] Despite Ponsonby's pleas to Morel, the UDC Executive's manifesto substantially followed the latter's position. Even though it did advise the French and German governments to accept the Dawes Plan, the bulk of the statement was filled with arguments to show that the whole plan was nothing less than an overwhelming disaster.[36] To emphasize the UDC's decision to recommend acceptance as evidence of a change of heart, rather than as a reflection of dissatisfaction with the direction of British policy, tends to underrate the depth of the disagreements on foreign policy within the labor movement.

The reaction of some of the leaders of the Trades Union Congress made it apparent that dissatisfaction with the handling of reparations was more than the aberration of a tiny minority. When a delegation visited MacDonald to discuss industrial questions, he himself brought up the Ruhr. Ben Tillett expressed surprise that in no single government report, British or other, had it been noted that German workers had ten percent deducted from their wages for the purpose of reparations. MacDonald pointed out that he had twice emphasized the point in recent speeches, but suspicion continued. At the TUC's annual meeting in September, the left-wing president of the Congress, A. A. Purcell, censured the Dawes Plan for concentrating economic power in the hands of a small group of money lords. Rejecting the argument that the German workers themselves were anxious that the scheme of settlement be adopted without delay, he scornfully suggested that in the same way it might be said "that the Russian people accepted the burdens imposed upon them by their Tsarist rulers, and asked for more!" His denunciation of the reparations settlement was accompanied by a call to British workers to join in the international antiwar days scheduled for September 20 and 21. Preparing the way for a resolution instructing the General Council to convene a special congress to decide on industrial action in the event of the danger of war, Purcell urged the TUC delegates to proclaim that they dared to refuse to associate with war movements or warlike preparations. Suspicion that the MacDonald government was abandoning long-standing Labour policies clearly colored the deliberations of the TUC.[37]

The government for the most part continued to muster support in the parliamentary mainstream of the Labour party. In those circles represented by the Independent Labour party and the Union of Democratic Control, however, the dissatisfaction over the Ruhr arrangements was simply an accompaniment to unflagging criticism of the manner in which foreign policy was conducted. During the war, the UDC had come into existence mainly for the purpose of combatting the secret diplomacy its leaders held responsible for the coming of the war. E. D. Morel, in particular, had searched the archives as they were opened and had painted a picture of a small group of European leaders, pursuing their purposes and making commitments completely without the knowledge of the people whom they supposedly represented. Under his prodding, first the UDC, then the ILP, and finally, in somewhat more general terms, the Labour party itself had become advocates of what was termed the democratic control of foreign policy. Various groups within the labor movement had their own interpretation of democratic control, but for Morel and the UDC it meant following the example of the United States and creating in the legislature a Foreign Affairs or Foreign Relations Committee for the oversight of governmental operations. It also meant the insistence that all treaties, agreements, and commitments of an international character should be placed before Parliament, so that it might exercise control in a systematic and open fashion. In the years after the war, opposition to secret diplomacy and advocacy of parliamentary control found their way into the rhetoric of the Labour party, in language centering about the notion of "democratic" conduct of foreign policy. By 1924, for example, whatever might have been their differing views of the government's handling of external affairs, the General Council of the Trades Union Congress and the Executive of the parliamentary Labour party agreed to join in a deputation to the prime minister, requesting that time be given in the House for consideration of the motion laid down by Morel and others: "That, in the opinion of this House, no diplomatic arrangement or understanding with a Foreign State, involving, directly or indirectly, national obligations shall be concluded without the consent of Parliament, and no preparations for co-operation in war between the naval, military or air staffs of a Foreign State shall be lawful unless consequent upon such arrangement or understanding; and this resolution shall be communicated to all States with which we are in diplomatic relations and to the League of Nations."[38]

Now that a Labour government was in office, the time appeared to have arrived to put Labour's propaganda into practice. As early as April 1, Arthur Ponsonby informed the House of Commons that in the future all treaties and agreements by which Britain might be bound in certain circumstances would be placed before both houses of the legislature for twenty-one days, so that any party could demand a discussion through the normal processes of Parliament.[39] The concession appeared to be a minor one to those who had campaigned for much stronger steps. Almost immediately, Morel wrote to Ponsonby to congratulate him on striking the first blow for the UDC policy, but regretting that the statement only promised to lay all treaties before the House. It said nothing about secret clauses, nor did Ponsonby speak of promoting a bill or resolution pledging the government to conduct open diplomacy. To the argument that any future government could reject the pledge, Morel replied that it would be courting public disaster to do so. As it was, unless a measure was passed pledging Britain to open diplomacy, the nation would be as badly off as before the moment Labour left office.[40]

To this Ponsonby replied that if he had not rushed his statement through, unsatisfactory though it might have been, nothing at all could have been done in the present session. As for a bill, Ponsonby paraded all the objections—it would have to be preceded by an address to the crown, it would take a whole session and be "riddled by constitutional lawyers," and in the end it would be a poor affair. In any event, he later wrote to Morel, he had come to the conclusion that no spectacular demonstration or resolution could really help. Surely the UDC existed for more than the establishment of the one reform. Democratic control meant education, watchfulness, discussion, and parliamentary intervention as much as passing a resolution about treaties and agreements. Although the agitation for further action continued, the realities of office ensured that the statement of April 14 was as far as the Labour government was prepared to go.[41]

If there were substantial differences on the handling of reparations and on open diplomacy, there were none when the Draft Treaty of Mutual Assistance came up for consideration. The draft treaty had been drawn up in part by Lord Robert Cecil and had been accepted by the League Assembly in 1923. Signatories were to obligate themselves to come to the aid of victims of "aggressive war" and the League Council was to decide when aggression had occurred. Military assistance was to be limited to states in the same region as the injured party and a measure of disarmament was to begin within two years. The proposals, which reflected the French approach to the issue of security, in general had a harsh reception in Great Britain, often for very different reasons from those in the Labour circles where they were almost unanimously suspect.

Meanwhile, as Labour ministers settled into office early in 1924, the Advisory Committee on International Questions, among its other concerns, had taken up the draft treaty. The ubiquitous Morel combined with G. Lowes Dickinson, who had been one of the first proponents of a League of Nations during the war, to prepare a long memorandum urging an alternative policy upon the Labour government. Noting that no practical definition of "aggressive" and "defensive" was possible in connection with acts of states, they stressed the impossibility of elaborating international arrangements based upon interpretations that could never find common acceptance. The League of Nations, Morel and Dickinson argued, was useless if its main function was not to abolish war. Yet the draft treaty would perpetuate, under the aegis of the League, the system of sectional military alliances whose essential purpose was to prepare for war and to maintain and perfect armaments. Instead they recommended dissociating the Labour government from the policy of the treaty; admitting Germany and Russia into the League; working to secure in advance the support of the dominions, Japan, and smaller powers, as well as the moral support of the United States, so that when the time came the opposition of a single power could be contested. If France were to leave the League, for example, the French people might bring in a government that would apply for readmission. There were risks, but they must be taken. A far more terrible catastrophe than that of 1914 was only a matter of time, unless the League did become an effective instrument of peace. If the showdown had to come, it was better that it should come while a government was in power in Britain whose peaceful purpose was unquestionable.[42]

Within a few weeks, Professor James T. Shotwell, an American political scientist, had provided for the Advisory Committee a careful assessment of the Morel-Dickinson document. He agreed, first of all, that to call upon the League, "in the heat of an international crisis," to condemn one of its constituents as a criminal was a task it could not now, and probably never could, discharge. Obviously its decisions were liable to be influenced by political considerations as much as by considerations of justice. But neither did the Morel-Dickinson document, in criticizing the draft treaty, itself supply a useful alternative definition of aggression. It did not seem helpful to argue, as they appeared to do, that security would be achieved by the mere acceptance of the obligation not to go to war. It would be calamitous to drive France to secede from the League, nor would doing so necessarily leave France isolated on the Continent. Moreover, such a policy would put off for a generation all hope that America might take a more active part in solving Europe's difficulties. Shotwell noted that he thoroughly understood the general lines of both the British and American objections to the draft treaty, but he warned that absolutely nothing would be achieved if British and American policy made no compromise with the Continent. "It is on the Continent that a change in conditions must be made, and that change must proceed from the basis of existing circumstances. . . . France has made the *only definite* step. It is at least a basis for negotiation."[43]

The Advisory Committee as a whole came to its recommendations fairly cautiously. Only after three-months' consideration was it able to bring forth a report that in turn reflected the deep differences of approach among its members. Much of the report's assessment of the Treaty of Mutual Assistance followed closely the lines of argument sketched out by Morel and Dickinson. But, as a covering letter revealed, it became clear during the committee's discussions that there were two distinct and contradictory views among its members. One group favored not rejecting the treaty outright, but rather accepting it subject to certain amendments. The second view supported rejection, urging that the British government put forward alternative proposals. The committee was so divided that it decided to prepare for the government and for the national committees of the Labour party and the TUC two memoranda giving the detailed arguments and reasons for each view. As for its own recommendation, the committee's vote showed a very small majority of those who advocated acceptance of the treaty subject to the amendments specified in their analysis.[44]

The minority of the committee was persuaded by the Morel-Dickinson argument. Its members agreed that it was folly for the League to aim at widening the obligation to afford military assistance at a time "when the dangers of any such obligation are, in view of French policy, particularly acute." Further, the establishment of the old system of hostile alliances under the League would be absolutely fatal to that body itself and to any hope of enduring peace and eventual disarmament. Urging absolute rejection, its advocates complained that the proposed treaty took for granted the general policy of dividing Europe into Leaguers and non-Leaguers, of differentiating between the victorious and defeated states. Step-by-step the memo repeated the advice of Morel and Dickinson, accepting their supposition that the moral effect upon public opinion throughout the world would be enormous if a Labour government were simply to declare its willingness to submit all disputes to arbitration and to abandon war. Like their guides, this group seemed quite willing to force a French withdrawal from the League, even while it professed not to believe that France would stand out against "the entire civilized world." In any case, they too agreed that the risk from French defection was minor when compared with the risk of ruining the League system.

The proponents of acceptance with amendments warned of the perils of an outright rebuff after years of work. If the treaty could be used to satisfy French demands for security, it could be a valuable instrument to induce her to change her general policy and accept a reasonable settlement with Germany. But, they emphasized, the government must make it clear that it would approve the draft treaty only with amendments.

The most important amendment must be an attempt to get a *definition* of aggression into the treaty. The Advisory Committee's majority suggested the following: Each state should agree to submit a dispute either to the International Court or other court of arbitration or to the Council or Assembly of the League. It should further agree to take no warlike action for three months after adjudication and decision. Any state should be able to cite any other before the Council or court, and any state that refused to use the procedure or to appear when cited would be the aggressor. Finally, if one state complained, the court or Council should decide in four days whether aggression had been committed. There was a series of other proposed amendments: the abandonment of "complementary" or regional treaties or at least a provision forbidding such treaties from nullifying the general guarantee and definition of aggression; strong provisions for the League to have the power to fix the measure of reduction of armaments, in the last resort by majority vote; and no acceptance until Germany and Russia were in the League and the Council. Even if the scheme were adopted, there were other policies to be pursued further that might mitigate the dangers many people feared in the treaty scheme: the effort to get the United States into the League; a British declaration of willingness to sign treaties with any other states to submit all disputes to some form of compulsory arbitration; the abandonment of Britain's share of reparations; even a reduction of arms by Britain without waiting for the other powers.[45] Much of this was a reiteration of notions that had long been at the heart of Labour's international propaganda. But what was most striking in the majority position on the Advisory Committee was its response, as yet somewhat tentatively and even awkwardly shaped, to the fear that any League body might use its power to identify an aggressor in an international dispute for its own political purposes. The linking of willingness to submit any such dispute to some form of international judgment with the definition of aggression had within it much that was to be found in the later Geneva Protocol.

Given Ramsay MacDonald's skepticism about military alliances and his suspicion of the use of force, he hardly needed the urging of the Advisory Committee to move toward a rejection of the draft treaty. As early as April 3, the Committee of Imperial Defense had reached conclusions that were used to form the basis for the prime minister's letter to the secretary general of the League of Nations explaining Britain's inability to accept the premises of the League document. The CID maintained that for the British Empire the naval, military, and air commitments would be almost unlimited. If the obligations of the treaty were to be scrupulously carried out, they would probably involve an increase rather than a decrease in British armaments. The British navy would certainly always be the first force to be called upon. As Canada had already pointed out, it would be very difficult, in the case of the British Empire, to apply the provision that no other party would have to cooperate other than those of the continent in which operations would take place. Further, the CID explained, under the terms proposed it would be impossible to prepare necessary military action in advance and time would be lost in the appointment of a High Command, while suggested defense arrangements would merely be going back to the old system of alliances. Above all, the committee objected that no adequate definition was provided for an "act of aggression" and indeed to the fact that the draft treaty involved an undesirable extension of the functions of the League Council. Presently, under Arti-

cle XVI, the Council could only recommend action. The treaty would give it
the power to decide various matters, but it was clearly not an appropriate
body to entrust with control of military forces in operations against any state
or states.[46] Although the assumptions of the military professionals had little to
do with MacDonald's own reasons for mistrusting the draft treaty, they provided a solid, as well as conventional, case for rejecting the proposal without
qualification.

For once, on the issue of the draft treaty, there was virtual unanimity in the
labor movement. Even those who had argued the case for amendment of the
proposal were unalterably opposed to accepting the treaty as it stood. The
Labour government's most outspoken critics on the left agreed with what
they conceived its policy to be, even as some of them made it clear that they
understood the concerns that had influenced the architects of the treaty.
Thus, even before MacDonald sent his letter to the secretary general of the
League rejecting the proposed treaty, the *Bradford Pioneer*, which supported
the Independent Labour party, commented on how difficult it would be to
abandon the whole scheme out of hand. With all its faults, the treaty was the
only practical proposal that might lead to a measure of disarmament. In
addition, it would be perilous for the leader of a political party that insisted
that France's security could be obtained only through the League summarily
to reject the first and only proposal the League had ever put forward for
achieving any sort of security or disarmament.[47]

In another corner of the Labour press, it was perhaps not surprising that
the *New Statesman* should be enthusiastic about the government's approach
to the security issue, even if its approach was rather different from that of the
northern paper. The *New Statesman* stood completely behind MacDonald,
applauding the courage of his letter to the secretary general of the League
rejecting the approach of the treaty. Accepting his criticisms as absolutely
valid, it further commented that a reduction of armaments, which seemed so
urgent in other quarters of the labor movement, was hardly of much consequence. If all the armed forces of the world were cut back by half, or indeed
by three-quarters, the nations could and would pursue their quarrels just as
effectively and viciously, so long as their relative strength remained unaltered.
"And nobody," it concluded, "has any suggestion for altering that."[48]

For its part, after the emergence of Edouard Herriot in France, the *New
Leader*, the most thoughtful of the Labour papers, indicated its acceptance of
the fact that mutual security, based in case of need on mutual military aid,
represented some progress, even if it was not that for which the Labour party
stood. Once the draft treaty had been rejected, H. N. Brailsford anticipated
that the government might hold out the possibility of some alternative plan

for affording France the security that otherwise she would seek in the sub-jugation of Germany and the military domination of Europe. In rejecting the treaty as it stood, the government had the support of the great mass of the Labour party, but unhappily the difficulty of French security still remained.[49]

Even so committed a pacifist as UDC stalwart Helena Swanwick made it clear that she understood that support for the Treaty of Mutual Assistance was tempting because the alternative, in the eyes of the French, was "the policy of militarism, revenge, resentment." But she argued that the temptation must be resisted, because what it really contemplated was military preparation, gener-ally on a "partial" or alliance basis, for action against a state that was judged the aggressor by the League Council. What, then, was the definition of an aggressor? The best proposal, thought Mrs. Swanwick, was that the state or states that refused to submit a quarrel to the League's award should *ipso facto* be considered the aggressor. "Does anyone think," she asked, "we are within measurable distance of having such a definition not only accepted but hon-estly acted upon? Acted upon perhaps by a State having, at the bidding of the League, to attack one of its own Allies?" Perhaps a first step in that direction might be made when all the states had signed the Optional Clause of the Court of International Justice, agreeing to abide by its decision. Even to expect such agreement, let alone to anticipate that mortal men could decide what constituted "aggressive policy" and perhaps thus unchain a major war, was to live in "the land of moonshine." The treaty, she concluded, would turn people's minds away from the only true foundation of peace, disarmament, and subsequent confidence in an impartial tribunal to which all nations voluntarily submitted.[50]

Mrs. Swanwick's evaluation was merely a somewhat extreme statement of the position of the Union of Democratic Control. From the beginning, that body rejected the approach of the draft treaty, urged signature of the Optional Clause of the statute establishing the Permanent Court of International Jus-tice, and insisted that real disarmament was the only path to lasting peace. From the UDC's point of view the refusal of the British government to enter into any defensive treaties and to concentrate upon making the League of Nations an all-inclusive and impartial body was a giant step in the right direction.[51]

The Labour government's outright rejection of the draft treaty in late July created considerable resentment among other members of the League. To the practical men at Geneva, Labour's expression of idealism in its communica-tion to the League of Nations was so much "hot air" and seemed to under-mine the possibility of dealing with the problem of security.[52] When Mac-Donald, fulfilling the commitment he had made to Herriot at the London

Conference, reluctantly went to the League Assembly in September, there were many fences to mend. He had to explain the reasoning behind his government's negative position. For this purpose, he raised two major questions about the League proposal: "Are the guarantees contained therein sufficient to justify a state in reducing its armaments? Are the obligations to be undertaken toward other states of such a nature that the nations of the world can conscientiously engage to carry them out?" After parading a long list of illustrations to show why the answers to both questions were negative, he then suggested that in some way arbitration must be used as an approach to the assignment of responsibility for aggression. The suggestion was little more than that, but the speech as a whole was a resounding success, not only in Geneva but at home as well.[53] Even the skeptical Brailsford was impressed. Herriot's response to MacDonald, that arbitration was not enough and that arbitration, security, and disarmament were inseparable, echoed recommendations that some within the Labour party's Advisory Committee had begun to explore.[54] Brailsford commended the two leaders not for speaking well but for speaking frankly. That was a shocking breach of all the conventions, he observed, and an immense advance in the international life of Europe. It could not have happened if Poincaré and Curzon had remained in office.[55]

The success of a speech, however, did not necessarily mean the success of a policy. The fundamental gulf between the French and the British positions could not be removed by MacDonald's eloquence.[56] There was, as the *New Statesman* somewhat wryly noted, a large difference between acceptance of the principle of arbitration and agreement on how it was to be applied in practice.[57] After hurried and somewhat hectic negotiations, MacDonald and Herriot agreed to sponsor a resolution calling for a disarmament conference as soon as possible, while they left it to the relevant committees of the League to work out proposals for a new approach to the prevention of aggressive wars. In the discussions, the Czech Beneš and the Greek Politis made perhaps the most important contributions, but Arthur Henderson and Lord Parmoor, the British delegate to Geneva, played conspicuous parts.

The role of Henderson in particular requires some elaboration. From about 1922, as has been noted, both he and MacDonald had argued for changes in the international system that had emerged after the war. Both were advocates of some form of arbitration to take the place of the devastating recourse to war that had plagued the nations of the world since time immemorial. But MacDonald often tended to substitute a somewhat vague reliance upon the development of an international spirit for a willingness to face the obvious inadequacies of the international arrangements that characterized postwar Europe. In Harold Laski's words, he supplied an atmosphere of "pacific emollience" to a turbulent European situation.[58] Henderson, whose role in the formulation of Labour's foreign policy grew steadily, augmented Labour's emphasis on disarmament, arbitration, and the use of the League to promote peaceful settlement with an understanding that these desirable measures ultimately would rest upon the willingness of the powers to accept the obligation of enforcement. From the beginning, he had warned the labor movement that disarmament would be impossible until there was assurance that all members of the League would come to the assistance of any victim of aggression. In a sense, despite the drama of MacDonald's initiatives toward the French, it was Henderson who undertook to lead the Labour party closer to the concept of security demanded by the French. While he clearly did not share the French insistence that preponderant power must be maintained by the wartime victors, he recognized that a European community based on friendly understanding was an ideal far from realization. Accordingly, he conceded that at least some concessions to the requirements of security would be necessary. In a sense he too was preparing the way for what came to be called the Geneva Protocol.[59]

In the Third Committee of the League Assembly, which dealt with security and the reduction of armaments, Henderson, according to Lord Parmoor, acted with great skill to reconcile British and French views. He argued successfully that to deal with war, to get rid of it unconditionally, required a scheme by which arbitration took the place of war for the settlement of disputes, by which armaments were limited and cut down to the lowest level upon which the League members could agree, and by which the sense of insecurity was removed through mutual undertakings to support a state that was the victim of unlawful aggression.[60] The new initiative proposed that some form of peaceful settlement—"arbitration"—be the bridge joining the conflicting purposes of disarmament and security. Refusal to submit a quarrel to one of the vehicles of international judgment would automatically constitute aggression and bring into play the sanctions of the League. Finally, the terms of the agreement were not to come into effect until a disarmament conference had met and adopted a scheme for the reduction of arms.

Before the work of the committees was submitted to the Assembly, it was discussed by the British cabinet. Parmoor was instructed to insist that the results be put in the form of recommendations to the respective governments rather than firm commitments. When the proposals came to the floor of the Assembly, both Parmoor and Henderson made vigorous speeches in its support. Henderson by all reports was particularly effective. He admitted that the proposed protocol contained some provisions he would have preferred to see omitted. The scheme had been adopted as it stood because as yet a full measure of confidence in the "cohesion, the peaceful intentions and the moral authority" of the League had not been established. Until that full measure of confidence had been secured, some states would continue to think that military force was an indispensable condition of their national security. What the protocol did do, he insisted, was to suspend the use of force until the last moment, when it was required to protect the community of nations against the criminal action of an aggressor state. And any military action would be taken under guarantees preventing any individual nation from using it for its own individual advantage. Despite all the demurrers, however, Henderson recognized that in existing conditions force might be a necessary instrument of international organization.[61] Firmly supported by the British delegation, the Protocol for the Pacific Settlement of International Disputes was accepted by the Assembly in early October and immediately signed by France and nine other countries.

As in the case of the Treaty of Mutual Guarantee, the British service departments were opposed to the Geneva Protocol. The Admiralty was especially concerned. Seconding the caveats of Admiral Beatty, Lord Chelmsford, the First Lord of the Admiralty, warned of possibly serious differences with the dominions over League jurisdiction in such matters as immigration. More to the point, the Admiralty feared the sanctions provisions in the proposal. It could not be content, Chelmsford wrote to the cabinet on September 27, unless it were specifically understood that nothing should preclude a movement of the Fleet in self-defense. The inability of the Fleet to move to a strategic position might involve the destruction of the Empire. Further, although aggression was defined in the League document, it appeared impossible to define what would be a threat of aggression.[62]

Both MacDonald's biographer and the historian of the first Labour government have described how divided its members were on the promise of the protocol. Despite the enthusiasm of Henderson and Parmoor, MacDonald was no better than lukewarm about sanctions, believing that security was more likely to be achieved by the improvement of the "atmosphere" than by any hard and fast legal formulas. Haldane supported the service leaders in opposition to the commitments contemplated. Wedgwood, Ponsonby, and probably Snowden, clinging to earlier articles of Labour's faith, were not prepared to accept that progress toward disarmament required the prior organization of international force. The leaders of the Labour party had come a long way in the years since the war, but for various reasons many of them were not yet ready to abandon the slogans and theoretical postulates that had served the propaganda purposes of an earlier time.[63]

When Henderson returned to Britain from Geneva he began immediately to press for acceptance of the Assembly's proposals. Both in the country at large and later in Parliament, he was candid in his advocacy. Even when he played down the coercive features of the protocol, he made clear his belief that the possible use of international force could not be evaded—at least not for the foreseeable future. In his own constituency of Burnley, for example, he hailed the protocol as an instrument that made reason, justice, and law the first line in dealing with the differences between nations, but also warned that those nations were pledged to use their force to make their decisions effective if peaceful accommodation failed and sanctions had to be employed.[64]

By the time the League proposal was submitted to Great Britain for its action, the Labour government was in its last days. As a result, most of the public discussion of its faults and its merits came after the Tories had rebuffed it and took place in a greatly altered political environment. Such early comments as did appear reflected little probing evaluation of the terms of the protocol. As was so often the case, the most penetrating assessment came from the pen of H. N. Brailsford. Although he greeted it as "the biggest and happiest thing which has happened in the world since the peace was marred at Versailles," he called attention to its defense of the status quo.[65] The plan that had been developed at Geneva, he wrote, was a plan for the prevention or outlawry of war. For that purpose, it was, perhaps, the best code that conservative wisdom could devise. It might banish war, but did it make any adequate provision for the need of change in the life of states? One fatal reservation marred the promise to refer every dispute to arbitration. The French text recalled the provision in Article XIX of the League covenant, that the Assembly of the League might declare that existing treaties stand in need of revision. To that provision the French had added the explicit reservation that the Assembly alone was competent to declare that such a need existed. In other words, Brailsford warned, in any future dispute that arose, the Council or the court could only apply or interpret existing treaties. It was, in short, in the power of any one delegation at the Assembly—"of the Poles, for instance, or the Serbs"—to forbid the civilized world to alter one comma of the sacred treaties. He implied that a sanctionist policy might well involve action against a state that preferred to risk war rather than accept a status quo it considered unjust or unbearable.[66] For the moment his concerns were scarcely noted, but later, as Labour party strategists sought to restructure its policies to the purposes of a party in opposition, considerable attention was given to the question of peaceful change.

Brailsford's caution was reflected in the views of some of the key protagonists of the Labour Left, whose reluctant acceptance of the need for sanctions he displayed in the pages of the *New Leader*. C. R. Buxton of the ILP, for example, while he minimized the coercive features of the protocol, did not dispute the fact that sanctions posed a serious obligation. In a world that had not yet embraced pure pacifism, the price was worth paying, he concluded, for a scheme that provided for the reference of every international dispute to judicial, arbitral, or conciliatory settlement.[67] Even Helena Swanwick of the UDC, who had been, like Buxton, a British delegate to the Fifth Assembly, agreed. Despite her previous arguments against any kind of sanctions, she was in no doubt early on that, unless the powers could get the international sanction of force, they would neither reduce their armaments nor abandon the policy of the balance of power. It was not, then, a question of force or no force; it was a question whether force should be subjected to law or remain anarchical.[68] Swanwick, like so many others on the left, was quickly to revert to a full-fledged pacifism, emphasizing disarmament and arbitration, not as programs to go along in parallel with the guarantee of security, but rather as the magic formulas to provide by themselves for the safety of the nations. For the moment, some of their fears were stifled by the prospects of breakthrough promised by the protocol. Shortly, however, deep misgivings about the use of force were to reemerge in substantial sections of the movement as Labour reverted to its role as Opposition critic of a sitting government.

When the Labour party Conference met in early October, the position of MacDonald's government had become even more vulnerable. At that conference, he took the occasion of his presidential address to maintain that if Labour had been at Paris in 1919 reparations would have had a very different complexion. As it was, he expressed satisfaction with what had been accomplished. The general agreement of the nations, Germany included, was to accept the Dawes Report and see how it would work. He warned, however, that vigilance was required. German employers were using the need to pay reparations as an excuse to reduce wages, increase hours, and intensify the slavery of German workers. He urged the labor movement not to lend its countenance to "one of the ordinary excuses capitalism is always seeking to increase its grip on the lives of the workers." When the parliamentary report was made to the conference, it reiterated MacDonald's own view that the London agreement had been the first substantial step taken since the War to promote an atmosphere of conciliation and to open the way to a restoration of the peace and international amity of Europe.[69]

But even at the Labour party Conference, where support for the actions of the government was the official posture, a number of local resolutions not only proposed the condemnation of the Dawes Plan, but insisted, in evident challenge to the strategy adopted by the government, that the League of Nations could not deal with such an issue and that a "conference of the working-class organizations of the world" must be called as a means of avoiding armed conflict in the future.[70] Unlike the case at the TUC's annual meeting a month earlier, however, the critical statements represented a small minority of the delegates present and found no outlet in the accepted pronouncements of the Labour party.

By October, Labour's leadership was under siege. Tangled negotiations with the Soviet government and the mishandling of the Campbell case, involving a Communist editor accused of urging soldiers not to turn their guns on fellow workers, were the occasion, but not the reason, for the fall of the minority Labour regime. Seen in retrospect it is evident that both matters were blown up out of all proportion. Recognition of the Soviet regime had long been a benchmark of Labour orthodoxy. Not only the uncritical George Lansbury and his various colleagues on the left, but also the moderates within the labor movement, believed that the true pacification of Europe required that Russia be brought once again into the mainstream of European life. Most of Labour's leaders had little use for the Soviet system. They had taken a major role in rebuilding the Second International as a rival to the Soviet-sponsored Third International. They had few illusions about the character of the Russian government, but they agreed with their more radical supporters that the Russians, like the Germans, must become major players if the economy and the politics of Europe were to be normalized. MacDonald's decision to grant recognition was supported by virtually all of the Labour party, but it was also accepted by most of the Liberals, and even by a substantial group among the Conservatives.[71] Nevertheless, the specific steps that Labour took toward recognition opened the way for a controversy that prompted the Liberals to abandon their support of MacDonald's government and prepare the way for a Tory takeover.

In recognizing Russia, the British government also agreed to a conference, to be held in London, that would attempt to settle the various outstanding differences between the two countries. For months, beginning in April, negotiations dragged on. On the British side, in part because MacDonald was deeply engaged in dealing with the Reparations Conference and a crisis in Ireland, Ponsonby, his undersecretary, led the discussions concerning a possible treaty. The two main issues were a commercial agreement and some settlement of the Tsarist government's obligations to British bondholders that had been repudiated by the Bolsheviks. For their part, the Soviet negotiators demanded a loan to be guaranteed by the British government.

It is not necessary to review the tortured process of negotiations. The Russian delegation was badly organized and appeared hardly to be in a position to make major binding commitments. Ponsonby was harried and appar-

ently less than skillful in handling his recalcitrant counterparts. As they became more difficult he turned to colleagues outside the government for help.
On July 31 he wrote to E. D. Morel suggesting that Morel telegraph the chief
Russian negotiator, Christian Rakovsky, in Moscow in words to the effect that
in view of present circumstances, Morel and his friends urged the Russians to
do their utmost to conclude agreement. If George Lansbury could send a wire
too, he added, it might help. MacDonald was kept informed, but it seems
evident that his attention was largely directed elsewhere. In any case there is
nothing to indicate he was aware of Ponsonby's overture to Morel and others
on the Labour Left. When discussions broke down in the early morning of
August 5, the news was made public. Then a group of M.P.'s, led by Morel and
A. A. Purcell, the left-wing chairman of the TUC conference, offered their
good offices to Ponsonby in reviving the deliberations with Rakovsky. In the
light of Conservative and Liberal charges that the government had caved in to
a ramp of pro-Soviet extremists in the Labour party, it is of some interest that
the initiative for intervention with the Russians first came from Ponsonby.[72]
At any rate, the arrangements were reported to the House of Commons on
August 6. The two documents in which they were outlined were quite unex-
ceptionable. In a commercial treaty the British opened their export credit
scheme to the Russians, while the latter gave most-favored-nation status to
Britain. More unusual was the granting of diplomatic immunity to an un-
determined number of persons of the Russian Trade Mission to Britain. In a
second agreement provision was made for further negotiations between the
Russian government and British bondholders. When the outcome of these
discussions was approved by the holders of at least half the capital value of the
bonds, and when other outstanding claims were settled, a general treaty
would come into effect. Then, and only then, was Britain committed to guarantee a loan.

In Labour circles that had consistently argued for normalization of relations with the Russians, the agreements were greeted as a "victory snatched
from defeat."[73] Purcell and Morel prepared a long economic argument in
support of the treaties, insisting that there could be no stable peace in Europe,
no effective League of Nations to ensure it, no substantial decrease in the
burden of armaments unless Britain's relations with the rest of the world
became normal. For the British Empire, in particular, friendly relations with
Russia were essential. The authors contended that it was hardly necessary to
point out that the British were in constant commercial, political, and strategic
contact with Russia in the Near East, the Middle East, and on the Indian
frontier, and that the state of friction between the two governments in recent
years had involved them in much unproductive expenditure.[74]

In the mainstream of the movement, the Labour party issued a pamphlet, introduced by Ponsonby, arguing the need for stability and hailing the treaties as a cure for unemployment. Its general thesis was that the agreement settled everything it was possible to settle at the present time. J. R. Clynes later commented that Russia had been changed from a dangerous outcast threatening everyone's peace into a country once more pursuing diplomatic methods. And even Philip Snowden, who was subsequently caustic about the mistakes of his colleagues in negotiating with the Russians, admitted that when the formula was submitted to him he had no objection to it if it were a face-saving device to prevent the conference from complete collapse.[75]

Whatever the satisfaction of the labor movement with the Russian initiative, it was resolutely opposed by virtually all of the Conservatives and a significant sector of the divided Liberals. The former argued that the proposals must be debated by the House of Commons before being signed, a dubious constitutional stand but one that was useful politically in helping force the Labour government out of office. The similarity to one of the key elements in the propaganda of the UDC will be evident. As for the Liberals, Lloyd George took the lead in opposition, evidently seeing in the issue the opportunity to strengthen his leadership and perhaps even unite his fragmented party.

Ironically, substantial elements in all the parties were agreed that recognition of the Soviets must soon be conceded. It was the other aspects of the Labour documents that triggered violent disapproval. But the maneuvering of the various parties, granted that it was rooted in sharply divergent views of how to deal with Bolshevik Russia, was perhaps more closely related to internal electoral politics than to the ultimate direction to be taken in British foreign policy. When a storm of criticism over its handling of an essentially trivial incident was added to the Russian imbroglio, the days of the Labour government were numbered.

The Campbell case evolved because both the politically inexperienced Attorney General, Sir Patrick Hastings, and Ramsay MacDonald himself handled it badly. Hastings had first agreed to the prosecution of the editor of the *Daily Worker* for urging soldiers to refuse to use their arms either in a "class war" or a military war. After a group of Labour M.P.'s protested, pointing out that the author, J. R. Campbell, was a disabled war veteran and that in any case he was simply arguing against the use of troops in industrial disputes, Hastings decided to abandon the prosecution. When questions were raised in the House, MacDonald's reply that he had not been consulted and had first learned of the prosecution from the press was, in the balanced words of his biographer, "untrue and unconvincing. . . . an appalling blunder." From that moment on, the last days of the government played themselves out as all parties maneuvered with an eye on forthcoming elections. When polling took place, Labour was turned out of office, but the Liberals who had withdrawn their support were the real losers. Reduced to a fraction of their former numbers, they were to find themselves increasingly on the fringes of a two-party system in which the Tories and Labour were the major players.[76]

Despite its stumbling over the Russian treaties, the first Labour government's conduct of foreign policy has generally received high marks from students of the period. Inheriting the dangerous occupation of the Ruhr by French and Belgian troops, Ramsay MacDonald had moved with skill and tact to build upon the initiative of the Baldwin government in helping to set up the Dawes committee to make recommendations about reparations. If the arrangements he brokered did not result in a permanent accommodation of postwar obligations, they did for a time ease Franco-German tensions and dramatically improve relations between France and Britain. When he went to Geneva as the first British prime minister to attend a session of the League of Nations Assembly, his address made a profound impression, not because it contained any substantive proposals, but because it was eloquent in its plea for the development of the international institutions of the future. Yet Mac-Donald's view of those institutions continued in part to reflect the attitudes that had dominated the labor movement since before the First World War. Despite his undoubted pragmatism in trying to persuade his followers of the limits imposed on any government by the existing international system, he maintained a deep suspicion of the use of force in international affairs and when it was proposed as a sanction in a system of international security was reluctant to accept it. He believed deeply that it was a "harmless drug to soothe nerves" and that force was merely to be used as a deterrent.[77] For the most part, he placed more emphasis upon a somewhat vague development of the international spirit than upon the need to initiate the Labour party and its allies into the real nature of the international world that figured so prominently in their rhetoric.

On the other hand, Arthur Henderson, whose direct role in the execution of foreign policy in this early period was limited, increasingly played the part of Labour's tutor on international questions. As early as 1917, he had warned in *The Aims of Labour* that "moral force must be supplemented by joint organised power—military, economic and commercial" and able to enforce the decisions of a proposed League of Nations.[78] From its inception he realized the potential of the Advisory Committee on International Questions and employed it effectively to help marshal the arguments for a strong international organization backed if necessary by the sanction of military force. From time to time, Henderson too slid back into the rhetoric of earlier formulations, as in the case of his controversial Burnley speech of 1922. On balance, however, he took the lead in envisaging the possibilities of a new collaborative security system and in outlining what it might require of the British people. From 1924 on, he was to play a more and more important role in shaping the changing approach of the labor movement to international affairs.

CHAPTER 6

ALTERNATIVES TO LOCARNO

In the field of foreign affairs, the leaders of the Labour party used their years of opposition between 1924 and 1929 to chart a course that would characterize the second Labour government and that, notwithstanding all the wrong turns and self-delusions of the early thirties, emerged as the policy of the Labour party in the years just before the outbreak of World War II. Despite the Labour Left's move toward the high-minded if startlingly optimistic pacifism of "disarmament by example," Labour's mainstream politicians were encouraged to champion a full-fledged League of Nations policy by their counselors in the Advisory Committee on International Questions. In that body, the proponents of disarmament by international agreement along with arbitration, conciliation, and the judicial settlement of international disputes gradually won relatively broad support. There was less consensus about the employment of force, especially military force, to back up international decisions, but, as the advocates of international sanctions came increasingly to the fore, Arthur Henderson, Labour's future foreign secretary, used their arguments to bolster a position he had long since accepted.[1]

Despite the generally favorable assessment of the first Labour government's conduct of foreign policy, there was widespread conviction in sections of the labor movement that the experience in office had been a failure. Disgruntlement tended in particular to focus on Ramsay MacDonald. In the course of time Ernest Bevin, of the powerful Transport and General Workers' Union, led a movement to remove him from the leadership of the parliamentary party. Not for the first time, such an attempt was frustrated by Arthur Henderson, who continued to be certain that with all his faults MacDonald was indispensable as the public leader of the party.[2]

Once the impracticability of jettisoning MacDonald became apparent, Bevin concentrated upon urging that the leaders of the party pledge never to take office again without a majority in the House of Commons. Nothing that the great mass of British working people wanted, he argued, could possibly be put through the legislature by a minority Labour government, and the compromises required would destroy the confidence of the very people sending it to the House to represent them. Bevin's case, which he put most forcefully at the Liverpool Conference of the Labour party in September 1925, reflected his political inexperience at the time as much as it did the dogged insensitivity that often characterized his later career. He did not understand, or at least was unwilling to admit, that the Labour party's capacity to govern was as much an issue as any unqualified achievement of particular Labour programs. MacDonald and his colleagues rejected Bevin's argument outright and it was demolished at the conference, by J. H. Thomas, among others. Nevertheless, the overwhelming vote against refusing to serve unless in the majority could not conceal the tensions that were constantly to plague the party in the course of the next few years.[3]

Bevin did not stand alone in the trade union movement in his opposition to much that the late Labour government had attempted. In particular, the Dawes Plan, which many had labeled a triumph for the skillful diplomacy of MacDonald, was anathema to sections of organized labor. At the Trades Union Congress in 1925, several aggressive trade union leaders, who had always regarded the "Experts' Report" as a capitalist scheme to enslave the workers of Germany and of Britain as well, succeeded in forcing through a number of resolutions of condemnation. At the heart of the campaign were such radical figures as A. J. Cook of the Miners' Federation, but the vote of the delegates made clear that he spoke for much of the industrial movement when he denounced the reparations settlement as the instrument of the "Anglo-American financiers." To be sure, prominent trade unionists rallied to the support of the Dawes Plan, arguing both at the TUC and at the Labour party Conference that it was the best solution that could be achieved and that it would contribute to the long-run pacification of Europe. It was clear, however, that the cautious and compromising posture of the labor movement's political guides did not have the enthusiastic support of some of its most powerful players.[4]

It would be a mistake, however, to pick out the relatively few serious attacks and assume that there was widespread dissent in the trade union movement. After 1925, for example, there was virtually no discussion of international affairs at the annual Trades Union Congress. The watershed appears to have been the failure of the General Strike of 1926, which not only riveted trade union concerns on industrial questions, but also tended to draw the rank and file generally away from the extremism that had accomplished so little. At the 1926 TUC the failure of the General Strike and the problems of the continuing miners' strike were of course the principal concerns. International affairs were virtually ignored. As late as 1928 almost the only TUC consideration of foreign policy came in Ben Turner's presidential address, in which he tackled the problems that disarmament might cause employees in the armament industries. He concluded that it would be cheaper to pension employees fully and well than to continue the "unholy system" of depending upon perpetual preparation for war to ensure employment for British workers.[5] Aside from Turner's comments, attention to the external world was conspicuous by its absence. Such neglect no doubt reflected trade union indifference to issues of foreign policy when immediate working class interests were not at stake. At the same time, while it would be difficult to demonstrate, it suggests that union spokesmen were beginning to abandon their thoroughgoing rejection of the postwar settlement and to move closer to the political leaders who counseled cooperation with other governments and the fullest possible use of existing international machinery in the quest for a just and peaceful world.

On the other hand, among politicians of the Left, particularly in ILP circles, a substantial number of key figures were sufficiently disillusioned with the 1924 experience of office to parallel Ernest Bevin's maneuvers by unsuccessfully attempting to give the party organization a greater role in the election of its leader. During the next several years the gulf between the ILP and the official Labour party began to grow. Because so many nominal members of the ILP had served in the 1924 government, the fissures were less evident than were revealed in the aftermath of defeat. Step by step that group began to lose its middle class element.[6] Philip Snowden's resignation has already been noted. Between 1924 and 1926 both Charles Trevelyan and C. R. Buxton transferred their parliamentary candidatures from the ILP to Divisional Labour parties. Shortly thereafter H. N. Brailsford was removed from the editorship of the *New Leader* and then driven from the ILP itself. Clifford Allen, who had been perhaps most responsible for the revival of the ILP in the early twenties but who was close to MacDonald, likewise was forced out.[7] MacDonald himself, who had edited the ILP's *Socialist Review* before taking office, had grown so far from ILP policy that there was no question of his resuming that post, even though his formal break was not to come for some time.

The internal conflicts within the ILP revolved about the question of relations with the official Labour party. Its quarrel was primarily on issues of domestic policy. In the words of one observer, it "was gradually becoming aware of one of the vital weaknesses of the British Labour Movement—its lack of a philosophy of action."[8] Gradualism and the theory of inevitability were criticized as the philosophical justifications for timid policy. By 1926, the ILP leaders, having either driven away or alienated the advocates of moderation in their ranks, had adopted, in the policy statement *Socialism in Our Time*, a clearly radical program that assumed the imminent downfall of the capitalist system. Its promotion of a Living Wage policy, a notion that was to find some favor in later generations, appeared utopian to most of the unions and to the parliamentary Labour party, driving the ILP farther and farther from the mainstream of Labour party policies.

The alienation of the ILP tended to ensure the success of the foreign policy moderates within the ranks of Labour. As differences of perception became increasingly marked, such middle-of-the-road League of Nations supporters as Will Arnold-Forster, Philip Noel-Baker, and Hugh Dalton were convinced that a viable international order would require, in the foreseeable future, the sanction of some kind of force. As their recommendations became more frequent in the memoranda of the International Advisory Committee and in the wider public media, they clashed with views held not only by the ILP but generally by those in the labor movement who feared the abuse of sanctions in the hands of existing governments or who, for pacifist reasons, repudiated recourse to arms in any circumstances.

To be sure, once the Tory government of Stanley Baldwin had taken over, the ILP shared many of the positions assumed by the mainstream Opposition critics. The government was accused of embroiling Great Britain in a conflict of East against West, first, by its bullying policy toward Egypt; next, by its challenge to Japan in the revival of the Singapore naval base so rightly abandoned by the previous Labour government; then by destroying the effort to link Russian recovery to British prosperity; and finally by its "revival" of the doctrine of the balance of power. In short, the ILP strategists urged their speakers to emphasize that the government "has embarked upon a voyage which may end in the shipwreck of civilisation."[9]

The 1924 government's mishandling of the Zinoviev Letter, which purported to demonstrate interference in British affairs by the Communist International, prompted a wave of criticism once Labour was out of office. Not only the ILP, but the more heterogeneous members of the Advisory Committee on International Questions found fault with the machinery for the conduct of foreign affairs. Many in the labor movement attributed the government's fumbling responses to charges made during the election campaign to the officials in the Foreign Office. As a result, several Advisory Committee memoranda urged that a future Labour government carry out extensive changes in the Foreign Office and in the decision-making process itself. In particular, George Young insisted, the position of principal private secretary, currently a civil servant, should be given to an experienced Labour party member and should be subordinated to that of the political parliamentary secretary. For Philip Noel-Baker and Arthur Ponsonby, the rather unlikely pair who jointly authored another memorandum, it was unacceptable that the Committee of Imperial Defense, overloaded with service members, should virtually determine the course the government pursued on matters of political importance. Their reform suggested either the complete abolition of the committee or the creation, in its place, of a standing committee of the cabinet to consider questions of defense on behalf of that governing body. Such a group could consult with military experts, but would remain directly responsible to the cabinet itself.

The proposals for reform implied that a future Labour government might find it troublesome to carry out its policies if permanent officials and service leaders were opposed. MacDonald gave serious attention to the proposals, commenting to a close colleague, for example, that if distrust of the personnel of the Foreign Office was justified, then a Labour government, when strong enough, should aim to remodel the whole office. Short of that, nothing could be satisfactory and any short-term expedients would destroy the efficiency of the office.[10] Quickly, however, he judged the proposals to be "both subversive in principle and impracticable as a business proposition" and rejected them decisively. Although the Advisory Committee followed up with some watered-down recommendations, even these were ignored when Arthur Henderson became foreign secretary in the next Labour government.[11]

Meanwhile, the Advisory Committee was busy addressing some of the issues that had begun to be raised about the Geneva Protocol even before the fall of the Labour government. The committee's minutes of February 11 made the recommendation that the party stand by the proposals of the League Assembly on the ground that they furnished the only practical plan for obtaining disarmament and substituting arbitration for war as the method of settling disputes. Britain should do everything in its power to facilitate the acceptance of the principles of the Protocol for the Pacific Settlement of International Disputes and the holding of a disarmament conference. The party should strongly oppose accepting any form of limited military alliance. If the simultaneous ratification of the protocol by Germany, France, and Britain could not be attained, then certain modifications might be necessary. Britain might insist that recourse to war in certain circumstances be permitted or that, in light of her relations with the United States, the rights of the League Council be limited in bringing into operation the provisions of the protocol regarding disputes with nonmembers of the international body. As for the argument, widely circulated by a variety of groups in Great Britain, that the protocol would freeze the status quo, the committee suggested that the arbitrators of disputes under its terms might be given the responsibility, under Article XIX of the covenant, of suggesting the reconsideration of treaties that had become inapplicable or of international conditions whose continuation might endanger the peace of the world. Certainly, the Advisory Committee's memorandum assumed, no British government would agree that the League Assembly should have the right to revise treaties, for example, by a four-fifths majority.[12] Labour's advisors were clearly struggling with the same problems of sovereignty and change that were currently being addressed by the new foreign secretary, Austen Chamberlain. For the most part, their recommendations for the Labour party's propaganda posture while in opposition were followed by the leadership, though with different emphases as time went on.

As Chamberlain embarked upon the policy that led from the almost immediate rejection of the Geneva Protocol to the compromises of the Locarno agreements of 1925, the parliamentary Labour party, in its turn, attempted to use the Geneva Protocol, which it had never ratified, as a weapon with which to challenge the strategies of the government.[13] Early on, MacDonald noted that the King's speech at the opening of Parliament did not completely throw over the protocol, but merely reported that the government was still considering it and would consult with the dominions—precisely what his own government had been preparing to do. As time went on he became more insistent that Labour would never have signed the protocol, even if it had had the power to do so, without further consideration and consultation. What was important was how the case was put before the dominions. And if the Tories scrapped the protocol, what were they going to substitute? The old system? To do so would be to go back to what happened before the war—"a policy which gives no security for peace and no opportunity for the complete co-operation of nations in the world's affairs."[14]

Once Chamberlain had informed the League of Britain's rejection, the details of Labour's posture in opposition began to emerge more clearly. In the debate on the Consolidated Fund Bill that took place on March 24, Henderson led off for Labour and, after a fairly extensive discussion, MacDonald summed up. Not for the first time, the differences in personality and policy of the two men tended to be the most revealing elements in Labour's parliamentary rhetoric. However much MacDonald had distanced himself from the millennialism of the Labour Left, it is possible to argue that his defense of the Geneva Protocol as promoting a "new habit of mind. . . . the habit of thinking of arbitration" reflected ideas and ideals that had persisted in Labour circles from well before the war. During the debate, as he was so often to do in the months ahead, he deprecated any emphasis on the sanctions in the League

Assembly's proposal and urged that the protocol had been intended to make the nations of Europe consider a "new system of security" based on the scrapping forever of the old ideas of military pacts and military alliances.[15] While he was much more prepared than many on the left to make use of the new instruments of international cooperation, he continued to share with them suspicion of force and an unwillingness to accept that any international organization might require more than the goodwill of its members in order to be effective.

Henderson's approach was quite different from that of MacDonald. Although some scholars have emphasized his minimization of the coercive features in the proposal being spurned by the Tory government, what is striking to a later observer is the extent to which he was willing to go beyond the pacifism and quasi pacifism that had characterized most of Labour's thinking since before the war.[16] Instead, he emphasized what he called "pooled security" in punishing aggression. However much members of the House might consider that the protocol required revision, whatever its faults or deficiencies, its great advantage was that it recognized the importance of getting rid of war as an instrument of *national* policy. Arbitration, broadly defined, provided the substitute for brute force. Already the League covenant required that members assist each other "loyally and effectively." The protocol provided for solving disputes through the Permanent Court of International Justice, an arbitral award, or a unanimous decision of the League Council. It added no new obligation that did not now exist. Only when peaceful settlement was refused would the sanctions of League policy come into effect.

A more cogent criticism, which Henderson acknowledged, was the charge that to accept the protocol would be to accept the freezing of the status quo. But, he argued, the protocol created no new obligation to use armed force to *maintain* existing conditions. Its only innovation was a requirement not to change them by means of force. If Article XIX of the League covenant was not sufficient to provide for peaceful change, then surely the way to proceed was to revise the protocol to make such change possible.[17] Henderson's most effective supporter in the debate was the relatively new M.P. Hugh Dalton, who emphasized in particular that none of the obligations of the protocol, "none of the sanctions, none of the machinery, none of the resort to arbitration," would have come into effect at all until a measure of disarmament had been achieved. If disarmament failed, the whole protocol would fall to the ground.[18]

While the efforts of the parliamentary Labour party were of no avail in the House of Commons, they were paralleled by a campaign to persuade readers of the labor press of the practicality of the Geneva Protocol. As Austen Chamberlain proceeded in the negotiations that eventually resulted in the Locarno agreements, the official *Labour Magazine* took up the battle. In January it published a series of articles that were obviously part of an effort to keep the idea of the protocol alive. The most striking contribution was that of the veteran G. N. Barnes, who contended that the Geneva scheme would give reality to Article XVI of the League covenant. Although Barnes emphasized his belief that economic sanctions would do the job, he was one of the few advocates who did not retreat from the possible necessity for military action to implement the decisions arrived at by the proposed procedures.[19]

Several months later, the same periodical carried a piece by Noel-Baker, who had served with Lord Robert Cecil at the League Assembly and was beginning to emerge as the Labour party's leading expert on the Geneva Protocol. Noel-Baker attempted to address the objections of "those persons of advanced views" who were unwilling to accept the provisions of the protocol until the injustices of the present territorial and political status quo had been removed. If nations waited for perfect territorial arrangements they would wait forever. The League system, with its minorities guarantees and with its work to break down economic barriers, could solve many of the worst effects of even inequitable boundaries, but this could happen only if the League could grow and develop and be free of the threat of war—which was exactly what the protocol was meant to achieve. The world, he pleaded, could not wait for perfection; it must make a beginning while that was possible.[20]

Shortly thereafter Noel-Baker published a substantial volume outlining the genesis, purposes, terms, and limitations of the Geneva Protocol. More than any other proponent he tackled directly the reluctance of the dominions and traditionalists at home to accept the notion of compulsory arbitration of nonjusticiable disputes, those that could not readily be referred to the Court of International Justice. Arguing that the nature of the international system made it likely that such compulsory arbitration would be more a safety valve than a normal method of procedure, Noel-Baker nevertheless insisted that in principle such an approach was not wrong. The only alternative was the retention of the right of war. But it would be difficult for Britain to insist upon that right if all the other members of the League were anxious to give it up and get rid of war altogether.

Noel-Baker was even more blunt when he took up the sanctions provisions of Article XI of the protocol. They made plain beyond dispute, he reported, the obligation of every signatory state to give military assistance to a victim of aggression; they provided criteria to judge whether the obligation was being fulfilled; and they obliged signatories to cooperate in sanctions whenever the

League Council might demand them, thus removing the quasi liberty of members of the League under the covenant to judge for themselves and perhaps take no action. Were the authors of the protocol moving too fast, as many contended? He did not think so. They had taken risks, he maintained, because they judged that governments had in a few short years learned to trust the international institutions through which they had already done so much. That was the essence of the matter. "Those who believe that international institutions can be made and have been made to work, want now to go forward," he concluded. "Those who doubt it hesitate."[21]

Noel-Baker's opinions merit attention. He was becoming more and more active in the Advisory Committee on International Questions and important, it seems clear, in supporting Arthur Henderson as the latter refined his own convictions about the changes required in the conduct of international affairs. In the not-too-distant future, when Henderson became foreign secretary in the second Labour government, Noel-Baker was to serve as his parliamentary private secretary. Along with Hugh Dalton, he was to have an increasingly significant role in the fashioning of Labour's international policies.

The deep-rooted ambivalences in the Labour press documented the fact that the views of Dalton, Noel-Baker, or even Henderson were far from solidly established in the labor movement. Despite Ramsay MacDonald's dissatisfaction with the *Daily Herald*, that paper more or less followed the line taken by Labour's leadership as it struggled with the stance it should take toward the policies of the Baldwin government. Thus it gave space to an article by Alfred Zimmern, already a respected commentator on international affairs, who argued that the Geneva Protocol did little more than ensure that changes in the status quo should not be altered by violence. That was not to freeze the existing order, but rather to open up ways for exploring peaceful methods to improve it.[22]

On what may be called the right-wing, neither *Clarion* nor the *New Statesman*, nominally supporters of the League of Nations, showed any enthusiasm for the Geneva Protocol. The former outlined all the well-publicized reservations that would have to be insisted upon by Britain before any such document could be accepted, while the latter affirmed that the document was dead even before it was born. Had not Lord Parmoor failed to realize and express the inevitable British view—"we are not ready to bind ourselves to employ, at the behest of the League, all our naval and military strength merely to preserve the status quo"—many misunderstandings would have been avoided. That Britain should undertake so rigid an obligation was inconceivable.[23]

On the Left, *Lansbury's Labour Weekly*, which for a brief period challenged the primacy of the *New Leader* in Labour circles, tended to mourn, not the death of the Geneva Protocol, but the manner in which it had been executed by Austen Chamberlain. Noting that both Henderson and MacDonald candidly admitted the imperfections of the original document, the paper warned that while there might have been good in it, there was also "much dangerous stuff." The paper continued to be suspicious all through 1925 because the protocol's generalities as to disarmament and the like "covered a multitude of sins as to particular military alliances." Although like its sponsor, George Lansbury, it was suspicious of any use of military force, it conceded, as the shape of the Locarno Pact began to emerge, that the protocol could, "at considerable cost," be supported by Labour. The pact must, under any circumstances, be opposed.[24]

Among the ILP publications, the *Bradford Pioneer* at one point gave Henderson and Parmoor praise for helping to frame the protocol, while at the same time wondering whether the League was presently inspired by no more than Liberal ideas. If so, then Socialists, in this field as in others, must not repudiate those ideas but "transcend" them.[25] Perhaps more characteristic of the rejectionism in some ILP circles was *Forward*'s bitter denunciation of any treaty guaranteed by capitalist or ruling-class statesmen. In the words of one of its contributors, "The fatuous faith in the League of Nations idea which so many Labourists profess is as rotten a reed to lean on as pure and simple pacifism."[26] And *Socialist Review*, after asserting that the Geneva Protocol was in danger, warned that foreign policy seemed again to be directed toward a parceling of the world between the Great Powers. The parliamentary Labour party, the *Review* contended, had frittered away debating points without bringing out the fundamental differences between the Labour policy and that of its opponents.[27]

Rather more complex were the reactions of the *New Leader*, for the moment still under the gifted editorship of H. N. Brailsford. Brailsford had no illusions, in particular, about the different Franco-British interpretations of the protocol. What the French wanted, he wrote, was guarantee of the Polish frontier, and this they found in the protocol. But Brailsford professed to be puzzled by Ramsay MacDonald's position. Quoting an interview reproduced from a Jamaican paper by the *Daily Herald*, he noted how the Labour party leader had expressed views about the League of Nations that contradicted each other violently: "He declares himself (though some reservations may be necessary) a wholehearted supporter of the Geneva Protocol. So, needless to say, are we, but no one can deny that it puts a heavy strain on the League. . . . It assumes that adult nations have learned enough from the Great War to prefer arbitration, for the future under the League's guidance. . . . And yet, when a simple juridical issue arises between ourselves and the 'independent'

Government of Egypt . . . Mr. MacDonald begs us not to overtask the League or 'to feed the baby on beef.' The strain, he tells us, would break it up."[28]

Brailsford's thoughtful support for the League, however much he was suspicious of the conventional statesmen who ran it, was a far cry from the slogans and battle cries of much of the Labour Left. Indeed, once it became clear that the Baldwin government would not have the Geneva Protocol at any price, he turned realistically to a consideration of another approach to the matter of security. If a western pact included Germany at the start, and on equal terms, and if it guaranteed her against invasions and aggressions from the French side, it might promote on a restricted local scale some of the ends of the protocol. But Brailsford predicted difficulties. How, for example, would such a pact define "aggression" and would it include the obligation of all its signatories to submit themselves in all cases to arbitration? Brailsford saw some reason to believe that Austen Chamberlain was holding out for the inclusion of Germany in any pact of guarantee, and also that he was resisting pressure from the French to extend a guarantee to their Polish and Czech allies. But the proposal, he concluded, must be judged, not by its terms alone, but also by the spirit that governed French policy. "France feels herself insecure only because she is resolved to exert a masterful dominion on the Continent."[29]

The more closely Austen Chamberlain and his continental counterparts approached the realization of a new security pact, the greater was the dilemma faced by the Labour party's strategists. From the beginning, there had been widespread suspicion in the labor movement of the terms proposed in the defunct Geneva Protocol. Obligations for the use of force, possible conflict with the United States, the reluctance of the dominions to have outsiders evaluate their "domestic" concerns, and mistrust of the capitalist governments represented in the League of Nations all provided an amalgam in which firm support for the commitments envisaged by the Fifth Assembly was at best very difficult. To illustrate, Philip Snowden published in the *Manchester Guardian* a violent attack on "uncritical supporters of the Protocol," which he described as a "mass of contradictions." The letter was particularly embarrassing to MacDonald, who saw it as serving no purpose except to do mischief. Indirectly replying to Snowden, he used his column in *Forward* to commend the protocol as the only avenue eventually leading to a revision of the wartime treaties. Nevertheless, he continued to keep open the question of whether Labour could in any circumstances support the alternative to the protocol being forged by Austen Chamberlain.[30]

Among the advisors of MacDonald and his colleagues, a majority of the Committee on International Questions insisted that in effect Chamberlain's anticipated pact would be a return to the old system of partial alliances against which the Labour party had so often protested. They counseled that the party should insist that no military guarantees come into force under any partial pact, and in particular that Britain have no military obligations what-soever unless and until (1) a general scheme for the reduction and limitation of the national armaments of all League members and any other participating states was achieved and (2) a general convention of mutual arbitration and guarantee on the lines of the Geneva Protocol "and of the kind suggested in the German Note of February 9" was agreed to by all members of the League and any other states that would participate.[31]

A minority of the committee, however, urged the parliamentary leadership to adopt a series of the usual tests—for example, that there be arbitration in all disputes, including those relating to the peace treaties, or that military guar-antees be given only to genuine victims of aggression decided by League Council machinery, or that no British guarantee be valid until there was agreement upon a scheme for the reduction and limitation of armaments—to apply to every pact brought before Parliament for its discussion. Unless each contemplated agreement was judged on its own merits, blanket opposition might prevent a whole series of desirable arbitration treaties from coming into effect.[32] Essentially the same advice was given to Ramsay MacDonald privately by Noel-Baker, who thought it desirable that the Labour party should not work to break down the government's negotiations but should insist that the military commitments that might result be made conditional upon the adoption of a scheme for general disarmament.[33]

When the Locarno agreements were presented to Parliament for ratifica-tion, it was the counsel of the minority of the Advisory Committee that was reflected. Labour tabled an amendment which, in the words of Tom Shaw, who moved it, "is the greatest concession ever made by a party towards the Government of the day." While the Opposition continued to believe that Chamberlain had had a much better instrument than the Pact of Locarno available when he entered office, the Labour party nevertheless agreed reluc-tantly to the ratification, warning that the real threats to peace lay not on the Rhine frontier with which Locarno dealt, but in the East. In particular, so long as Russia was outside, there would always be a danger for Europe.[34]

Having made the argument for the discarded Geneva Protocol in his own way both in and out of Parliament, Ramsay MacDonald now tried to make the best of what he could not change. Whatever the new Pact did or did not do, he told the House, it certainly achieved one or two things that somebody had to accomplish before any substantial advance could be made toward the paci-fication of Europe. It was neither an alliance nor a military pact. It brought

Germany into the League and at the same time removed certain technical difficulties in the way of complete commitment to international arbitration. Its change in psychology was almost miraculous, smashing down barriers of the mind that had kept peoples separated and making them see that there was some hope in Europe.

MacDonald then went on to develop the argument that was to be the Labour leadership's central rationalization for accepting the Locarno Pact rather than denouncing it as a betrayal of the hopes that had been placed in the Geneva Protocol. It was universally accepted on the Continent, he maintained, that the Pact was the first step to the protocol. "Every risk that was in the Protocol is here," he stressed, "every safeguard that is here was in the Protocol." He warned that without disarmament the risk from the Locarno Pact was greater than under the protocol, that attention must still be paid to the revision of wartime treaties, and that the relationship—or lack of relationship—of the agreements to the League of Nations itself was troubling. Putting his finger on the chief flaw of the new arrangements, he contended that war would not erupt because of the western frontiers. "The lighting of the match will take place," he predicted, "if it takes place at all, in Middle and Eastern Europe." All in all, MacDonald's speech was one of his best parliamentary performances of the period. Clearly he found himself in an "uncomfortable position," but hoped that increasingly Britain could find the security in the League of Nations that she had once looked for from her isolation.[35] The leader of the Labour party was attempting to say, as he had insisted a few days earlier to Arthur Ponsonby, who had criticized the generosity of his concessions to the government's policy, that "as an accomplished achievement Locarno might not be great, but that as an opportunity it was great."[36]

Ponsonby, along with Josiah Wedgwood, Richard Wallhead, and George Lansbury, was among the thirteen Labour M.P.'s who rebelled against both the Labour party Executive and the parliamentary party to vote against ratification.[37] Most of the dissident M.P.'s came from the ILP parliamentary group. Their dissatisfaction with the Locarno Pact in large measure reflected their unwillingness even to accept what they regarded as the excessive concessions made by the MacDonalds and the Hendersons to the existing order in Europe. A few months earlier, a British delegation, which included Wedgwood and Wallhead along with Clifford Allen, had abstained when the bureaus of the Labour and Socialist International and the International Federation of Trade Unions passed a resolution calling upon the entire Socialist and Labour movement in all countries to focus its efforts on the ratification of the Geneva Protocol. The heavily ILP British delegation had wanted ratification to come only after Germany and Russia were in the League and to tie its acceptance to the strengthening of the League's authority in matters relating to the peace treaties.[38] Short of that, they were unwilling to go along with the positions adopted unanimously by the non-British representatives in the international working class organizations.

Many of these same opponents of Locarno had resisted the Geneva Protocol because it made provision for the eventual enforcement of international decisions. Now, by way of contrast, they changed their argument. The motion they hoped to bring forward in Parliament reflected their self-deluding contention that the Geneva Protocol was a pacifist measure. Starting with the usual viewing with alarm at "the reversion of the present Government to policies which can only result in a renewed competition in armaments, and may lead to war," the motion then went on to declare entire opposition to the method of war as a means of settling international disputes. It regretted that the government had not adhered to the principles embodied in the Geneva Protocol. Branding the existence of national armaments for aggravating the possibility of war and jeopardizing the pursuit of a policy of peace, it urged the government to initiate a proposal not in favor of limiting or reducing armaments, but for their simultaneous abolition by all nations.[39]

The motion was never offered, but it reflected views that continued to dominate ILP thinking, whatever the efforts of some of Labour's leaders to move toward what they regarded as a more realistic posture. In any event, although many of Labour's M.P.'s were nominally associated with the ILP, the overwhelming majority of the parliamentary party, including most of the ILP members, voted for approval.

On the morrow of ratification, the New Statesman solemnly intoned that such opposition as there was to the agreements was obviously negligible. Apart from the moral results of the Locarno Conference, the important fact for the New Statesman, which had earlier damned the Geneva Protocol because it stereotyped the status quo, was that Germany had consented to join the League of Nations.[40] Indeed, many in the labor movement followed the lead of party officials in seeing Germany's acceptance of her western frontiers and the likelihood that she would soon become a member of the League as worth the cost of accepting, at least for the time being, Chamberlain's approach to international security.[41]

Such expressions of the "Locarno spirit" as were to be found in the ranks of Labour were actually considerably more reserved than implied by the New Statesman's sanguine effusions. In short order, the limited euphoria over what Hugh Dalton later described as "a nine days' wonder which led nowhere" tended to disappear. Chamberlain's awkwardness in handling the entry of Germany into the League was widely regarded in Labour circles as one more piece of evidence of his vulnerability to the cunning of France and her followers.[42] More important in the light of later developments, Labour's criticism of Locarno's failure to address the danger of conflict in central and eastern Europe went to the heart of the weakness of the new arrangements.

Labour's search for a new position was not easy and soon it began to explore realistic alternatives to the Locarno agreements. As early as March 1926, MacDonald, whose qualified acceptance of Locarno had expressed the official view of the Labour party, was having second thoughts. The spirit of Locarno as a gesture was admirable, he told the House of Commons, and it was a great achievement, but its method was fundamentally wrong. For it had gone back, as the French newspapers clearly saw at the time, to the old idea of European alliances—a fatal blunder. The League had been left in confusion and sadness, and British prestige had been seriously lowered.[43] Now it was necessary, he wrote in *Socialist Review*, to reverse Chamberlain's policy "of having no policy except to accommodate others."[44] But aside from ringing the changes on the phrases "arbitration and disarmament," he was reluctant to be very specific about what Labour would substitute for the approach of the Tory government. That reluctance was a matter of policy. As he later told Arthur Ponsonby, he thought it would be a mistake to formulate with any finality an "exclusive formula" regarding Labour's peace policy: "We are in the fortunate position of enjoying so much confidence, both at home and abroad, that when we get into office we shall continue—in relation to whatever may be our circumstances—to pursue a policy of settlement and peace, and it would be most short-sighted of us to do anything to disturb that confidence."[45]

The Labour press, particularly the ILP instruments, had no such compunction about political strategies. Stalwarts like *Bradford Pioneer, Forward*, and *New Leader* gave relatively grudging acceptance to Locarno for a brief moment, then reflected a growing disillusionment and bitterness. *Forward*, for example, professed to see the Locarno documents as wretchedly drafted, obscure and ambiguous, contradictory and redundant, loosely worded and full of loopholes, above all, misleading. The *New Leader*, where Brailsford, until forced out of the editorship in October 1926, had attempted to follow a balanced and indeed analytical approach, had real doubts whether the Locarno system could endure or whether even the League could survive the creation of new military alliances and the machinations of various of the powers. The Union of Democratic Control's *Foreign Affairs*, which had suffered a grievous blow when E. D. Morel had suddenly died in late 1924, continued under the editorship of Helena Swanwick to share many of the international viewpoints of the ILP papers. In a series of articles throughout 1925 and into 1926, *Foreign Affairs* still promoted the Geneva Protocol as an alternative to a failed Locarno system, castigated the British Empire as the major block to the realization of arbitration and disarmament, and attacked Britain's role in the disreputable game of the old diplomacy. "The Locarno spirit," in the words of Arthur Ponsonby, "has turned out to be poison."[46]

As time went on, despite an occasional, almost nostalgic revival of earlier rhetoric, the Geneva Protocol was largely abandoned and Labour turned to other instruments for the achievement of its ends. Chief among those ends was the search for some avenue to achieve the disarmament that bulked so large in the hopes of the labor movement. Here too there were as many definitions as there were factions in the movement itself. The sterile maneuverings that passed for discussions of disarmament both before and after the establishment of the Preparatory Commission for the Disarmament Conference have been described again and again in all their futility and tediousness.[47] The point that needs to be emphasized is that there was no inevitability about the Labour party's move toward the moderate center in foreign affairs.

The ILP in particular moved steadily toward the position of advocating a form of unilateral disarmament. As the group drifted away from the path being followed by the parliamentary leaders of the Labour party, Ramsay MacDonald, clinging tenuously to his ILP membership while others were abandoning any illusion of unity in the labor movement, was frustrated. He confided to his diary that the control of the ILP was getting into bad hands, "men with spites and grievances, retailers of cheap thoughts, with no constructive capacity; assailers who think that by a few Acts of Parliament they are to move from Capitalism to Socialism in their own time." For him, the proper ILP conception should be that change in form followed change in "moral desires," a gradualist position that simply exacerbated the impatience of many ILP activists.[48]

The public press of the ILP divided a good part of its attention in the year or so after Locarno between castigating Austen Chamberlain for his reestablishment of the old diplomacy and for his bumbling over Germany's entry into the League of Nations.[49] Occasionally, one or another of the papers echoed the demand of the ILP's leaders for total international disarmament by mutual agreement, but for the most part the press seemed content to make its points by reporting the details of the various battles undertaken by the political movement.[50]

The shifting position of the ILP on the issue of disarmament was nicely illustrated at its annual conference in 1926. There a move essentially to censure Labour's parliamentary group was defeated, but not before J. Southall of Birmingham City had had his say. He pointed out that of 154 Labour M.P.'s,

106 were members of the ILP. They were in a position to present to the House of Commons a definite ILP policy, but instead most of them accepted the direction of the official Opposition leadership. As a result, whenever the ILP did attack the Tories, government spokesmen simply looked up the record of the Labour government and said that they were following the lead of Ramsay MacDonald.

While the attack on MacDonald was rejected, it reflected the growing alienation from his leadership within the ranks of the ILP. What was accepted, in any case, was a long composite resolution introduced by long-time activist Fenner Brockway. After parading the usual castigations of militarism, imperialism, and war and branding modern capitalism a constant menace to peace, it called, among other things, for the complete revision of the peace treaties, the cancellation of all war debts, the reorganization of the League of Nations to include all nations, and the establishment of friendly relations with Russia. It supported the acceptance of arbitration for all disputes, justiciable and nonjusticiable, and finally asked Britain to take the initiative by making a proposal to the other nations for immediate universal disarmament by mutual agreement. As yet, the ILP acknowledged the need for Britain to work with other nations in seeking to achieve the abolition of the means for violent conflict. But at the same time, "simultaneously with the advocacy of this policy of constructive peace," the resolution, which was accepted by the conference, called upon the workers to make clear to their governments that they would meet any threat of war by organizing general resistance, including the refusal to bear arms, to produce armaments, or to render general material assistance.[51]

Perhaps not surprisingly, given the role of its own annual conference as the place in which the rank and file often let off steam, the Labour party Conference, toward the end of 1926, not only adopted the Executive Committee's composite resolution welcoming the admission of Germany into the League and its support for the League's Preparatory Commission's work toward a World Disarmament Conference, but also accepted, without any discussion, a resolution introduced by Brockway and seconded by Arthur Ponsonby that repeated the war resistance call of the ILP.[52] Several years later much the same point of view appeared, as might have been anticipated, in George Lansbury's presidential address to the conference, when he insisted that the only way to peace was in the simple formula, "Throw down your arms."[53] These pacifist proclamations were treated by the Labour party's leaders as essentially ceremonial gestures, contributing to the good feelings of the delegates at the annual meeting, but hardly the stuff of practical politics. Once passed, they were ignored and played little part in the thinking of MacDonald or Henderson or indeed of their most influential advisors on international policy.

As for the ILP, it grew increasingly out of touch with the main currents of Labour policy, a fringe group on its way to eventual disaffiliation from the party. As time went on its emphasis shifted increasingly from disarmament by mutual agreement to what was called "disarmament by example." In December 1926, for example, ILP officials and M.P.'s made up most of the speakers at a war resistance rally held in the Royal Albert Hall in furtherance of the Peace Letter campaign that had become Arthur Ponsonby's passionate commitment. A pamphlet, *Why We Will Not Fight!*, summarized the arguments of Ponsonby, Fenner Brockway, J. H. Hudson, Lansbury, and others, although with the exception of the *Daily Herald* and the *Manchester Guardian*, the press as a whole ignored the meeting.[54] Ponsonby's own pacifism was encouraged by a variety of correspondents, both British and German, and he soon was able to persuade himself that in the second quarter of the twentieth century no civilized people would support their government in launching an aggressive war.[55] In an important paper in the *Journal of the Royal Institute of International Affairs*, he argued that the natural consequence in public policy of the individual pledge of refusal to take part in war was national disarmament. "It was not taking the gun out of the man's hands that mattered; it was getting out of his head the idea that made him want to use the gun. That was the whole point."[56]

Ponsonby likewise attempted unsuccessfully to persuade the Union of Democratic Control, of which he had been one of the founding members, to take a stand against the use of military sanctions in any circumstances. The showdown came at the Annual General Meeting of the UDC in the spring of 1928. At its last meeting, the UDC Council had adopted a resolution that was now being questioned by key members of the organization. The resolution so clearly reflects Ponsonby's position that it merits quotation in full: "That in the opinion of this Council no effective progress can be made towards the abolition of war so long as the sanction of force is preserved in the Covenant of the League of Nations; it therefore proposes that Great Britain should take the initiative in a declaration in favour of the final abandonment of the war weapon in any circumstances whatever, thus bringing to the forefront the proposal for the amendment of the sanctions clauses of the Covenant and inviting by example the other nations to outlaw war." When the resolution was submitted to the annual meeting, it was opposed by J. A. Hobson, Will Arnold-Forster, and Delisle Burns. An attempted compromise by several members, who announced their support on the assumption that the resolution meant not abandoning but foreshadowing the abandonment of the war weapon by agreement, was repudiated by Ponsonby. His position was then defeated when the UDC narrowly adopted an amendment declaring it undesirable to restrict the membership and activities of the organization by a decision on the question of sanctions.[57] This further attempt to finesse the issue was unsatisfactory to Ponsonby. Within a short time he resigned from the Executive of the UDC and resisted all efforts to persuade him to change his mind.[58]

The UDC meanwhile pressed for all-out arbitration of international disputes, without reservations, welcomed the Russian proposal for complete disarmament, and urged that steps be taken to prohibit the private manufacture of arms and munitions and their sale either privately or by governments. Helena Swanwick, as editor of *Foreign Affairs*, continued indefatigably to make the arguments for what the UDC considered to be a more rational approach to international diplomacy, but it seems fair to conclude that with Morel's death much of the fire disappeared from the organization.[59]

As for Ponsonby, while he was moving rapidly away from the basic positions of leaders such as Henderson and MacDonald on the issue of arms, he nevertheless continued to support the main lines of party policy in the House of Commons. When MacDonald was unable to attend, he sometimes substituted in presenting the views of the Labour party on foreign affairs.[60] As late as 1929, when Labour had returned to office, he explained his position to the secretary of the Sheffield branch of the ILP, who wrote to remind Ponsonby, as parliamentary representative of the ILP, that their policy was to vote against all war credits. Ponsonby's reply was revealing. He was in favor of a personal pledge against war service, he wrote, and supported the public policy of disarmament by example. But he insisted that he must be absolutely free as an M.P. to promote "the best procurable" official policy of peace. Although he and many others had worked fairly hard on the subject, he knew that the majority of his countrymen were not in agreement with his view on disarmament and he doubted that a majority of the Labour party were. He had taken part in demonstrations and supported resolutions of a very drastic character that amounted to support for complete disarmament. But so long as a Labour government showed a disposition to reduce armaments, to pursue a policy of peace, and to avoid all wars, so long in fact as he thought it was the best government for advancing toward his ideal, Ponsonby was not (even as a member of the rank and file and not the government) going to vote against the government simply because it would not go the whole way and abolish the military services at once. "As we all of us know quite well that the abolition of the war services at once is politically, economically and industrially impossible," he told his correspondent, "I do not think it would be fair of us to indulge in a vote which may endanger the existence of the only instrument at present available for promoting a real policy of peace."[61] He was trying to reconcile his deeply held beliefs with a duty to be responsible to his party.

While neither the ILP press nor its official leaders were perhaps as knowledgeable as Ponsonby, there too the struggle to maintain a coherent policy in the face of an intractable world was reflected. No longer served by such strong and informed journalists as Brailsford and Morel, the left was less coherent and patently began to be less effective a thorn in the side of Labour's official leadership. For example, the *New Leader*, already beginning its slide to journalistic mediocrity after the dismissal of H. N. Brailsford, continued to trumpet the ILP policy of suspicion of military sanctions and the call for universal disarmament by mutual consent. When the Disarmament Conference recessed in the early spring of 1928, the editor of that paper found it evident that for the Great Powers, disarmament talks were simply a concession to their simple-minded constituents, who, for some unknown reason, believed the story about the war to end war. "The great bulk of people of all nations would like to see an end to these dangerous armaments. The official classes want nothing of the kind. Some economy—yes, but disarmament, heaven forbid!" Similarly, to the *Bradford Pioneer* the attempt to find a basis upon which a real Disarmament Conference might be held had already failed. The British government was doing all that it could to destroy the League of Nations, which was now split into two camps, "the Big Nations, who sneer at it behind the scenes, and the Little Nations, who fear them, and want a League powerful enough to preserve their safety."[62] For the most part, the ILP press reacted day-by-day to events on the international scene, but there was little evidence of the systematic, if sometimes idiosyncratic, analyses that had characterized Brailsford's journalism, or for that matter the positions taken by Morel in the pages of *Foreign Affairs*.

By 1927, some of the ILP leaders were beginning the campaign to shift away from the policy of international collaboration in achieving a measure of disarmament. One step was taken at the annual conference, when a resolution reaffirmed the view that the next Labour government should propose to the other nations not partial disarmament, but total disarmament by mutual agreement. In his address as chairman, James Maxton, who was increasingly coming to the fore in the ILP leadership, expressed his hope that before long the organization would make up its mind that such negotiated disarmament was not enough. Disarmament by example, he quoted Arthur Ponsonby as arguing, offered a different method of approach. It meant that a nation, convinced of the inefficiency of force, would set out to reduce armaments on its own initiative without the prompting or general consent of others. Admitting that the first steps might have to be slow, for economic and domestic reasons, nevertheless Maxton called for the ILP to take the lead quite deliberately in facing in a new direction. As yet, the ILP retained the strategy of "mutual agreement." Logically, there was no quarrel between such a strategy and the war resistance resolution that the conference also reaffirmed, but their difference in spirit was evidence of the ambivalence that continued to characterize ILP international policy.[63]

By the time of the next ILP conference in the spring of 1928, Ponsonby introduced a resolution calling upon the Labour party to press for the British acceptance of a policy of disarmament by example. Referring back to Maxton's presidential address of the year before, Ponsonby declared that it went further than any proposal made so far. The Labour party, in particular, had missed one of the greatest opportunities. Great Britain should now go to the League of Nations and say that it was going to abandon the war weapon and had decided not to use the method of force. Others would then follow. As for the argument that nations must be prepared to meet the unprovoked attacks of the aggressor, the fact was that the "aggressor" was a myth. He did not exist. Some discussion and a few minor amendments ensued, but the ILP felt comfortable enough with disarmament by example to pass the resolution without any trouble.[64]

For the most part, the Baldwin government showed little interest in achieving more than the immediate foreign policy objectives indicated in 1925.[65] Its apparent unwillingness to strike out in new directions and the persistence of the "old diplomacy" gave all elements of the Labour press the opportunity to criticize, although for the most part there was little painstaking suggestion of alternatives beyond the simplified slogans designed to influence popular support. The failure of the "Coolidge" conference on naval limitation, slow progress of the Preparatory Commission for disarmament, and suggestions of an Anglo-French bargain on land and sea forces all elicited angry comments across the range of Labour's relatively few media representatives. In the assignment of blame to Austen Chamberlain and his colleagues there was little to choose between, say, the *New Statesman* and the *New Leader*, *Clarion* and *Forward*, the *Daily Herald* and the *Bradford Pioneer*. Headlines like "The Vicious Circle," "The Disarmament Failure," "A Militarist Victory," or "Will the League Die?" dotted their pages throughout the life of the Tory administration.[66]

In similar fashion, when Labour M.P.'s rose to criticize Chamberlain in Parliament, there was substantial agreement among them. However much they might differ on productive approaches to international peace and security, their parliamentary performance continued to be consistent in its condemnation of Tory policies. An example was in a full-dress debate on November 24, 1927, introduced by MacDonald with a motion that summed up Labour's charges: "That this House deplores the lack of preparation by the Government and the military character of the British delegation which seriously contributed to the failure of the recent naval conference at Geneva, the slow progress being made by the League of Nations Preparatory Commission for the Disarmament Conference, and the refusal of the Government to accept the principle of arbitration and promote a scheme of international security guaranteed by the League of Nations." The defeat of the motion and the acceptance of an amendment commending the government for its actions were, to be sure, inevitable. Perhaps the most memorable formulation in the debate was Lloyd George's description of the Preparatory Commission as an "algebraic farce." "No wonder," he commented, "they have not discovered the 'X.'"[67] As for the Labour argument, when Noel Buxton pointed to the facts that disarmament had not proceeded and that there were urgent dangers in various parts of the world as proof of the failure of the Locarno treaties, he was not only mirroring MacDonald's own arguments, but also those of such participants in the debate as J. M. Kenworthy and H. B. Lees Smith, who often found themselves otherwise at odds with the tactics of the leader of the Labour party.

In the course of his own comments, MacDonald carefully avoided spelling out the details of Labour's peace program except to place great stress on the importance of substituting arbitration for conflict in the resolution of disputes. The absence of specificity did not escape Chamberlain, who asked whether MacDonald was arguing for arbitration without sanctions or plus sanctions. The leader of the Opposition had not committed himself because the answer was evident, Chamberlain said. Why could not the protocol, asked the foreign secretary, be brought into effect among all the nations that wanted it, without the British Empire? Because in that case the British Navy would not be at the disposal of the League, which showed the onerous burden Britain was being asked to assume. Any tightening of the covenant would lead to an increase of sanctions and a new and dangerous obligation to apply them without discretion.[68]

As has been noted, MacDonald as a matter of practical politics did not want to be too specific in spelling out the details of international policy. At the same time, though on occasion he paid lip service to the concept of sanctions, he was genuine in his conviction that peace and disarmament depended not upon the substitution of international for national force, but on psychological change. "Do not let us babble so much about security," he urged the House of

Commons late in 1928. "Only by establishing peace, as an alternative to force, can security be achieved."[69]

During the last two years of the Tory government's tenure, the "American question" came to play a dominant role in Chamberlain's diplomacy.[70] The "Coolidge" negotiations of 1927, which broke up in a dispute over cruiser tonnage and numbers, were simply one of many indications of the American determination to achieve naval parity with Britain. While Chamberlain was determined to pursue relations with the United States as quietly and unobtrusively as possible, his very caution opened the way to a barrage of Labour censure. Not only the haggling over the size and numbers of cruisers to be permitted, but the continuing American differences with the British on blockade and the rights of neutrals in time of war provided opportunities to make points against the government.[71]

To be sure, there were those in the Labour party who feared that to raise the issue of free seas in Parliament would provide ammunition to the advocates of unchallenged naval supremacy. One of his correspondents, for example, advised MacDonald that the suggestion that the Labour party proposed to challenge Britain's position on "freedom of the seas" would give the moribund Navy League a new lease on life and a cry that would be as effective against Labour as the Zinoviev Letter.[72] While for the time no major parliamentary campaign was mounted, the phrase, however vaguely defined it sometimes might be, was the slogan under which some substantial criticism was mounted. On the basis of a preliminary draft authored by Arnold-Forster, the Advisory Committee developed early in 1928 a pamphlet that was not issued until May 1929.[73] Published with a foreword by MacDonald, it maintained that the Labour party stood for the complete renunciation of the right of private war and private blockade and called for full acceptance of the "new doctrine" of freedom of the seas, that is, that the high seas should only be closed by international agreements for the enforcement of international covenants. To elaborate, this official statement of Labour position held that the development and the codification of international law should be made on the assumption that private war and private blockade, instead of being a legitimate exercise of national sovereignty, were international crimes. All of this, the document concluded, was logically a part of Labour's policy of all-out arbitration, pooled security, and disarmament to the level strictly required for the maintenance of order.[74]

Other American initiatives on the international scene provided vehicles through which Labour could press for its version of an international policy while at the same time continuing its attack upon the Baldwin government. Thus, when Frank Kellogg, the American secretary of state, skillfully diverted a French proposal for a Franco-American agreement to abandon war between their countries as an instrument of national policy into a broader international proposal, Labour took up the idea. In the House of Commons, MacDonald urged the government to respond favorably, since acceptance would certainly bring America closer to the practical peace problems of Europe and influence Anglo-American relations for a long time to come. If only the big nations of Europe could be brought to say, "We will eliminate war from our national policy" and mean it, then 98 percent of the peace difficulties would be solved. The worst approach, he declared, would be to accept Kellogg's proposals but with various reservations. He argued that to take refuge, for example, in the differences between "League of Nations" formulas and those proposed by Kellogg would be one of the greatest tragedies of history. In replying to MacDonald, Chamberlain welcomed the American initiative but took pains to insist that Great Britain had never in the past treated war as an instrument of policy and to point out that before the government could act it must consult with the dominions.[75]

From the beginning, the Advisory Committee was favorably disposed to the American proposals. Both J. M. Kenworthy and Leonard Woolf, for example, responded to the sense of resolutions, proposed in Congress by American Senators William E. Borah and Arthur Capper, which spelled out their respective views of an agreement to outlaw war. Although the Advisory Committee found things to criticize, particularly in the Borah resolution, nevertheless it urged support. Woolf had no doubt that the proposals were in complete accord with the Labour party's position and with the system developing in the League. He saw them as the most hopeful sign to come from America since 1919. He urged that the government be pressed to declare its willingness to enter into an agreement with the U.S. along the lines of the Capper Resolution, which proposed a treaty between the United States, France, and others outlawing war. They should conclude an all-out arbitration treaty, defining an aggressor as a nation that, having signed, refused to submit to arbitration, conciliation, or judicial settlement. Furthermore, they should agree that nationals not be protected by their governments in giving aid and comfort to an aggressor.[76]

The Borah resolution was far more general than Capper's, and a subcommittee, which included Arnold-Forster and David Mitrany, indicated its agreement with the Capper approach rather than that of Borah. Finally, the various comments were drawn together in a thoughtful assessment that reflected few illusions about the practicality of the proposals. It was clear from Secretary Kellogg's speech of March 15, the memorandum pointed out, that the Americans were not yet ready for the approach of Senator Capper and an all-out treaty for pacific settlement of all disputes. For the present they insisted on retaining the right to maintain a deadlock, but at least were willing to go so far as to renounce the right to begin a private war. The subcommittee urged a cordial welcome without asking provocative questions as to whether it was sincere or an American electoral stunt.[77] From the outside, too, Lord Robert Cecil of the League of Nations Union discussed with MacDonald the best ways to persuade the government seriously to consider the American initiative.[78]

Until the British government responded to Kellogg late in May, the Labour press gave reluctant support to the idea of outlawing war. Both the *New Leader* and the *Daily Herald* would have preferred a simple approval of the Russian proposal, made some time earlier, for completely scrapping armies, navies, and air forces. The latter pointed out that so far from outlawing war, the Kellogg Pact legalized it exactly in those spheres where it was likely to arise. In *Clarion*, too, "W. G." pointed out that the proposals did not outlaw war in any sense, although they might encourage the United States indirectly to cooperate with the League, and Robert Blatchford, while he did not undervalue the American initiative, warned that it would not achieve disarmament and thus would not abolish war.[79]

The skepticism of these few examples of the press was well warranted. When the British government published its reply to Secretary Kellogg, the Labour press virtually threw up its collective hands. In so doing, it merely mirrored the reaction within the Advisory Committee on International Questions and from the leadership of the various wings of the labor movement.[80] A few examples will illustrate. The *Bradford Pioneer*, which had greeted the original proposals as a new start in the solution of the war problem, saw Britain's reservations, giving her "the right to go to war when and where she sees fit," as making a farce of the whole matter.[81] The *New Leader* used the same word in describing Chamberlain's reply and was equally caustic in pointing out that Kellogg's own interpretation in no way restricted or impaired the right of any nation to decide entirely on its own responsibility whether any given circumstances required it to wage war in self-defense. If so, the Kellogg Pact was not worth the paper it was written on.[82] *Forward* simply pointed to disquieting rumors of a "military alliance" with France and the lack of accomplishment of the Preparatory Commission to heap scorn on those holding special services and prayers of thanksgiving for the outlawry of war.[83] After the signature of the Kellogg treaty by fifteen nations on August 17, *Foreign Affairs* summed up the general Labour view: "Not even the most enthusiastic supporters of this avowedly anti-war pact are able to claim for it anything more than a certain moral value, and even that, it is generally conceded, has been greatly impaired by the most disquieting reservations formulated by the French and British Governments."[84]

The unanimity within the labor movement in castigating the Tory government barely concealed the growing alienation of the ILP. By June of 1928, the so-called Cook-Maxton Manifesto clearly signaled the sharpening of the split between the Labour party leadership and that of the ILP. It had nothing to say about foreign policy, yet because it continued the process of isolating the ILP, it had the effect of reducing the influence of the party's most radical foreign policy advocates and strengthening the middle-of-the-road center. Although there was a serious attempt to present a common front as Labour prepared for the election that would have to take place in 1929, the differences even on matters of foreign policy could not be concealed. In particular, the ILP stand for "disarmament by example" could hardly be ignored even though there was public agreement on the government's responsibility for the inadequacies of the Kellogg Pact, the deadlock in disarmament negotiations, the failure of the Three-Power Naval Conference, the unwillingness to accept the principle of freedom of the seas, the increasing antagonism to Russia, and the attempt to hamper the League of Nations by slashing its budget.

For most of the mainstream experts of the Labour party, the idea of unilateral disarmament was the very midsummer of madness. The formula of "arbitration, security, disarmament" that had characterized the Geneva Protocol continued to be at the heart of their proposals for the improvement of the international order. Like MacDonald, but in more concrete detail, Noel-Baker, Arnold-Forster, and Dalton labored to promote a set of ideas that recognized the realities of international politics and could be shaped in conjunction with other powers. Like him, they hoped for the disarmament that many in the left wing of the labor movement believed could be achieved almost at the stroke of a pen. But they insisted that it could only be built gradually and on the basis of a viable international system. In a variety of ways—in books and pamphlets, private correspondence and Advisory Committee documents—they advanced the notions that disarmament in the abstract was a chimera; that no nation would give up the instruments of its protection in the absence of a guaranteed substitute; that "arbitration," that is, peaceful methods of dispute settlement, could only be effective in the near term if there was the sanction of international force behind it; and that only in the long run might the habit of pacific settlement minimize the need to use force. They distinguished between the use of force by individual nations to promote individual purposes and its employment in support of the international community. Although he was frequently in touch with Noel-Baker and used the counsel of these members of the Advisory Committee quite systematically, MacDonald was never persuaded by their argument for the indispensability of sanctions. On the other hand, these advisors appear to have captured the confidence of Arthur Henderson, whose own opinions on the role of international force increasingly reflected their recommendations in the second half of the decade.

Among the extensive writings of this group of advisors was a substantial volume authored by Noel-Baker and issued by the Hogarth Press of Leonard and Virginia Woolf. Looking forward to the task of the Preparatory Commission for the Disarmament Conference, he warned that great patience would undoubtedly be needed. In logic and in common sense, only one plan deserved consideration—the general adoption of the terms of disarmament imposed upon the ex-enemy states by the peace treaties. But, however deplorable the fact, such a plan was outside the realm of practical politics at the present time. Were the difficulties too serious to be overcome? Noel-Baker insisted that they were not. If the governments moved carefully, perhaps taking a first small step to curtail a great expansion of air forces, then further progress was virtually assured. Calling upon the British government to make a draft proposal, he urged the patience, compromise, and unremitting effort that would make the adoption of any definite comprehensive scheme of disarmament, "however small its first reductions," a great and decisive victory for the League of Nations.[85]

A somewhat different avenue to the conclusions reached by Noel-Baker appeared in a substantial pamphlet sponsored by the Women's International League and also published by the Hogarth Press. In "The Victory of Reason," Arnold-Forster discussed the alternatives to warfare upon which disarmament would have to be based. He described the arbitration principle and outlined the growth of arbitration from the time of the Anglo-American Jay treaty of 1794 all the way to the provisions proposed in the Locarno Agreements of 1925. In dealing with legal disputes under the League of Nations, he commended the Optional Clause of the Permanent Court of International Justice, which bound its signatories to submit all justiciable disputes to The Hague. Most significant, Arnold-Forster tackled head on the troubled issue of the use of force to compel acceptance of the jurisdiction of the court or indeed of the League Council in other cases. Only by tying up sanctions with an international system in which they were least likely to be required could they be made a tolerable burden to the guarantor or an acceptable insurance to the guaranteed. That meant "an international system in which the right of private war had been surrendered and all-inclusive arbitration has been accepted." The two were inseparable. Those who maintained that an international sanction of some sort was desirable as a backing for the arbitration they considered so essential should also be ready to maintain that all-inclusive arbitration was the only reason by which to justify the use of sanctions. "Except for the defence of the principle and practice of arbitration," he concluded, "the use of the fearful weapon of an international sanction is intolerable."[86]

Much of what Noel-Baker and Arnold-Forster were urging was reiterated and then developed by Dalton in an extremely important book published in 1928. In the light of his later part in the management of foreign affairs between 1929 and 1931 and his central role in the 1930s in leading his party away from the fruitless Utopianism of the Left and the self-defeating pacifism of a Lansbury and his supporters, *Towards the Peace of Nations* was a key statement of the position increasingly being advocated by the young intellectuals to whose advice Arthur Henderson in particular was turning a sympathetic ear. Cogently summing up both the present state of Labour's attitudes and its policies, Dalton outlined the direction in which he believed it was necessary to aim. Taking his stand on support for the League of Nations, he was more sweeping than was usually the case in Labour circles in his view of the contemporary scene. Between the prewar international anarchy and a possible world state, the League was a compromise and, perhaps, a transition. An inevitable transition, if the world state was destined to be born; a pale substitute, if it was forever unattainable. But "this League, full of promise and full of imperfections," was a fact, and a world state, as yet, was not. It was the most ambitious piece of international machinery ever to have been built and it deserved close and objective study.

Dalton noted that by now to be a supporter of the League, especially when it was doing nothing in particular, had become a sign of respectability. That very fact had tended to arouse socialist suspicions. In some quarters, the League had come to be regarded as a device for stabilizing capitalism and as a diversion from the central task of establishing socialism. Those who held such views were grievously mistaken, for the League was only an unusually elaborate piece of international machinery. Its value would depend upon who handled it and upon the spirit and motives and competence with which it was handled. "Its character will be determined by the character of the Governments of the States which are its members, and of public opinion within these States."

In sharp disagreement with large segments of the labor movement, he rejected the idea that revision of the existing frontiers of Europe was a necessary condition of future peace. The fact must be squarely faced that in no state which would be required to surrender territory under any such revision would public opinion presently agree to such surrender unless defeated in another war. The practical policy was to take existing frontiers for granted and to aim not toward their revision, but toward their obliteration. If justice were done within the present frontiers, if communication and trade and personal intercourse were facilitated, the "itch may be soothed" and frontier revision come to seem less impossible and less important.

International stability, Dalton held, could be enormously increased by the practical acceptance of the principles, though not necessarily of all the details, of the Geneva Protocol, by all-round disarmament, all-out arbitration, and guaranteed, "though largely consequential," security. It depended also on a substantial growth in economic prosperity, which could be most quickly achieved by measures of "economic disarmament" and in particular by a general lowering of tariffs. Certain disturbing factors needed close watching— the problem of national minorities, the New Russia, "hovering, a suspicious outcast, on Europe's Eastern flank," the New Italy, "flushed with Fascist wine."

Most significant of all, Dalton pulled no punches in addressing the issues of international coercion, so troubling to many of Labour's supporters. Bluntly, he declared that "playing ostrich" was both a dangerous and a cowardly game. Some provision for sanctions and for coercive action, however discreetly they might be kept in the background and however sparingly they might be used in practice, was a logical requirement of any legal system. "We cannot trust solely to men's good nature not to murder their neighbours," admonished Dalton, going on to warn, "To think, as some sentimentalists appear to do, that we can build a new international order without any sanctions whatever, is not to think at all."

To be sure, Dalton admitted, any move forward required a change of political leaders, no less than of policy, in more than one country, but in any event the threat of military sanctions would have to be held in ultimate reserve. Not only that, but while it was reasonable to assume that in some cases the application of economic sanctions would be enough to bring about a speedy and peaceful solution, the strongest of all economic sanctions was blockade and it was hard to see how this could be enforced without military force behind it. Given the present state of mind of a large part of the world, it was simply not possible to eliminate military sanctions from the covenant.[87]

Dalton's almost brutal directness was a refreshing display of realism not very often evident among many of his colleagues and constituents. Along with Noel-Baker, Arnold-Forster, and occasionally Norman Angell, he continually struggled to turn the labor movement away from the vague sentiments and slogans that had served it as policy when its status as a political force was more or less inconsequential.[88] Now, after the brief experience of 1924 had brought home to some of the leaders of Labour the complexities of dealing with the fears and needs of other peoples, their case for embracing the "new diplomacy" seemed more and more compelling to some of those leaders, not the least of whom was Arthur Henderson.

It is unlikely that large numbers of readers were persuaded by the arguments of Noel-Baker or Arnold-Forster or Hugh Dalton. But, because in the mid-twenties their recommendations were at the heart of the advice given by the Committee on International Questions to the Labour party's Executive, it is clear that their views were given serious attention within that body. Often, indeed, when the recommendations of the Advisory Committee were accepted by the leadership they found their way into public documents designed to influence the labor movement and, in the best of circumstances, a wider constituency. An example is a memorandum by Arnold-Forster on "All-Inclusive Arbitration," which concluded that a large body of public opinion supported "the acceptance of, as well as submission to," the judgment of reason in all international disputes. As evidence, Arnold-Forster listed a number of organizations that had recently passed resolutions urging signature of the Optional Clause of the Court of International Justice, among them the League of Nations Union, the Union of Democratic Control, the Women's International League, the Women's Peace Pilgrimage, the National Council for the Prevention of War, the Federation of League of Nations Societies, the International Conference of Disabled and Ex-Service Men, as well as a host of other women's organizations. Their efforts, he maintained, had helped spread a reasoned belief in all-out arbitration as a practical proposition.

The first two sentences in the conclusion of Arnold-Forster's paper declared, "It will have been seen that the Government have hitherto neglected every opportunity for advance beyond the position of the Covenant. Perhaps it would be fair to add that the Labour Party has neglected some opportunities for urging such advance."[89] When the memo appeared as a pamphlet it was virtually unchanged, except for the second sentence of the conclusion: "The Labour Party, on the other hand, reaffirms its support for the principle of all-inclusive pacific settlement, as embodied in the Protocol."[90]

Whatever the changes for purposes of public propaganda, Arnold-Forster's memorandum and pamphlet signalized a further step in the evolution of the Labour party's thinking. Its leaders and its publications continued on occasion to support the general principles of the Geneva Protocol and from time to time even repeated their grudging acceptance of the Locarno treaties as moving toward the ultimate achievement of those principles.[91] Increasingly, however, emphasis was placed on other initiatives, such as signature of the

Optional Clause, now seen as a useful first step in achieving the aims of the protocol.

As early as February 1927, the Labour party offered to the Labour and Socialist International the draft of a model arbitration treaty prepared by the Advisory Committee. Three days later Fridtjof Nansen of Norway submitted to the Third Commission of the League Assembly a model all-out arbitration treaty based upon the Labour draft, although that fact was not publicized. In a series of memoranda, the Advisory Committee examined and refuted the objections of the Baldwin government to the initiative from Geneva, both in the case of justiciable and of nonlegal disputes. In the former case, the claims that public opinion in Britain could not be trusted to accept submission of all kinds of legal disputes, that Parliament might not honor an award going against Great Britain, that British interests were worldwide and hence the dominions were involved, and that some foreign countries could not be trusted all suggested that the government believed that everyone was to blame for its recalcitrance except itself. Point by point, the Advisory Committee subjected the Tory rationalization to ridicule, noting, among other arguments, the extraordinary number of societies of various sorts who had declared their support for signature of the Optional Clause dealing with disputes in questions of international law.

As for the government's view that in nonlegal disputes a procedure of conciliation was all that was at present possible, the committee pointed out that since Britain had rejected the Geneva Protocol, many countries had made bilateral treaties providing for arbitral judgment in nonlegal disputes if conciliation should break down. The government, it concluded, was deliberately shutting its eyes to the manifest possibility of advance beyond the position of the League covenant: "In their anxiety to keep open the gap in the Covenant [ultimately making recourse to war acceptable], they obscure what others have done to close it, whether by accepting arbitral judgment or by merely renouncing the right of private war."[92] Although the Advisory Committee considered the Labour draft to be superior to that of the League, particularly since it admitted no reservations, the group advised that in any forthcoming election manifesto the "General Act"—the proposal of the international body—be accepted as a whole. Every effort should be made to use the new treaty as a valuable weapon and to expose to the electorate the government's shameful record of opposition to the worldwide movement in favor of all-inclusive pacific settlement. "Full acceptance of that principle," the Advisory Committee admitted, "is far from being enough to secure either peace or justice; but it is an indispensable condition of both."[93]

The issue of coercion, in particular, came to the fore in the Advisory Committee when Charles Buxton raised the question whether it should reconsider its attitude on the whole question of military and naval sanctions. As a member of the League, he pointed out, the British government was already committed, under Article XVI of its covenant, to take actions that in some cases might involve it in war against an aggressor. The same undertaking, in more definite form, appeared in Articles XI, XII, and XIII of the Geneva Protocol. While he maintained that he had not yet made up his mind, and indeed had earlier reluctantly accepted the need for force in the abortive Geneva Protocol, Buxton listed a series of reasons for rejecting sanctions, including the opposition of the United States; the doubtful cooperation of the dominions; the growth of out-and-out pacifism in the Labour party itself as evidenced in the resolution of the party conference in 1926; and the fact that steps taken since 1924 on disarmament and arbitration gave rise to the hope that more might be done with them, even without the use of military or naval threats. To him it appeared doubtful whether the Labour party as a whole would ever support military or naval action even in a "League war."[94]

Two important responses were drafted by David Mitrany and Arnold-Forster. The former agreed with Buxton that the subject should be studied, not only because of its inherent importance, but because it might split the labor movement unless conflicts were resolved in time. Asking whether sanctions were really necessary, Mitrany concluded that they could not be rejected without danger of breaking up the League, since the countries favoring them were those most in fear for their security. To reject sanctions entirely, therefore, would be to give up hope of early disarmament. Just as domestic order required support, he repeated, so was it doubtful that the League could keep the peace without sanctions. "Public opinion can do a great deal," he warned, "but not with dictators or irresponsible political cliques; these are the elements most likely to give the League work, and with them the League will carry weight only in so far as it can dispose in case of need of real power." Mitrany believed that as a minimum all League members must agree to economic sanctions, that is, to sever all trade and economic relations with the country declared an aggressor by the League, but he proposed to leave "active" sanctions optional, with members being free to agree in advance with the League Council about the help they would render in certain definite contingencies. Because no nation was likely to give military aid unless its own interests were closely involved, he insisted that his proposal was a realistic one and clearly justifiable.[95]

Arnold-Forster's reply, as was to be expected, was much less compromising. Noting that Buxton's paper raised two points, the total abolition of any sanctions or the discarding of only international military and naval pressures, he rejected both outright. Total elimination would be impossible without smashing the League, for to suppose that Britain could convert the present League to abolition or, with much the same human material, build a better League on its ruins was to make very large assumptions. And even if all that could be achieved, the real problem of sanctions would still remain. Clearly, it was idle to pretend that a war in breach of the covenant, or of the terms of the protocol, would never again occur. Future wars, too, would be labeled wars of defense and there must be some way to deal with them. Whether for dissuading a would-be attacker, or for stopping an attack once begun, or for assuring and assisting the attacked, a sanctionless League would be in a position so much worse than a League with a sanction that the sanction must be regarded as indispensable. Effort should be therefore directed not to abolishing the use of force, but to making the instruments used to resist recourse to private war as unobjectionable as possible.

Arnold-Forster went on to insist that if the League were to have a sanction at all, it should be effective, tolerable as a burden to its "guarantors," and acceptable as an assurance to the guaranteed. Admitting and then discussing the difficulties presented by the various kinds of pressure, he used willingness to submit to arbitration as the key to determining when even military sanctions were justified. In summary, Arnold-Forster declared himself to share Mitrany's view that for one cause, and only one, should it be possible to invoke adequate public support for an international sanction, the cause of all-out arbitration. Resort to private war was a crime, while nonresistance to private war was impracticable. International resistance to the war maker was a lesser evil than national resistance. So instead of trying to eliminate sanctions altogether, Labour should concentrate upon trying to reduce the moral, political, and technical difficulties of their use, above all by tying them to an international system in which they were least likely to be required. In such a system the causes of war would be courageously taken in hand, for example, by the use of Article XIX of the League covenant, and the right of private war wholly renounced.[96]

The three important Advisory Committee papers exemplified, with the exception of the root-and-branch pacifism advocated by an Arthur Ponsonby, the range of positions that still divided the various sections of the labor movement. For his part, Arthur Henderson, who continued publicly to advance the Geneva Protocol as the instrument of what was later to be called collective security, mirrored many of the arguments that surfaced in the Advisory Committee. In an important article prepared late in 1927 for *Labour Magazine*, he castigated the Conservative government not only for rejecting the Geneva Protocol, but for obstructing every move toward the achievement of compulsory arbitration as a substitute for war. The Tories, he charged, "want to be free to choose the course which, in given circumstances may be most likely to enable them to gain their ends. They do not believe in the outlawry of war."

Henderson denied Austen Chamberlain's charge that the protocol would commit Britain to a universal guarantee that, if required, might split the Commonwealth, emphasizing that its provisions took into account the geographical position and particular situation of its members. But while he downplayed any automatic compulsion to bring military, naval, and air forces to the active assistance of victims of aggression, he nevertheless agreed that Britain must support the League or get out. Those who opposed the resuscitation of the protocol itself, or some new treaty embodying the same system, should understand that, because of Britain's "special burdens," the British Commonwealth of Nations must either become equal and effective members of a League that had made war an international crime or contract out of the system entirely. To do so would be to become an empire that might maintain peace within its borders but was organized for war against all other states. That, he argued, was the road to conflict and the ultimate destruction of the Empire.

As for coercion, he insisted that a disproportionate emphasis on the sanctions clauses of protocol and covenant had been skillfully promoted by those who disliked the idea of the all-inclusive pacific settlement of international disputes. The system envisaged was one in which the fear of war would be removed, in which machinery for peaceful settlement was prearranged and available, in which treaties might be revised in an atmosphere of goodwill, and in which competitive armaments would be abolished. How soon such disarmament might take place, and to what extent, was uncertain. But he argued "with absolute assurance" that the final goal of disarmament would be achieved more quickly under the protocol system than under the covenant, and that it would never be achieved so long as the British Empire was regarded as a unitary system whose homogeneity would be imperiled by the protocol or the literal fulfillment of covenant obligations. As a practical politician, Henderson played down the difficulties in the sanctions provisions of both protocol and covenant in ways that his advisors did not feel compelled to adopt, but the increasing urgency of his commitment shone through even the somewhat pedestrian phrases that often characterized his public statements.[97]

Although MacDonald remained the major spokesman for Labour on foreign affairs as the coming election increasingly dominated politics in late 1927 and 1928, Henderson's growing attention to international issues foreshadowed his future role in the next Labour government. In a sense, as his biographer has noted, MacDonald's concern was to avoid a repetition of 1914, the lesson of which seemed to be that if there were arms they would eventually be used. Accordingly, even though he recognized the French need for security, he stressed disarmament rather than the notion of an armed pact to deter war.[98] Henderson, on the other hand, increasingly came to believe that disarmament without the prior provision of concrete guarantees for the protection of threatened nations was a chimera and that those who did not recognize the connection were simply deceiving themselves. In the light of his perceptions, along with those of such people as Noel-Baker, Arnold-Forster, and Dalton, it may be appropriate to revise modestly the judgment of W. M. Jordan, in his important *Great Britain, France and the German Problem*, to the effect that the notion of collective security remained an alien on British soil throughout the decade that followed the war.[99]

Both MacDonald and Henderson served *ex officio* on a subcommittee appointed by the National Executive to draw up a new statement of the Labour party's program for the future. At least three drafts, by Oswald Mosley, Ellen Wilkinson, and most importantly by MacDonald himself, reworked by R. H. Tawney, went through a variety of maneuvers finally to emerge as "Labour and the Nation," whose style was clearly Tawney's, while the conception was unmistakably MacDonald's.[100] Both on the domestic side and in its consideration of international questions, the document, which was presented to the annual conference of the party in October 1928, testified to the ambivalence within the labor movement. Domestically, for example, the scourge of unemployment was not mentioned, and at the Birmingham Conference the Executive had to fight off the attacks on that issue of the ILP leaders who were becoming ever and ever more frustrated by the MacDonaldite policy of cautious gradualism. On the international side, "Labour and the Nation" likewise elicited criticism, at one point leading an impatient MacDonald to declare that he was rather tired of hearing about the wonderful Soviet proposal for complete disarmament. "Where is it?" he asked. "My friends, do not be misled by words. The Soviet Government made a proposal which they had to run away from."[101]

The foreign policy planks in the document outlined the positions that Labour had evolved in the years since the war, but touched only gingerly on such controversial questions as the sanctions behind any international decisions on war and peace. Instead, "Labour and the Nation" was content to call for the renunciation by international treaty of the use of war as an instrument of national policy—the policy of the Kellogg Pact—and the negotiation of international compacts through the League of Nations. It advocated the reduction of armaments by international agreement and then bowed to the sanctionists by adding "to the minimum required for police purposes." Most concretely, it demanded the immediate signature of the Optional Clause accepting the jurisdiction of the Permanent Court of International Justice in all justiciable disputes. Beyond that the Labour manifesto was very general, calling for economic cooperation and the systematic use of the League of Nations. Published as a pamphlet, it was used as the centerpiece of Labour's case in the months leading up to the General Election.[102] On balance, Sidney Webb's assessment, that "Labour and the Nation" was not likely to be an improvement on "Labour and the New Social Order," issued at the end of the war, was accurate.[103]

As Britain approached closer and closer to a General Election in the early months of 1929, Advisory Committee members were convinced that if a Labour government came into power it could achieve substantial results more quickly in the field of foreign affairs than in home affairs. An important memorandum suggested prompt measures that might be taken, dividing them into those already adopted as part of the Labour party's program and those not yet adopted but recommended by the committee as worthy of consideration. Among the first were immediate signature of the Optional Clause, adherence to the League Assembly's General Act of Conciliation, Arbitration, and Judicial Settlement, withdrawal of British reservations to the Kellogg treaty, acceptance of the new doctrine that the high seas and international waterways should only be closed by international action for the enforcement of international covenants, resumption of diplomatic relations with Russia, an effort to secure immediate withdrawal of all Allied troops from the Rhine and at the least those of Britain alone, and the immediate reversal of the policy of building a naval base at Singapore. This substantial array of Labour policies was augmented by recommendations as widely ranging as those for a single minister of defense with cabinet rank to support for women candidates for the Foreign Office and the diplomatic service.[104] A number of the suggestions were indeed to be implemented during the next two years, while others were either rejected or disappeared in the complicated real world of international give and take.

Of the two key architects of Labour's foreign policies when it again took office, MacDonald was never comfortable with an emphasis upon force. He thought in terms of changing outlooks, of the psychology of peace, and quite consistently belittled accent upon coercion. Henderson, on the other hand, fairly early on came to accept the view that countries such as France would never consider themselves to be secure unless there was some concrete guarantee behind international decisions. As a politician appealing to a divided constituency, he sometimes joined in downplaying the likelihood that armies and navies might have to be employed as instruments of international action. But more than any prominent Labour figure he struggled to implement the reasoning of the champions of economic and military sanctions in the policy initiatives of his party. When he took over the Foreign Office after Labour's success in the election of May 1929, he came prepared with a concrete and coherent program that had been elaborated and refined during the years of opposition. In a modest way, its insistence upon collective security implemented through international institutions looked more far-sightedly into the future than any of the faltering orthodoxies it proposed to replace. The repercussions of the Great Depression, no less than the failures of the 1920s, made it certain that his program would become another of the twentieth century's lost causes. In its time, however, it was a responsible and realistic alternative to the more customary approaches that characterized Britain's approach to foreign policy for most of the decade after the First World War.

CONCLUSION

When the Labour party formed its second minority government after the election of 1929, it came prepared with an international program that reflected the strong element of realism gradually infused into Labour thinking during the preceding decade. "Labour and the Nation," whatever its ambiguities and compromises, evidenced an understanding that any British program must take into account relations with the United States and reach a measure of common ground with the governments of France and of other European nations. Circulated among the officials of the Foreign Office, it was used as a blueprint by Arthur Henderson, the new foreign secretary, as he struggled doggedly to augment British use of the instruments of international cooperation, particularly through the League of Nations. That struggle, in a Europe of economic depression and political disintegration, has been thoroughly described by David Carlton in his perceptive study of the foreign policy of the second Labour government.[1] But the process by which Henderson and his colleagues shaped their blueprint tells us much about the paths not taken in the interwar years—and perhaps something about subsequent struggles with similar issues.

The foreign policies pursued by Labour at the end of the 1920s had been hammered out in an atmosphere of almost constant tension. After the First World War, Labour's embittered reaction to the settlement imposed by the victorious Allies encouraged the view that socialist cooperation with the capitalist and imperialist governments could only be self-defeating. For a time, few of Labour's key figures challenged that view and even fewer pleaded for compromise and an attempt to work within existing institutions in the struggle to avoid another terrible conflagration. Gradually, as it began to be evident that Labour might for the first time be able to form a government, those leaders began to seek a basis for a viable Labour posture on international affairs. Despite their disappointment over various aspects of the postwar settlement, some of them, Henderson above all, came increasingly to insist that international peace and security could only be achieved by faithful use of the machinery of the infant League of Nations. By the end of the decade, sterile repudiation of the entire existing European system gave way to an affirmation of the new international institutions at the heart of Labour's policy.

Labour's acceptance of a League policy evidenced its growing maturity as a potential wielder of governmental power. When there had been no possibility of having to take responsibility, party spokesmen could insist upon ideal solutions to international questions without having to bother themselves with the aims and the ideas of other nations. As Labour grew stronger and gradually took the place of the divided Liberals as the official Opposition, the unyielding certainties of an anticapitalist, anti-imperialist propaganda began to erode. More and more of the rank and file were willing to concede that a viable foreign policy required an informed concern for the needs of other nations and the willingness to work cooperatively through collective institutions in the search for compromise solutions to complex problems. Proximity to power quickened the rupture between the pragmatic mainstream of the party and its more ideological left wing, not only on domestic issues but on foreign policy as well. The "taming of Labour" had many facets in the years after the First World War.

For Arthur Henderson when he came to the Foreign Office, adherence to the Optional Clause of the League covenant, which provided for compulsory arbitration of justiciable disputes, and to the General Act of Arbitration, Conciliation, and Judicial Settlement, which extended arbitration even to nonjusticiable issues, was simply the rounding off of obligations already assumed under the League covenant and the Pact of Paris, recently accepted by the previous British government. He fought, unsuccessfully, in the cabinet to prevent the service departments, and especially the naval staff, as well as the dominions, from vitiating British adherence with reservations that undercut the purposes of the new agreements.[2] Ramsay MacDonald, on the other hand, was evidently more influenced by the advice not only of the military leaders, but also of correspondents from the outside, all of whom warned against excessive British commitments that might bring Britain into conflict with the United States over issues of freedom of the seas.[3]

The almost constant discord between MacDonald and Henderson, which Carlton has portrayed so well for the period of the 1929–31 government, rested, as he understood, on much more than personal antipathy.[4] Despite occasional flights of rhetoric, MacDonald was hardly more than lukewarm in his support for the League of Nations that Henderson regarded as the fulcrum of Labour's international policy. MacDonald's papers make clear that he gave serious attention to the analyses made throughout the 1920s by the ever-changing membership of Labour's Advisory Committee on International

Questions, but they also reflect his considerable disagreement with those like Noel-Baker, Arnold-Forster, and Dalton who came increasingly to the fore in that group toward the end of the decade. MacDonald was never a pacifist in the strict meaning of the term, and he frequently warned that it was impossible to disarm in a heavily armed world, but for the most part he was not a supporter of the initiatives to strengthen the coercive powers of the League.[5] His well-known reference to sanctions as a "harmless drug to soothe nerves" was more than a concession to the sensibilities of the more genuinely pacifist among his followers; it reflected views about international politics that he maintained fairly consistently throughout his career. However, even when he spoke eloquently about the illusion that national security could be guaranteed by military preparations, he acknowledged that in the world as it was force might be necessary as the ultimate guarantor of national policy. Certainly in practice he was less than whole-heartedly enthusiastic about most of the disarmament initiatives that surfaced during the 1920s. Despite the skillful pragmatism that characterized his tenure in the Foreign Office in 1924 and his negotiations with the United States during the second Labour administration, he appeared convinced that until there was a change in people's thinking there was little chance that they would give up the supposed security of substantial national military forces. He placed his greatest reliance, in the search for international justice and peace, upon the gradual development of a spirit of cooperation among the peoples of the world, even when he was somewhat vague about how such a spirit was to be achieved.

There are implications for the thirties, the years of the national government, in the issues that can be personified in the positions of MacDonald and Henderson. Clearly MacDonald remained closer to the earlier attitudes of much of the labor movement, indeed of the ILP that he had come to despise by the end of our period, than were the advisors to whom Henderson paid more and more attention as time passed. Seen in that perspective, there is a fascinating element of continuity between MacDonald's foreign policy attitudes before 1931 and those of George Lansbury as leader of the Labour party after the debacle of that year. MacDonald was contemptuous of Lansbury and the latter reciprocated the feeling. Lansbury was a pacifist and MacDonald was not. Yet both were highly suspicious of reliance upon force as the sanction behind international intercourse, both looked to some vague change in the hearts of people as the future guarantor of peace and security, and both, in their very different ways, captured some measure of their support from constituents who looked to them for assurance that Labour would have nothing to do with the bad old world of alliances, huge military establishments, and eventual war. MacDonald often disappointed his followers, especially those on the left, but his break with the party after 1931 should not conceal how much he shared with them the conviction that the growth of goodwill and understanding would supersede the use of force in international affairs. He played his part in cultivating the illusions that, during the thirties, permitted the parliamentary Labour party to substitute gestures like voting against military credits for facing up to growing international danger. There was little consolation in the fact that most of Labour's opponents lived in a world of even greater illusion. During the twenties they had taken it for granted that a healthy Germany was essential for the future prosperity of Britain herself, but, with the possible exception of the Locarno agreements, they had done little to appease effectively German resentment over the Versailles "diktat." Tragically, the policy of appeasement that might have preserved a struggling German republic during the twenties was adopted by the national government only after the triumph of Hitler's National Socialism, when the likelihood of collective resistance to the Nazi threat had faded in the shadow of Europe's economic distress and political disarray.

Henderson's posture also had implications for the future policy of the Labour party. Recent brief biographies by Fred Leventhal and Chris Wrigley have fleshed out the portrait of a much more complex figure than appeared in either the caustic dismissals in MacDonald's diary or the virtual canonization that characterizes the hagiography of a Mary Agnes Hamilton. Throughout the twenties Henderson's understanding of international issues continued to expand and his support for a powerful and effective international organization continued to grow. Although he shared much of the distaste of his Labour colleagues for the postwar peace settlement, he and J. R. Clynes were virtually the only leaders in the movement to place their support quickly and unequivocally behind the League of Nations and then to understand that it needed more than goodwill as a sanction if it were to be effective. He seems to have worked well with younger people—the testimony of Dalton and Noel-Baker and the observations of Beatrice Webb make that clear—and to have used their assessments and advice adeptly.

At the beginning of the postwar period, the new Advisory Committee on International Questions was customarily attended by members who often shared a skeptical negativism about international cooperation with the bulk of the labor movement. Gradually, in part because of Labour's growing experience with international affairs, in part because of skillful staff work by Leonard Woolf as secretary of the committee, the balance began to shift toward those members who argued that certain concrete obligations, including the possible use of military force to support an international organization, must be accepted as part of the price for peace and security. In contrast to some of their Labour fellows, men such as Will Arnold-Forster, Philip Noel-Baker, Hugh Dalton, and occasionally others such as David Mitrany accepted from early on the truism that any British government, Labour or otherwise, could only implement effective international policies in collaboration with other governments. They recognized the legitimacy, for example, of the French obsession with security even as they were critical of the French for the way they pursued their goals. They elaborated a policy for which Henderson became the chief advocate, recognizing a legitimate role for force in international affairs and sought to ensure that if it had to be used it would be employed in support of a strengthened League of Nations rather than as an instrument of national policy.

It is true, as has sometimes been pointed out, that neither Henderson nor his advisors were unwavering in their insistence that international sanctions were indispensable to a viable international order. Henderson frequently spoke, in public as well as in Parliament, as though he believed that the growing use of arbitration in international disputes could normally obviate the need for recourse to force. He was a tenacious champion of disarmament and worked tirelessly in and out of office to find formulas and understandings to make possible progress in reducing the weapons of war. Nevertheless, as I suggested many years ago, his position came closer, in the Britain of the 1920s, to a conception of an international order with teeth than that of any major politician in any party. Certainly no one in the leadership of the Tory party nor any of the political chiefs of the fragmented Liberals came measurably as close as he to making the case for what later came to be called collective security.

As in the case of MacDonald, the heritage of Henderson continued into the 1930s. Attention has often focused on the dramatic scene at the Brighton Conference of the Labour party in 1935 as Ernest Bevin rumbled slowly to the platform to denounce George Lansbury for "hawking his conscience round from body to body." After the collapse of the second Labour government in 1931, Lansbury became the leader of the Labour party and moved it in a pacifist direction quite out of keeping with the policies Henderson had pursued. Bevin's intervention was momentous, paving the way for Lansbury's resignation of the leadership and the abandonment of Labour's almost suicidal protest votes against the war estimates. But it was Dalton, Henderson's collaborator and second-in-command in the second Labour government, who consistently during the thirties carried the banner of collective opposition to the looming threat of Fascism, whether in its Italian or its more virulent German form.

Too many commentators have busied themselves looking for the mote in

Labour's eye for the claim to be made that Labour stood foursquare in the later thirties for international resistance to menacing aggression. What can be argued is that with all their reservations (and subsequent equivocations) the younger leaders of the Labour party, more nearly than their Tory rivals who held the reins of government, understood the dangers of the Nazi attack upon the international order and, eventually, also understood the importance of joining others in resistance to that attack. The heirs of Arthur Henderson in support of international collective security were among the Labour leaders who served so effectively after 1940 in the great Churchill wartime coalition. Subsequently, as they took over the reins of government in 1945, they played a significant role in still another effort to substitute international approaches to keeping the peace for the traditional reliance upon national strength alone, which had failed so devastatingly in the past.[6] Their competence to do so was in part a result of the preparations laid in the decade after World War I, as Labour found itself compelled, almost for the first time, to grapple with concrete issues of international policy.

If Labour's conclusions were often ambivalent and sometimes contradictory, they were arguably at least as realistic as the policies of the more traditional stewards of British politics. What might have been the history of Europe if policies based upon a collective defense of the legal international order had been embraced cannot be judged. All that can be said is that they were not adopted and Europe, to say nothing of the world, was compelled to endure the worst bloodletting in its history, hardly a recommendation for the paths that were followed in the interwar decades of decision.

NOTES

INTRODUCTION

1. See Winkler, *League of Nations Movement* and "British Labor."

2. Even so thoughtful a scholar as F. S. Northedge falls into the trap of oversimplification. Commenting on the interwar period, he notes that while leaders of the Labour party repeatedly called for a breach with traditional diplomatic practices and the adoption of a policy of collective security, the party never expressly proposed reforms in the League covenant so as to eliminate the principle of national sovereignty. But in fact, in 1924 and again in 1929 some of the leaders suggested changes in the covenant that disputed the basic traditionalism of the conventional British approach to the League. See Northedge, *Troubled Giant*, p. 619.

3. Hamilton, in *Remembering*, pp. 99–100, warns against seeing the twenties and thirties "under the uniform, oppressive climate of approaching catastrophe."

CHAPTER I

1. Reid, *Origins*, pp. 157–204, and Chapter 2 of Miller, *Socialism and Foreign Policy*, are still useful for the prewar problems of the party.

2. Marquand, *Ramsay MacDonald*, p. 285.

3. See Windrich, *British Labour's Foreign Policy*, esp. pp. 258–59, and Miller, *Socialism and Foreign Policy*, pp. 244–77.

4. Northedge, *Troubled Giant*, pp. 617–30; Reynolds, *British Foreign Policy*, p. 11; Medlicott, *British Foreign Policy*, pp. 86–92; Wolfers, *Britain and France*, pp. 331–43.

5. This phrase is used by Gathorne-Hardy, *Short History*, p. 50.

6. Aside from discussions of the Boer War, the standard accounts of the Labour party's early years quite properly have almost nothing to say about any other foreign policy matters. See Pelling, *Origins*; Bealey and Pelling, *Labour and Politics*; Poirier, *Advent*, and Reid, *Origins*.

7. McBriar, *Fabian Socialism*. Williams, *Fifty Years' March*, pp. 9–109, offers a convenient account of the constituent elements in the newly formed party.

8. Graubard, *British Labour*, p. 10.

9. See, as one example, 32 HC Deb. 5s. (Nov. 27, 1911): 75–80, 129–36. It is illustrative that Marquand, *Ramsay MacDonald*, pp. 164–67, devotes only a few brief pages to MacDonald's prewar views on foreign affairs and then only as an introduction to a discussion of his position during the war. For Hardie, see Morgan, *Keir Hardie*, Chapter 12.

10. E.g., *Report of the Annual Conference of the Labour Party* (1908), p. 81; (1909), p. 59; (1910), p. 14; (1912), pp. 98–99; (1913), p. 111; (1914), pp. 121–22. Henceforth *LP Annual*

Conference Report and similarly for Independent Labour party and Trades Union Congress.

11. Cole, *Second International*, 1:19–20; Morgan, *Keir Hardie*, pp. 260–62.

12. Review of Bullock and Shock, *Liberal Tradition*, in *New Statesman and Nation* 52 (Nov. 10, 1956): 596–97.

13. Many of these Liberals were far to the left of their Labour colleagues in Parliament in the decade before the war. Bealey, "Electoral Arrangement," 373.

14. Tucker, *Attitude*, p. 50.

15. Maddox, *Foreign Relations*, pp. 35–38.

16. Tucker, *Attitude*, p. 21.

17. The best study of these Liberals and a few others is Cline, *Recruits to Labour*. Still interesting is Garratt, *Mugwumps*, pp. 155–58.

18. Viscount Haldane, who was to be of considerable importance in Labour's first government, does not really fit into this group even though he was the most prominent Liberal to come over to Labour after the war. His growing sympathy for many aspects of the Labour program was nonetheless gradual, and his influence on the development of Labour's views on foreign policy was negligible until he took office as Lord Chancellor in 1924. For Haldane's own account of his move toward the Labour party, see *Haldane: An Autobiography*, esp. pp. 308–10. Other Liberals were not completely comfortable with their move toward Labour. See, for example, Hobson's comments in his *Confessions of an Economic Heretic*, p. 126, cited by Miller, *Socialism and Foreign Policy*, pp. 82–83, and Wedgwood, *Last of the Radicals*, pp. 139–40, 158.

19. Angell, *After All*, pp. 236–44.

20. Mary Agnes Hamilton goes so far as to say, perhaps with rhetorical exaggeration, "It is very largely owing to him that the Labour party was steered into the right path, so far as collective security is concerned." *Remembering*, p. 104.

21. Anderson, *Noel Buxton*.

22. Tracey, *Book of the Labour Party*, 3:227–31, and Anderson, *Noel Buxton*, esp. foreword by G. P. Gooch, pp. 5–10.

23. Ponsonby was the son of Queen Victoria's private secretary and the nephew of Noel and Charles Roden Buxton. Trevelyan was the son of Sir George Otto Trevelyan and the grandnephew of Thomas Babington Macaulay. See Morris, *Trevelyan*.

24. Swartz, *Union of Democratic Control*, is the standard study. Older accounts are Swanwick, *Builders of Peace*, and Trevelyan, *Union of Democratic Control*.

25. Swanwick, *I Have Been Young*, pp. 425–27.

26. Namier, "Diplomacy in the Interwar Period," p. 110.

27. In September 1919, for example, the UDC's Executive Committee of eleven members included four future ministers (J. R. MacDonald, F. W. Pethick Lawrence, Arthur Ponsonby, and Charles Trevelyan), the wife of a future minister (Ethel Snowden), and a future delegate appointed by the Labour government to the League of Nations Assembly at Geneva (H. M. Swanwick).

28. Morel was sentenced under a technicality of the Official Secrets Act for sending some of his pamphlets to Romain Rolland, then resident in neutral Switzerland.

29. A. Wallace (Secretary of the Dundee Labour party) to Morel, Feb. 2, 1924, E. D. Morel Papers, bundle no. 21. See also Gallacher, *Rolling*, p. 65–66.

30. For Morel, see Cline, *Morel.* Also Cocks, *Morel,* and Tracey, *Book of the Labour Party,* 3:326–28.

31. The most conspicuous exception was Arthur Henderson, who never joined the ILP.

32. It is characteristic that Snowden, who became alienated from the ILP considerably after MacDonald, should have finally resigned from the party in 1926 while MacDonald held on until 1930. Marquand, *Ramsay MacDonald,* pp. 450–62, places most of the fault for the break at the feet of the ILP and argues that MacDonald found it hard to sever the ties of some thirty-five years. At the same time, he notes that even late into the twenties, the ILP still had great influence on opinion in the Labour party and no leader wishing to retain his hold on the rank-and-file membership could afford to ignore its positions. The struggle, crystallizing around the ILP's "Socialism in Our Time," was concerned with the pace and the tactics of social and economic change, but it was accompanied by a constant counterpoint of argument over issues of foreign policy.

33. Brailsford, *War of Steel and Gold* and *League of Nations.*

34. Leventhal, *Last Dissenter,* p. 95, and Hamilton, *Remembering,* pp. 146–48. See also Koss, *Rise and Fall,* pp. 410–11.

35. From March 1919 until the spring of 1922, the *Herald,* under the editorship of George Lansbury, was unofficial and consistently on the far left of Labour opinion. In 1922 it came under the control of the Trades Union Congress and the Labour party, after which, with Hamilton Fyfe as editor, it became the exponent of official Labour party and TUC policy.

36. Maddox, *Foreign Relations,* pp. 74–77.

37. Of the Labour M.P.'s successful in the election of 1918, forty-nine of the fifty-seven were sponsored by trade unions.

38. Even Clynes did not seem to Beatrice Webb to have the qualities of leadership required by the times. "Clynes," she wrote in her diary, "is not a great Parliamentary leader but he does not disgrace the party as Adamson did—that is about all you can say" (Beatrice Webb Manuscript Diary 36 [Jan. 4, 1922]). Margaret Cole has published the diary for the years 1912–32 almost in its entirety. I have used some materials Mrs. Cole did not publish and also materials that have been printed. See Cole, *Beatrice Webb's Diaries, 1912–1924* and *1924–1932.*

39. Cole, *Beatrice Webb's Diaries, 1924–1932,* Feb. 5, 1927, pp. 130–31. For Woolf, see Wilson, *Woolf.* Also Meyerowitz, *Woolf,* and Woolf, *Downhill.*

40. Tracey, *Book of the Labour Party,* 3:69.

41. Dalton, *Call Back,* pp. 101–2.

42. Tracey, *Book of the Labour Party,* 3:134–35.

43. For examples see Sacks, *MacDonald in Thought and Action,* esp. Part 5, "International Arena," pp. 470–567.

44. Marquand, *Ramsay MacDonald,* esp. pp. 164–237 and 329–56, and Cole, *Beatrice Webb's Diaries, 1924–1932,* p. 112. Hamilton, *Remembering,* pp. 104, 120–30, and Tracey, *Book of the Labour Party,* 3:214–18, are interesting as insiders' views after the Labour party split in 1931.

45. The following paragraphs are taken almost verbatim from my essay on Henderson in Craig and Gilbert, *Diplomats,* pp. 312–13. See Leventhal, *Henderson,* for an overall assessment. *Henderson,* a biography by a close and admiring collaborator, Mary Agnes

Hamilton, is still of some use. See also her *Remembering*, esp. pp. 251–52; Lloyd in *New Statesman* 10 (Oct. 26, 1935): 591–92; and Cole, *Makers*, pp. 256–60.

46. Cole, *Beatrice Webb's Diaries, 1924–1932*, p. 16.

47. Beatrice Webb was one of those who early on recognized the importance of the Advisory Committee and parallel groups. In her typically astringent fashion she noted in her diary on Jan. 30, 1920: "These Labour leaders, stupid though they may be, feel far more responsibility for the administration of subject races and foreign affairs generally than any former H.M.G. And the activities of the dozen or so Advisory Committees of the Labour Party, with their determination to discover facts and formulate policy on all sorts of technical questions, is only another sign of a new type of politics—the initiation of social change from outside the recognized machinery of government." Cole, *Diaries, 1912–1932*, p. 174.

48. Maddox, *Foreign Relations*, p. 102. Also Advisory Committee, "Minutes," n.d., Labour party Archives.

49. A typical problem shows up in the minutes as early as February 1919. "The meeting called for Tuesday, February 18 at 2:45 p.m. did not take place, owing to lack of attendance."

50. Maddox, *Foreign Relations*, p. 100, lists the following as more or less active participants in the work of the committee: C. R. and Mrs. Buxton, Noel Buxton, Sidney Webb, Norman Angell, H. N. Brailsford, George Young, Dr. Hugh Dalton, E. F. Wise, G. D. H. Cole, G. Lowes Dickinson, David Mitrany, W. N. Gillies, Charles Trevelyan, J. A. Hobson, J. Ramsay MacDonald, Leonard Woolf, A. J. Toynbee, Arthur Ponsonby, Bertrand Russell, E. D. Morel, Mrs. H. M. Swanwick, C. Delisle Burns, Dr. E. Bentham, and Prof. C. R. Beazley. To these should be added from the minutes a few other names, not necessarily of members, but of participants: H. Duncan Hall, Rex Leeper, R. C. K. Ensor, J. L. Hammond, E. M. H. Lloyd, Josiah Wedgwood, Seymour Cocks, Sidney Olivier, and Oswald Mosley. The list is not an exhaustive one.

51. Advisory Committee, "Preliminary Memorandum," p. 2.

CHAPTER 2

1. This chapter is an enlarged and substantially revised version of my "British Labour Party and the Paris Settlement," in Beaver, *Some Pathways*, pp. 111–48.

2. Winkler, *League of Nations Movement*, pp. 167–98; Brand, *British Labour Party*, pp. 43–60.

3. E.g., *British Citizen and Empire Worker*, Feb. 1, 1919, p. 46 ("The League of Nations plan is still too nebulous to be understood by the ordinary man, but the hint that the German colonies may be under its control sent an uncomfortable shiver down the back of many of its advocates in this country") and Feb. 6, 1919, p. 1 ("the trouble over the German colonies nearly wrecked the Conference. . . . both in France and England there is grave scepticism as to the practicability of the scheme, and its enunciation in this shape has done not a little harm to the slowly emerging ideal of a League of Nations"). Damning with faint praise was a standard tactic.

4. *Clarion*, Oct. 4, 1918.

5. *Bradford Pioneer*, Oct. 11, 1918.

6. "Labour Party" (unnumbered Labour party leaflet); "Why Labour Supports a League of Nations"; "Why I Shall Vote Labour."

7. "Why Women Should Join the Labour Party."

8. Advisory Committee, Minutes (May 30, 1918). Present at the first meeting were Sidney Webb, Leonard Woolf, G. Lowes Dickinson, H. Duncan Hall, G. D. H. Cole, Major Gillespie, C. Deslisle Burns, and Arnold Toynbee.

9. "League of Nations," Advisory Committee (1918). Other memoranda as the war drew to a close dealt with "Freedom of the Seas," "Colonies," "Reform of the Foreign Services," and, after the armistice, "Intervention in Russia."

10. G. N. Barnes, who had remained in the Coalition cabinet after the affair of the Stockholm Conference, was a member of the British delegation, but Labour did not regard him as its representative.

11. Van Der Slice, *International Labour*, p. 313.

12. Brand, *British Labour's Rise to Power*, pp. 150–52.

13. Swanwick, *Builders of Peace*, pp. 114–18. Signatories were Fred Bramley, C. R. Buxton, F. Seymour Cocks, J. A. Hobson, F. W. Jowett, J. R. MacDonald, E. D. Morel, F. W. Pethick Lawrence, Arthur Ponsonby, Ethel Snowden, H. M. Swanwick, and Charles Trevelyan.

14. *Labour Leader*, Jan. 9, 1919. Even when the Birmingham Trades Council warned against a "Capitalist" League, it went on to pass a resolution congratulating President Wilson for his support of the League idea. *Herald*, Jan. 11, 1919.

15. *Herald*, Jan. 18, 1919. Shortly before this time the *Herald* was credited with a sale of about 100,000. It resumed daily publication in the new year. Other papers supportive of Labour had an even more modest circulation. The *New Statesman*, for example, had a weekly sale of approximately 3,000 and very likely commanded less general influence than, say, the *Nation* or the *Spectator*. Koss, *Rise and Fall*, p. 343.

16. Leventhal, *Last Dissenter*, pp. 152–54.

17. *Herald*, Jan. 4, 1919.

18. *Forward*, Oct. 5, 1918.

19. *Labour Leader*, Jan. 9, 1919.

20. *Herald*, Jan. 11, 1919.

21. *Labour Leader*, Jan. 9, 1919.

22. See Van Der Slice, *International Labour*, pp. 309–42, for a useful account of the Berne Conference and its aftermath.

23. "Notes on Procedure at the International Labour Conference," Advisory Committee (1918).

24. It will not escape notice how strikingly similar these proposals of Brailsford are to some of the patterns that have emerged in the European Community over the last several decades.

25. Brailsford, *Parliament of the League of Nations*.

26. MacDonald in *Forward*, Feb. 8, 1919.

27. *LP Annual Conference Report* (1919), p. 18.

28. Van Der Slice, *International Labour*, pp. 303–4.

29. On the other hand, there were those on the right of the labor movement to whom even their leaders, let alone a MacDonald, were unrepresentative. See, for example, *British*

Citizen and Empire Worker for Feb. 13, 1919: "Mr. MacDonald himself is no longer a member of Parliament, nor likely to be again; Mr. Henderson, his pliable tool and puppet, is also a private individual once more. The Germans could not help recognising that these men no longer counted in English politics, and were therefore not worth wasting time on. Mr. Thomas, it is true, was also there, but Mr. Thomas is not a pacifist, and does not like being deluded; and he seems to have left as soon as he could."

30. *LP Annual Conference Report* (1919), pp. 14, 196–97; Labour party, "International Labour and Peace," p. 4; *Herald*, Feb. 1919; Independent Labour party, "International Socialism and World Peace," pp. 1–2. Wilson apparently considered very seriously the socialist project for minority representation, but his advisors could come up with no scheme that seemed practical. Seymour, *Intimate Papers of Colonel House*, 4:313. See also Marquand, *Ramsay MacDonald*, pp. 248–49.

31. *LP Annual Conference Report* (1919), pp. 197–98. The full text of the program of principles in the Berne resolution follows:

1. The right of all nations to determine their own fate and to determine to which State they will belong within the League of Nations.

2. In disputed territories any nationality question will be referred to a popular consultation under the control of the League of Nations, whose decision shall be final.

3. The protection of nationalities, forming a minority or majority in a country, to be secured by a minimum of national rights determined and guaranteed in its application by the League of Nations.

4. When new States are formed or territories become part of already existing States, the League of Nations should take steps by means of treaties of commerce and free communication to guarantee the vital economic interests of all nations affected by the new creations.

5. The right of the League of Nations, after consultation by plebiscite, to satisfy any new claims of nationalities or parts of nationalities which desire to modify their frontiers.

6. Protection of the populations of dependencies, protectorates and colonies to be assured by the League of Nations, which should take steps to prepare the native populations as rapidly as possible for the exercise of the rights of full self-determination, through the founding of schools, grants of local autonomy, by the freedom of the press, the right of holding meetings and of forming associations, together with other political rights.

32. See, for example, *Herald*, Jan. 25, 1919, which complains that "the first act of the preliminary Peace Conference has been to try to assure that the covenants of peace shall be not open and not openly arrived at. . . . its decisions are being taken in secrecy without the knowledge of the people whose destinies are thus being settled for generations."

33. *Labour Leader*, Feb. 20, 1919; *New Statesman* 12 (Feb. 1, 1919): 361; *Herald*, Feb. 1 and 8, 1919. See also, Brand, *British Labour's Rise to Power*, pp. 151–52.

34. *New Statesman* 12 (Feb. 22, 1919): 436–37, and 12 (Mar. 22, 1919): 540–41, but not without criticism of details; "Rob Roy" (Dr. J. Stirling Robertson), *Forward*, Feb. 22, 1919. Robertson's views often differed from those of the editor of *Forward*.

35. *Labour Leader*, Feb. 20, 1919; *ILP Annual Conference Report* (1919), pp. 37–41.

36. Brailsford had used the epithet in the *Herald* on Jan. 4, 1919, p. 4.

37. *Labour Leader*, Feb. 27, 1919; Marquand, *Ramsay MacDonald*, pp. 248–49.

38. *Herald*, Feb. 22, 1919.

39. *Forward*, Feb. 22, Mar. 1, 1919; *Bradford Pioneer*, Feb. 21, 1919.

40. *U.D.C.* 4, no. 5 (Mar. 1919): 305.

41. Swanwick, *Builders of Peace*, p. 119.

42. Bridge, "Pan-Anglo-Saxonism and the League of Nations," *Socialist Review* 16 (Apr.–June 1919): 166–71. Earlier, on Feb. 1, 1919, the *Herald* had optimistically declared, "Our policy is the establishment of an international authority whose decrees would in practical fact never need to be backed by physical force."

43. *Clarion*, Mar. 14, Apr. 18, 1919.

44. *British Citizen and Empire Worker*, Feb. 6, 20, 27, 1919.

45. Advisory Committee, Minutes, Mar. 4, 1919.

46. *LP Annual Conference Report* (1919), pp. 23–25; *Herald*, Apr. 3, 5, 1919; Trades Union Congress and Labour party, "Amendments to the Covenant of the League of Nations," pp. 3–15.

47. *New Statesman* 13 (May 3, 1919): 109.

48. Graubard, *British Labour and the Russian Revolution*, pp. 64–144.

49. *LP Annual Conference Report* (1919), p. 26; *Herald*, Apr. 5, 8, 1919; *Labour Leader*, Feb. 20, May 22, 1919. At the Independent Labour party's annual conference, the resolution calling for the withdrawal of all Allied armies was introduced by Arthur Ponsonby, who had recently joined the ILP, and carried without discussion. *ILP Annual Conference Report* (1919), pp. 73–74.

50. *LP Annual Conference Report* (1919), pp. 17–18.

51. Van Der Slice, *International Labour*, p. 335. See also LSI Permanent Commission, Amsterdam, Apr. 1919, LSI Apr. 1, 1929, Labour party Archives.

52. LSI Permanent Commission, LSI Apr. 1, 1929, Labour party Archives; *LP Annual Conference Report* (1919), pp. 206–11; Labour party, "International Labour and Peace," pp. 15–17.

53. Van Der Slice, *International Labour*, pp. 343–75.

54. *ILP Annual Conference Report* (1920), pp. 9–10.

55. *LP Annual Conference Report* (1919), p. 216.

56. Ibid., pp. 212–13; Labour party, "International Labour and Peace," pp. 19–20.

57. *LP Annual Conference Report* (1919), p. 217.

58. Henderson, "Labour and the League of Nations," in Tracey, *Book of the Labour Party*, 3:91–94.

59. Advisory Committee (1919). There is no title on this memorandum, but a penciled note at the top of the first page reads, "May 1919. Peace Terms. Norman Angell."

60. Ibid., (n.d.) [1919]. This is a typewritten, not mimeographed, memo with no title, but with "Policy towards Germany" penciled across the top.

61. There is no direct indication of who prepared Henderson's material, but the internal evidence makes the source quite clear.

62. Henderson, "Peace Terms," pp. 18–19.

63. Beatrice Webb Manuscript Diary 35 (May 10, 1919): 3694–95.

64. Swanwick, *Builders of Peace*, pp. 121–22.

65. *Forward*, May 17, 1919.

66. *Labour Leader*, June 19, 1919.

67. *New Statesman* 13 (May 10, 1919): 129.

68. *Herald,* May 17, 1919; Postgate, *Life of George Lansbury,* p. 192. For an assessment of the *Herald's* importance during this period, see Schneer, *George Lansbury,* esp. pp. 150–51.

69. *E.g.,* Philip Snowden at a meeting to protest the terms of peace held at Essex Hall, London, May 30. *Labour Leader,* June 5, 1919.

70. *Clarion,* May 23, 30, 1919.

71. The *New Statesman,* however, thought that the modified peace terms were an improvement and hoped that the German government would accept them quickly in order to pave the way for further revision. *New Statesman* 13 (June 14, 1919): 249.

72. An interesting sidelight on MacDonald's public emphasis on Germany's plight is provided by Sidney Webb. Writing to his wife from Southport, Webb noted: "Ramsay MacDonald is here, in his usual form. He says the socialists all over Europe, whilst hot against the Peace Treaty, are also indignant with the Germans, and wish to take a 'European' attitude about the peace terms, rather than a pro-German one, protesting against the Treaty on the grounds that it does not rebuild the economic life of the world, and provide for general industrial reconstruction.—This is his usual good sense in council and in criticism. It is a pity he is not more constructive." Sidney Webb to Beatrice Webb, June 23, 1919, Passfield Papers. MacDonald himself had written publicly a few months before about "that terrible document of the League of Nations," the Draft Covenant. *Forward,* Mar. 1, 1919.

73. *LP Annual Conference Report* (1919), pp. 111, 139–42.

74. Tucker, *Attitude,* p. 66; Brand, *British Labour's Rise to Power,* pp. 162–63.

75. *LP Annual Conference Report* (1919), pp. 127–32; *Daily Herald,* July 23, 1919.

76. 117 HC Deb. 5s. (July 3, 1919): 1232–34.

77. Ibid., 118 (July 21, 1919): 959–64.

78. Ibid., 1031–33, 1118–19. The debate on the Anglo-French alliance took place after the vote on the treaty.

79. *Labour Leader,* July 31, 1919.

80. *New Statesman* 13 (July 19, 1919): 382.

81. *Daily Herald,* June 28, 30, July 4, 1919.

82. "New Triple Alliance," *Daily Herald,* July 2, 1919.

83. The first issue appeared in July 1919. Its name had been suggested by Ramsay MacDonald. Trevelyan to Morel, Mar. 3, 1919, cited in Wuliger, *Idea of Economic Imperialism,* p. 411. See also, Cline, *E. D. Morel,* pp. 121–22.

84. *Foreign Affairs* 1 (July 1919): 1–2.

85. "Peace Treaty," *Daily Herald,* June 30, 1919.

86. *Socialist Review* 16 (July–Sept. 1919): 200–201.

87. A letter to the editor of the *Manchester Guardian,* reprinted in the *Railway Review,* demonstrated how widely the feeling was shared. Subscribing to the view that "it is a settlement opposed to every ideal for which Labour stands," were, along with George Lansbury, C. T. Cramp of the National Union of Railwaymen, Robert Williams of the National Amalgamated Labourers' Union, Robert Smillie of the Miners' Federation, and John Bromley of the Locomotive Engineers. Cramp and Williams also served on the National Executive of the Labour party, but evidently the leadership of the most powerful trade union groups in Great Britain were no less disillusioned by the peace settlement than were the leaders of groups like the ILP or the UDC. *Railway Review,* July 4, 1919.

88. "Labour and the Peace Treaty. An Examination," pp. 13–14.

89. Ibid., p. 11.

90. Ibid. A much shorter pamphlet, also entitled "Labour and the Peace Treaty," collected together conference resolutions, party manifestos, and speeches in Parliament outlining the case against the treaty.

CHAPTER 3

1. Angell, *Peace Treaty*, p. 12.

2. Ibid., p. 69.

3. These proposals were based upon the assumption that the League constitution would be rapidly reformed along the following lines: (1) The powers of the Assembly, particularly in checking and revising the acts of the Council, to be increased. (2) Veto of Council decisions by one of its members to be abolished. (3) Provision for appeal by a state against decisions of the Council. (4) Provision for representation in the League of "non-governmental parties" in the constituent states. Without such revisions, Angell predicted that the League would invoke increasing hostility from all the sincerely democratic forces of the world. See ibid., p. 97 and footnote.

4. Ibid., pp. 142–43. Like Keynes, Angell placed considerable emphasis on the "transfer problem," making much the same argument as appears in *Economic Consequences of the Peace*. See Angel, ibid., pp. 18–23.

5. *LP Annual Conference Report* (1919), pp. 218–24; Marquand, *Ramsay MacDonald*, pp. 254–55.

6. Raymond Postgate is correct in stressing the importance of the *Herald* in the immediate postwar years in the light of the weakness of the parliamentary Labour party and the lack of unified leadership in the trade union world. See Postgate, *Life of George Lansbury*, pp. 195–96, 198.

7. *Daily Herald*, Nov. 22, 1919. Also Oct. 14, 1919.

8. Ibid., July 30, Aug. 11, 1919.

9. *Foreign Affairs* 1 (Sept. 1919): 1. The signatories of the UDC statement were C. Roden Buxton, J. A. Hobson, R. C. Lambert, F. W. Pethick Lawrence, J. R. MacDonald, E. D. Morel, Arthur Ponsonby, H. B. Lees Smith, Ethel Snowden, H. M. Swanwick, Charles Trevelyan. Most were recent Liberal converts to Labour and most were now members of the ILP.

10. *Forward*, Dec. 27, 1919.

11. *Foreign Affairs* 1 (Dec. 1919): 2.

12. MacDonald diary, Aug. 7, 1920. A little earlier he had noted that he had just finished a "terrible week of Executives"—Labour party, UDC and ILP—commenting that he was depressed by the ILP meeting. "Pointless talk & heartbreaking revelation of slackness. My first real meeting as member of N.A.C. after many years. Deterioration very marked." Diary, May 27, 1920. PRO 39/69/1753.

13. *Socialist Review* 16 (Oct.–Dec. 1919): 314.

14. *Labour Leader*, Nov. 20, 1919.

15. Ibid., Oct. 16, 1919.

16. LSI 3/206 (Oct. 30, 1919) and LSI 3/287 (Nov. 12, 1919). Labour party Archives.

17. "Draft Memorandum on the Proposed Alliance with France," Advisory Committee (1919), pp. 1–3.

18. 121 HC Deb. 5s. (Nov. 17, 1919): 697–701, 761–62.

19. "Labour and the Proposed Alliance," Advisory Committee (1919), pp. 1–2.

20. Tucker, *Attitude*, pp. 43–44.

21. Graubard, *British Labour and the Russian Revolution*, pp. 64–113, has the fullest account of Labour's Russian policy in this period.

22. *Labour Leader*, May 27, June 24, 1920.

23. Ibid., May 13, 1920. The comments reflect the suggestions offered by party strategists to ILP speakers: "Point out that the League of Nations is a farce; real control remains with the Allies. Point out Polish attack on Russia should have been stopped by the League. Poland is a member of the League; but three Allied Premiers in practice superior to League." "I.L.P. Weekly Notes for Speakers," no. 56, May 13, 1920.

24. *Labour Leader*, Jan. 15, Mar. 18, Dec. 23, 1920; *Bradford Pioneer*, Dec. 10, 1920; Joseph King, "Political Crooks at the Peace Conference" (ILP Pamphlets, n.s., no. 29, 1920), pp. 14–15.

25. *Socialist Review* 17 (July–Sept. 1920): 204–5.

26. *ILP Annual Conference Report* (1920), pp. 52–53.

27. Brailsford, *After the Peace*, pp. 173–75.

28. Ibid., pp. 21–22, 47, 58–59, 159–60. It seems to me that A. J. P. Taylor is rather less than generous in describing Brailsford's lack of enthusiasm for the newer small states of Europe. To be sure, while Brailsford was one of the most knowledgeable western journalists about the Balkans and Central Europe, he had his blind spots: for example, with regard to the peasant problem, as F. M. Leventhal has pointed out. Imperialism was the touchstone of Brailsford's analysis and, whatever one may think of his views, its rejection in every circumstance gave to Brailsford's position a consistency sometimes not evident on the surface. Cf. Taylor, *Trouble Makers*, pp. 175–77, and Leventhal, *Last Dissenter*, pp. 153–58.

29. Brailsford, *After the Peace*, p. 79.

30. Ibid., pp. 87, 180–83.

31. *Foreign Affairs* 1 (May 1920): 16–17; 2 (Aug. 1920): Special Supplement, vii–viii.

32. Ibid., 2 (July 1920): 3. Morel's position was elaborated privately to a correspondent at Dundee, where he had been invited to become the prospective Labour candidate for the House of Commons. "You know what my view is—that Labour is building on sand so long as the foreign policy of the country is nationally uncontrolled; that the British working man cannot expect to secure decent conditions of existence so long as he supports, or tolerates, a foreign policy directed to the starvation and massacre of the Russian peasant and the German or Austrian artisan; nor can a better State or a better civilisation evolve until the working masses realise that their interests are common interests, and that war and the makers of war are the worst and most deadly foes of democratic emancipation." Since Winston Churchill was the incumbent M.P. for Dundee, Morel's further comments are of some interest. "I stand of course on the ILP's existing platform in every respect. But a struggle between Churchill and myself would inevitably resolve itself into a square fight on the issue of militarism and foreign policy. . . . The personality of Churchill—who incarnates militarism and a foreign policy making for endless wars—and my own in an

electoral contest would inevitably give predominance to those issues." Morel to D. Watt, May 12, 1920, Morel papers, bundle no. 21.

33. Morel to J. Ogilvie (Secretary of the Dundee Labour party in 1920), Sept. 30, 1920, Morel papers, bundle no. 21.

34. Morel, *Horror on the Rhine*, pp. 8–20, 22. Cline has pointed out, in *E. D. Morel*, pp. 123–25, that observers acquainted with the situation in Germany, including a number of Germans, criticized Morel for playing into the hands of the antidemocratic forces in Germany, confirming the denial of all responsibility for the war, and unwittingly promoting the revival of German militarism. Morel's associates tried unsuccessfully to persuade him to temper his rhetoric. Arthur Ponsonby, for example, wrote to him in 1923 (n.d.): "I have had a talk with my F.O. friend who is in the German department at the F.O. so he knows a good deal about what is going on. In the main he is entirely sympathetic especially with regard to French intentions and the French plot. But with regard to the black troops he said they had sent an officer to investigate & he reported that many of the cases could either not be traced or were found not to be fully substantiated. He thought therefore that the quotation of cases weakened the argument. The mere existence of Black troops in the area was quite bad enough in itself." Morel Papers, F8/123.

35. *Daily Herald*, Apr. 14, 1920.

36. Beatrice Webb's astringent comments on the Labour party's leaders were often unjust, but her comment on Lansbury was more than passingly accurate: "He has no constructive capacity—he cannot, in fact, distinguish between one type of society and another. But as a ferment for dissolving the present order of things by a strange combination of mystical love for men and an impatient iconoclastic fervour against all existing institutions—he is certainly most uniquely effective." Cole, *Beatrice Webb's Diaries, 1912–1924*, p. 84.

37. *Daily Herald*, Mar. 17, 1920. "Parliamentary government [in all of Central Europe] is clearly passing," wrote the *Herald*. "To it is succeeding a new phase, the struggle for power between the military and the workers. To that again, before settled conditions can supervene, must succeed a period of dictatorship—a dictatorship of the proletariat or a dictatorship of the generals." June 11, 1920.

38. Ibid., Mar. 29, Apr. 7, 14, 1920.

39. Ibid., Apr. 8, 10, 17, 1920.

40. Ibid., June 17, 27, Nov. 12, 13, 23, 1920.

41. Graubard, *British Labour and the Russian Revolution*, pp. 83–114.

42. 114 HC Deb. 5s. (Apr. 9, 1919): 2167.

43. *TUC Annual Conference Report* (1920), p. 62.

44. *LP Annual Conference Report* (1920), p. 112. See also p. 132 for similar comments by Tom Shaw of the Textile Workers.

45. *New Statesman* 15 (Apr. 17, May 1, June 5, 12, 1920): 30, 94–95, 241, 265.

46. *Clarion*, Jan. 30, Apr. 9, 1920.

47. Ibid., May 14, 1920.

48. 127 HC Deb. 5s. (Mar. 25, 1920): 652–53; 129 (May 20, 1920): 1676–81; 133 (Aug. 16, 1920): 675–76; 136 (Dec. 22, 1920): 1826–32.

49. Josiah Wedgwood and Joseph Kenworthy (later Lord Strabolgi) were most noteworthy. Kenworthy, who at this time was still formally a Liberal, in particular harped away on

the need for a League of Nations military force. Oswald Mosley, who spoke out for disarmament in February, is reported as arguing that "If we allow all these miniature Napoleons, who exist in every country, to continue to strut across the European scene with their weapons in their hands there will never be peace." Ibid., 125 (Feb. 12, 1920): 314–23, 338–41; 127 (Mar. 22, 1920): 157–63; 127 (Mar. 25, 1920): 710.

50. Lord Robert Cecil, for example, in acknowledging Clynes's work in support of the League of Nations, commented: "If the cause of the League of Nations had received as great assistance from the party to which I belong as it has received from the Labour party, it would be in a better position to-day in this country." Ibid., 129 (May 20, 1920): 1682.

51. *Resolutions for the Twentieth Annual Conference of the Labour Party* (1920), pp. 13–15; *Agenda for the Twentieth Annual Conference of the Labour Party* (1920), pp. 20–21.

52. *LP Annual Conference Report* (1920), pp. 132–41, 202–3. The International Labour and Socialist Congress at Geneva took much the same line in July. British Labour was represented, among others, by MacDonald, Webb, Noel Buxton, and even Thomas, but not by Clynes or Henderson. See p. 223.

53. "Letter from Henderson" (1920); "Interview [with W. H. Hutchinson]" (1920); Toynbee, "Draft Memorandum" [May 13, 1920, revised and issued, May 17, 1920]. All memoranda of the Advisory Committee.

54. B[urns], "Notes on the League" (1920) and "Draft Notes on European Federation" (1920), Advisory Committee. Criticism of the mandates and a positive Labour alternative appeared in a pamphlet published about this time. Labour party, "Empire in Africa," esp. p. 20. Similarly, Leonard Woolf contributed two carefully developed pamphlets, issued by the Labour party, which concealed, publicly at least, the pessimism running through the private discussions of the Advisory Committee, "International Economic Policy" and "Mandates and Empire." Charles Roden Buxton identifies several authors of Advisory Committee pamphlets in "We Told You So," *Labour* (Oct. 1937): 34.

55. "Letter to the Executive Committee," Advisory Committee (1920).

56. A characteristic outburst appears in a letter from Morel to Count Max Montgelas, May 24, 1921:

I can well understand your irritation with British Labour. But I have much more cause to be irritated with it than you have! . . . It has never contained among its leaders intellectuals of even second-rate or third-rate type. . . . It has been with, as I say, the exception of the small Socialist I.L.P. movement within it, a purely Trade Union manual labourers' movement, seeking one thing and one thing alone—increased wages and betterment of industrial conditions. And the only influence since the war broke out which is "intellectualising"—in the international sense—this vast mass of ignorance is the influence wielded by our small group. . . . We are educating it daily, and have been. No books on international affairs and no writings of anyone on international affairs have ever been read as my writings are read by Labour. But, even so, we are only touching the fringe. That fringe, of course, leavens gradually the mass. But you have no conception of the enormous difficulties we have to face. In the first place, there is the old jealousy of the "intellectual"—Henderson, Clynes, Thomas, etc. are intellectually far inferior to Ponsonby, Trevelyan, Hobson, and so on. They are jealous.

Morel papers, bundle no. 19.

57. The Morel papers contain a voluminous correspondence between Morel and Montgelas, the prominent German revisionist. The latter's judgment of Morel's role in the "war guilt" question may be seen in the following excerpt from a letter written in 1924: "The other news is very good also. Official retraction of the responsibility avowal. That this step has been possible is largely due to *your* indefatigable efforts. Without your persevering work it would have been risky to undertake such a step, for German votes alone would never have stirred up the opinion of the world. . . . Will the other members of the U.D.C. including those who are now in office have the courage of saying what they really think about the origins of the war?" Montgelas to Morel, Aug. 30, 1924, Morel papers, bundle no. 19. Also Montgelas to Morel, Jan. 20, May 7, 29, 1921. Montgelas was associated with the more-or-less liberal Heidelberger Vereinigung, but Morel also depended for his "information" on German groups that were much more openly propagandistic. See Cline, *E. D. Morel*, pp. 125–27.

58. *Foreign Affairs* 3 (Nov. 1921): 66–67. The UDC resolution of protest against the partition is reproduced in Swanwick, *Builders of Peace*, p. 148.

59. *Foreign Affairs* 4 (Aug. 1922): 26.

60. Ibid., (July 1922): 12; (Sept. 1922): 53–54; Swanwick, *Builders of Peace*, pp. 139–40.

61. *Foreign Affairs* 2 (Jan. 1921): 105; (Feb. 1921): 120.

62. Ibid., (May 1921): 167; 3 (Mar. 1922): 131; 4 (Sept. 1922): 53; Swanwick, *Builders of Peace*, pp. 149–51. It should be noted, however, that while UDC resolutions paralleled the positions articulated by Morel, the organization did circulate materials whose tenor was not quite so starkly anti-French. The most important of these was a pamphlet written by Will Arnold-Forster and issued by the UDC in March 1922. Weighing France's intransigence against her legitimate craving for security, Arnold-Forster warned that every effort must be made to avoid any further widening of the Anglo-French breach. Neither the economic restoration of Europe nor the development of a real League of Nations was possible without French participation. Like Morel, Arnold-Forster opposed any alliance with France against Germany, as he rejected a unilateral guarantee to France without a corresponding guarantee to Germany. But, anticipating in a sense the future Locarno agreements, he raised the question of a *reciprocal* guarantee that would reassure both France and Germany. If such a document were submitted to the free judgment of Parliament, it might lead to a detente in European tensions and turn out to be an invaluable achievement. Arnold-Forster's emphasis, then, differed rather markedly from that of the majority of the leaders of the UDC. It is not surprising, therefore, particularly in the Advisory Committee on International Questions, to find him taking more and more moderate a position as the years passed. Cf. Arnold-Forster, "France, Ourselves and the Future," pp. 3–19.

63. *Foreign Affairs* 2 (Jan. 1921): 105; (Feb. 1921): 120; 3 (Sept. 1921): 35; (Dec. 1921): Special Supplement, i–viii; 4 (Sept. 1922): 53–54. The Morel papers contain a revealing characterization in a letter from the Rev. John A. Harris to Morel, Sept. 7, 1921, bundle no. 6: "Many thanks for your letter which has caught me in Geneva where I am watching this interesting institution, which I fear, has no attraction for you!"

64. In a letter to Charles Trevelyan on Oct. 13, 1921, Morel comments on sharing a platform with Gilbert Murray of the League of Nations Union, remarking that Murray's contribution to the discussion consisted of a melancholy and depressing account of what the League of Nations has done—or rather not done—on the question of disarmament.

"But a more complete exposure of the utter futility of the League, it would have been hard to imagine." UDC Papers, DDC 4/30.

65. *Daily Herald*, Jan. 27, 29, Mar. 3, 8, 12, May 3, 1921, Aug. 1, 4, 1922; *Labour Leader*, Jan. 27, 1921.

66. *New Statesman* 16 (Jan. 22, 1921): 462; 17 (Aug. 20, 1921): 538; 18 (Oct. 22, 1921): 61; *Daily Herald*, May 9, 19, July 22, 1921.

67. *New Statesman* 16 (Jan. 22, 1921): 462; 17 (Aug. 20, 1921): 538; 18 (Oct. 22, 1921): 61; *Daily Herald*, May 9, 19, July 22, 1921.

68. *New Statesman* 17 (July 16, 1921): 401–2; 17 (July 23, 1921): 433; 17 (July 30, 1921): 457; 17 (Aug. 6, 1921): 481; 17 (Sept. 10, 1921): 610; 17 (Sept. 17, 1921): 636–37; 18 (Nov. 19, 1921): 186, 189. In contrast, see, e.g., *Daily Herald*, July 12, 19, 1921, and Jan. 14, 25, 1922. Also *Labour Leader*, Jan. 27 and Sept. 15, 1921, and *Bradford Pioneer*, Feb. 17, May 12, 1922. Even *Clarion*, which like the *New Statesman* welcomed a naval agreement with the United States (July 15, 1921), found little to be enthusiastic about in the League of Nations (Sept. 16, 1921).

69. *Daily Herald*, Jan. 25, Feb. 8, July 30, 1921.

70. Ibid., Jan. 13, 20, Apr. 3, 4, 10, 27, 1922; *Bradford Pioneer*, Feb. 17, May 26, 1922; *Labour Leader*, May 4, June 15, 1922; *New Leader* (successor to *Labour Leader*), Oct. 6, 1922.

71. *New Statesman* 18 (Jan. 7, 1922): 385; 18 (Jan. 28, 1922): 461–62; 19 (May 22, 1922): 201.

72. *ILP Annual Conference Report* (1921), pp. 138–39, 142–43.

73. "I.L.P. Weekly Notes for Speakers," no. 111 (June 2, 1921), no. 117 (July 14, 1921); Tiltman, *J. Ramsay MacDonald*, p. 165.

74. "I.L.P. Weekly Notes for Speakers," no. 151 (Mar. 9, 1922), no. 160 (May 11, 1922); *ILP Annual Conference Report* (1922), pp. 52–55, 72, 84–85, 248.

75. Brockway, "How to End War," ILP Programme Pamphlet, pp. 3–14.

76. *ILP Annual Conference Report* (1922), pp. 83–84.

77. *TUC Annual Conference Report* (1921), pp. 278–81, 294–306; (1922), pp. 78–85, 89–90, 311–12.

78. *TUC Annual Conference Report* (1922), pp. 325–26.

79. Ibid., p. 58.

80. 139 HC Deb. 5s. (Mar. 10, 1921): 742–49; 139 (Mar. 24, 1921): 2875–76; and 141 (May 5, 1921): 1326, 1344–45.

81. *LP Annual Conference Report* (1921), pp. 233–34; *LP Annual Conference Report* (1922), pp. 32–33, 247–48.

82. Labour party, "Control of Foreign Policy," and Young, "Reform of Diplomacy."

83. *LP Annual Conference Report* (1921), pp. 200–201. The threat that Labour would not be bound in advance to any pact was looked upon by E. D. Morel as the most important resolution passed by the conference. *Foreign Affairs* 4 (Aug. 1922): 25.

84. *LP Annual Conference Report* (1921), p. 201. A tone of somewhat saddened disillusionment runs through the publications of all groups associated with the Labour party during this period. Thus, a resolution presented to the National Conference of Labour Women runs as follows: "The Conference expresses its regret that the League of Nations has failed so far to influence the world towards peace, and believes that this failure is due

to the fact that it has acted as a League of powerful governments instead of a League of Peoples. It believes that the road to peace is open, but that it can only be reached if the old system of the balance of power of great armaments, secret diplomacy, and profit-making trade and industry is set aside and the peoples of the world come together with mutual good will, ready to co-operate with one another for the common advantage of all." Labour party, "Agenda for National Conference of Labour Women . . . April, 1921," p. 14.

85. "Resolution for Submission to the Executive Committee," Advisory Committee (1922). See also "Anglo-French Agreement" (1922).

86. *LP Annual Conference Report* (1922), pp. 31–33.

87. Ibid., pp. 188–93.

88. Ibid., pp. 200–203.

89. See above pp. 78–79.

90. "Draft Report for the International Socialist Conference," Advisory Committee [1922], p. 1. See also "Draft Pamphlet on *Labour and the League of Nations*" [1921] and "Draft Pamphlet on Foreign Policy," [1921].

91. Henderson, "Labour and Foreign Affairs," esp. p. 9.

CHAPTER 4

1. Woolf, "Labour's Foreign Policy."

2. *Daily Herald*, Oct. 6, 1922.

3. Marquand, *Ramsay MacDonald*, pp. 269–70.

4. *Socialist Review* 20 (Oct. 1922): 152–53.

5. Henderson, "War against War."

6. The Belgians insisted that they had no political purpose for the occupation, but French motives were evidently more mixed. President Alexandre Millerand hoped for gains in security as well as reparations, but Raymond Poincaré was primarily concerned with reparations, in the sense of forcing Germany to acknowledge defeat and to make concessions to French needs. Officially, he denied any security motive. Orde, *Great Britain and International Security*, esp. pp. 48–49.

7. Buxton, "France and Her Ruins," *Socialist Review* 20, no. 107 (Aug. 1922): 82–91, and Buxton, "Opinion in France: The Root of the Trouble," *Labour Magazine* 1 (Sept. 1922): 201–2.

8. *Foreign Affairs* 4 (July 1922): p. 12.

9. "What We Think," *Foreign Affairs* 4 (Sept. 1922): 53–54.

10. Ibid., pp. 117–18.

11. MacDonald Diary, May 15, Sept. 25, 1924, PRO 30/69/1753 and Koss, *Rise and Fall*, pp. 439–40. The *Daily Herald*, early in the decade, came upon bad days and, in the words of Raymond Postgate, was "rushing to disaster." It was taken over by the Labour party and the TUC in 1922 and became the official organ of the labor movement. In August 1923 the paper nearly closed down. Lansbury, who had become increasingly unhappy as the paper moved from independence to an official status, resigned in February 1925.

12. See, for example, *New Leader*, Nov. 10, 24, Dec. 1, 15, 1922.

13. *Daily Herald*, June 3, Aug. 1, Sept. 1, 1922.

14. *TUC Annual Meeting Report* (1922), pp. 56–58.

15. Ibid., pp. 78–85.

16. Cline, *Recruits to Labour*, p. 83, cites Arnold-Forster's article, "Democratic Control and the Economic War," *Foreign Affairs* 1 (Mar. 1920): 10–11.

17. Arnold-Forster, "France, Ourselves and the Future," pp. 2–17.

18. Advisory Committee, Minutes, Dec. 14, 1922.

19. "Memorandum on Ruhr Situation," Advisory Committee Memorandum, 1923.

20. "Draft Manifesto," ibid.

21. "Labour and the Ruhr," pp. 7–8.

22. "International Situation," leaflet published in 1923 over the signatures of C. W. Bowerman and Arthur Henderson.

23. MacDonald, "International Scene: Our Foreign Policy," *New Leader*, Feb. 23, 1923.

24. MacDonald to Bonar Law, Jan. 29, 1923, MacDonald Papers, PRO 30/69/1167.

25. Orde, *Great Britain and International Security*, p. 48.

26. 160 HC Deb. 5s.(Feb. 15, 1923): 363.

27. Ibid. (Feb. 16, 1923): 496–510, 520–28, 543–54.

28. Ibid. (Feb. 19, 1923): 709–14.

29. Labour and Socialist International, 14/8/1 [Jan. 26–27, 1923], Labour party Archives.

30. Ibid., 4/4/7 [Mar. 26, 29, 1923].

31. Dorothy Buxton, "Why Are the French in the Ruhr?," *Socialist Review* 21, no. 114 (Mar. 1923): 114–22; Brailsford, "Invasion of the Ruhr," *Labour Magazine* 1 (Feb. 1923): 436–38.

32. A few exemplary reactions may be found in *Forward*, Jan. 27 and Feb. 17, 1923; *Bradford Pioneer*, Feb. 23 and Oct. 5, 1923; and above all in the *New Leader* almost constantly throughout that year.

33. *Daily Herald*, Jan. 22, 1923; *Nation*, Jan. 17, 24, 1923. See also the drafts in the Leonard Woolf Papers.

34. *New Statesman* 20 (Feb. 17, 24, 1923) and 21 (Apr. 14, 28, May 12, 19, 1923), among other comments.

35. An exception to the chorus of condemnation, almost needless to point out, was in *Clarion*, where Alexander M. Thompson opined that "the German capitalist brigands who caused the war are now deliberately and systematically shirking payment of their liabilities. They are defaulting bankrupts who are concealing their assets." Feb. 9, 1923. Also Jan. 12, 1923.

36. *Foreign Affairs* 4 (Mar. 1923): 185–86, 191–94; (May 1923): 223; 5 (Sept. 1923): 45–46; (Oct. 1923): 70–72. Morel articulated the same arguments from the public platform. See typewritten extracts for a speech on March 9, 1923, at a meeting to celebrate the victory in the General Election of members of the Executive Committee of the UDC. Morel Papers, bundle #21.

Ramsay MacDonald tried hard to keep Morel from acting as a loose cannon on the Ruhr issue. In an almost plaintive note of April 12, he asked Morel to "consider the position from the point of view of our relations with the French and Germans and also in relation to an alternative policy. Have we been wrong in trying to get a document presented which would re-open negotiations? My own position is that any attempt to pay reparations beyond a very modest figure will do damage for some time; but is the conclusion from that, that unless the Belgians, the French and the Germans accept that view, I stand apart and say to them, 'go to your own damnation'?" Morel Papers, F8/106, Apr. 12, 1923. Clearly, Morel *was* prepared to say "go to your own damnation."

37. Beatrice Webb Manuscript Diary 37 (Mar. 6, 1923): 3947.

38. *Foreign Affairs* 4 (Feb. 1923): 161.

39. Ibid., (Apr. 1923): 214.

40. Ponsonby, "Triumph of France and Its Significance," ibid., 5 (Oct. 1923): 63–64.

41. Dowse, *Left in the Centre*, pp. 74–75.

42. *ILP Annual Conference Report* (1923), pp. 44–45.

43. Ibid., pp. 24–25, 46–47.

44. Ibid., pp. 86–97.

45. *Principles of a Disarmament Policy*, Advisory Committee Memorandum, undated, but a further development of 278 (a) of the same title and dated 1923.

46. *Labour and the League of Nations*, Advisory Committee (1923), pp. 1–23.

47. *LP Annual Conference Report* (1923), pp. 12–14, 19–20, 184.

48. *TUC Annual Meeting Report* (1923), pp. 257–59, 417–19.

49. [Reply to Baldwin Statement on the Ruhr Situation], Advisory Committee Memorandum (1923).

50. The delegation to Hamburg included, of course, more than the leaders of the Labour party and the TUC. Among them were for the Labour party, Sidney Webb, F. W. Jowett, Dr. Ethel Bentham, and Susan Lawrence; for the TUC, J. B. Williams and J. Bromley. British members of the Executive of the Second International were Arthur Henderson, Ramsay MacDonald, Harry Gosling, and J. H. Thomas. William Gillies was secretary of the delegation. MacDonald was not present at Hamburg. Also represented were the ILP (whose delegation included H. N. Brailsford and C. R. Buxton among others), the Social Democratic Federation, and the Fabian Society (represented by Beatrice Webb).

51. *Hamburg International Socialist Conference. Suggestions for Draft Resolutions Proposed to be presented to the Organisation Committee by the British Section representing the British Trades Union Congress and the British Labour Party*, Labour and Socialist International 12/4/1, Labour party Archives.

52. Report of the Executive Committee, *LP Annual Conference Report* (1923), p. 12; Resolutions of the Labour and Socialist Congress Held at Hamburg, May 21st to 25th, 1923, pp. 8–10, LSI 12/1/14.

53. "Labour and the European Situation" (1923), pp. 1–2.

54. 146 HC Deb. 5s. (July 23, 1923).

55. *Socialist Review* 22, no. 119 (Aug. 1923): 51–52. Also 21, no. 113 (Feb. 1923): 4–5, and 21, no. 114 (Mar. 1923): 45–52, 99.

56. MacDonald's "Policy for the Labour Party," p. 134, and "Foreign Policy of the Labour Party," p. 17, both quoted in Miller, *Socialism and Foreign Policy*, pp. 106–7. See also MacDonald, "Foreign Policy of the Labour Party," pp. 20–24.

57. 160 HC Deb. 5s. (Feb. 19, 1923): 709–14; *Daily Herald*, Oct. 11, 1923; Henderson, "War against War."

CHAPTER 5

1. Despite a number of assessments of the politics of the mid-twenties, Richard W. Lyman's early study of *First Labour Government, 1924* still holds up; see Chapters 5–7.

2. Marquand, *Ramsay MacDonald*, pp. 294–95, 301–3.

3. Swanwick, *I Have Been Young*, pp. 373–74; A. Wallace (Secretary of Dundee Labour party) to Morel, Feb. 2, 1924, Morel Papers, bundle no. 21.

4. See, for example, MacDonald to Morel, Apr. 12, 1923, Morel Papers, F8/106. Also Ponsonby to Norman Angell in Apr. 1924, quoted in Angell, *After All*, p. 239. Sidney Webb later complained of the "perpetual misrepresentation" of nearly the entire newspaper press in its "quite unwarranted" suggestion that the Labour extremists had exerted improper influence on the government. Webb Papers 4, item 18, pp. 27, 30.

5. Ponsonby to Morel, Apr. 19, 1924, Morel Papers, F8/123.

6. The support of the *Herald* seemed a mixed blessing to Sidney Webb, who complained of the evident Communist sympathies of the paper, due to the sentimental weakness of George Lansbury and the real disloyalty of W. N. Ewer, W. Mellor, and others of the staff. Webb Papers 4, item 18, p. 30.

7. *New Statesman* 22 (Feb. 9, 1924): 500–501.

8. As late as the end of April, the ILP leadership was urging speakers to support the government "in its vigorous foreign policy of peace." "I.L.P. Weekly Notes for Speakers," no. 253, Apr. 24, 1924.

9. *New Leader*, Jan. 25, Feb. 15, 22, 1924.

10. Morel to James Thomson, Feb. 28, 1924, Morel Papers, bundle no. 7. Sidney Webb later commented on how little cabinet discussion of foreign matters took place. In a long memorandum later published in revised form as "First Labour Government" (*Political Quarterly* 32 [Jan.–Mar. 1961]: 9–18), he wrote that no memo examining a particular problem and discussing alternative policies was ever circulated and that only very occasionally were especially important or interesting dispatches circulated in print. "Substantially, the Cabinet left foreign affairs to the Foreign Secretary (who could not, in this Government, obtain the advantage or experience the check of consultation with the P.M.). See "Working of Government" in Webb's memo on the Labour government of 1924, Webb Papers 4, item 18, pp. 20–47. See also *Foreign Affairs* 5 (Mar. 1924): 167, and (Apr. 1924): 193–94, as well as typescript of a speech at Bradford in early 1924, Morel Papers, bundle no. 21.

11. *Daily Herald*, Jan. 3, 29, Feb. 11, 1924.

12. Ibid., Feb. 24, 1924.

13. Norman Angell, "France and Europe," *New Leader*, Jan. 25, 1924. Cline, *Recruits to Labour*, pp. 89–90, cites this article as well as "Pacifists and Cruisers," *New Leader*, Feb. 29, 1924 and Angell, *After All*, esp. pp. 242–43.

14. Young, "Can Labour Pacify Europe?," *Contemporary Review* 125 (Mar. 1924): 416–24.

15. The memo, dated Jan. 1924, was transmitted to MacDonald by Arthur Greenwood as Secretary of the Joint Research and Information Department of the TUC and the Labour party. It is found in PRO/FO371/9807.

16. "Labour, the League and Reparations," Advisory Committee (1924), pp. 1–6. This was a report of the subcommittee on the League of Nations, recommended to the full committee on Feb. 25 and accepted a few days later. See "Report on Memorandum no. 310" (1924) and "Permanent Court of International Justice" (1924). The last document in particular was noted by the prime minister's private secretary, C. W. Orde (in W 2855/338/98) and called to the attention of officials in the Foreign Office. See FO 371/10573/81–82.

17. Noel Baker, "Obligatory Jurisdiction," pp. 68–102, Noel Baker Papers, NBKR 4/485. See also his lecture at the London School of Economics, Oct. 7, 1924, later published as "Growth of International Society."

18. See, for a few examples among many, memos of Feb. 13, 1924 (C. W. Orde), June 28, 1924 (Hurst and H. W. Malkin), and July 29, 1924 (Orde, Haldane, with MacDonald minute), in FO 371/10573, pp. 33, 145–47, 156–57.

19. Foreign Office memorandum dated July 8, 1924, cited in CID 513-B (Sept. 1924), PRO 30/69/158. Enclosed with the same material is CID 518-B, in which the Air Staff agrees in general with the War Office assessment, but notes that it cannot agree to *any* buffer state having an Air Force stronger than Britain's. "The potentialities of French aircraft to attack England discount the value to us of a buffer State unless the British Air Forces are at least equally powerful to those of France."

20. Orde, *Great Britain and International Security*, pp. 58–59; Lyman, *First Labour Government*, pp. 160–62; Marquand, *Ramsay MacDonald*, 333–36. MacDonald explained to the House of Commons his desire to increase the representative character and authority of the League of Nations along with his unwillingness to tie a detailed exploration of the problem of security to the immediate reparations issue. See 169 HC Deb., 5s. (Feb. 12, 1924): 772–74 and 171 (Mar. 27, 1924): 1603–5.

21. 170 HC Deb., 5s. (Feb. 27, 1924): 608–12.

22. Lyman, *First Labour Government*, p. 169, cites Brockway, *Inside the Left*, p. 161, and Cole, *Beatrice Webb's Diaries, 1924–32*, Feb. 29, 1924, p. 11, for the view that Henderson's speech was an old one sent to him in an emergency because he had run out of speeches. But in fact the substance of the speech was fully in conformity with official Labour party policy, a policy that MacDonald as foreign secretary was on the verge of changing significantly. Both Leventhal, *Arthur Henderson*, p. 124, and Wrigley, *Arthur Henderson*, pp. 151–52, have sensible accounts of this tempest in a teacup. In a communication to MacDonald from William Gillies, Secretary of the Joint International Department of the Labour Party and the TUC, he points out for the two national committees that the repudiation of Henderson's statement on the revision of the treaty can be interpreted to mean that the Labour government has gone back on its policy as previously published. The document also reveals uneasiness about MacDonald's policy because it is causing the left wing and moderate movement in Germany to fear that the British government is unfriendly to Germany. The message from Gillies is in the MacDonald Papers, PRO 30/69/26.

23. Marquand, *Ramsay MacDonald*, pp. 335–36.

24. McDougall, *France's Rhineland Diplomacy*, pp. 366–68.

25. For a succinct statement of MacDonald's purposes, see Foreign Office to Treasury, Apr. 16, 1924, FO (old style) C6073/70/18, MacDonald Papers, PRO/30/69/96 and C11976/70/18, circulated to the cabinet on June 22, 1924, in PRO30/69/123, as well as his explanation to the cabinet on July 30, 1924, in CAB 23/48. For examples of his frustrations at the conference, see his diary entries for Aug. 11 and 15, 1924 in PRO 30/69/1753. See Nelson, *Victors Divided*, p. 259, and Schuker, *End of French Predominance*, pp. 171–382, 393. Also useful is Marks, *Illusion of Peace*, p. 54.

26. For example, *Daily Herald*, Apr. 10, July 19, Aug. 23, 1924.

27. *New Statesman* 23 (Aug. 23, 1924): 560.

28. *New Leader*, Aug. 8, 1924.

29. Lansbury to Beatrice Webb, Mar. 14, 1924, Webb Papers, 2, 4(h).

30. Beatrice Webb Manuscript Diary 38 (Aug. 30, 1924): 4103–4; MacDonald Diary, Aug. 13, 1924, in PRO30/69/1753. In his *Autobiography*, pp. 673–79, Snowden praises MacDonald's chairmanship of the conference while savaging the conduct of the French.

31. Brailsford, "France at the Crossroads: Is It Peace?," *New Leader*, Aug. 15, 1924, and Brailsford, "Half-Way to Peace: The Perilous Year in the Ruhr," *New Leader*, Aug. 22, 1924.

32. Lyman, *First Labour Government*, pp. 164–66, quoting *Socialist Review* (Oct. 1924): 98; Leventhal, *Last Dissenter*, p. 186; MacDonald Diary, entries of May 15 and Sept. 15, 1924, PRO 30/69/1753. During this period MacDonald speculated in his diary, not for the first time, about the need for a new political alignment. "Sometimes I think a new Party must arise. The Liberals get meaner & meaner & we respect the Conservatives more & more. They have a calmer sense & a bigger vision in their Parliamentary work." Diary entry of Mar. 2, 1924.

33. 176 HC Deb., 5s. (July 14, 1924): 133–72. See Lyman, *First Labour Government*, pp. 164–65.

34. Ponsonby to Morel, May 23, 1924, Morel Papers, F8/123.

35. *Foreign Affairs* 5 (May 1924): 217–18.

36. Ibid. (June 1924): 243.

37. *TUC Annual Meeting Report* (1924), pp. 69, 72–73. For the General Council's statements on the Ruhr, see pp. 256–59.

38. Ibid., p. 259; *LP Annual Conference Report* (1924), p. 56.

39. 171 HC Deb., 5s. (Apr. 1, 1924): 2003–5.

40. Morel to Ponsonby, Apr. 14, 1924, Morel Papers, bundle no. 21.

41. Ponsonby to Morel, May 1, 1924, Morel Papers, F8/123; *Bradford Pioneer*, July 25, 1924; *Daily Herald*, Sept. 11, 1924.

42. Morel and Dickinson, "Alternative Policy for a British Labour Government," Advisory Committee (1924).

43. "Memorandum on the League and Disarmament by Prof. Shotwell," ibid.; emphasis in the original.

44. Cover note in "Draft Treaty of Mutual Assistance," Advisory Committee Memorandum (1924).

45. Ibid. See also "Draft Memorandum prepared by the Special Sub-Committee," ibid.

46. Conclusions of a meeting held on April 3, circulated to the cabinet by Secretary Hankey on May 22, and forming the basis for MacDonald's draft letter of May 27–in CP 309 (24)–to the Secretary General. CP 311 (24) in CAB 24/167.

47. *Bradford Pioneer*, July 18, 1924.

48. *New Statesman* 23 (July 26, 1924): 456–57.

49. *New Leader*, June 27, July 25, 1924.

50. Swanwick, "Security and the Treaty of Mutual Assistance," *Socialist Review* 23 (Apr. 1924): 178–81.

51. Resolutions of the Tenth Annual UDC General Meeting, Mar. 14, 1924, reported in *Foreign Affairs* 5 (Apr. 1924): 204. When the government rejected the draft treaty, the Executive Committee of the UDC issued a statement supporting the action and insisting that the problem faced by mankind was that of substituting processes of arbitration and law for a "mechanism of self-destruction." Signatories to the statement included not only

such stalwarts as Morel, Swanwick, and C. R. Buxton, but also such relative moderates as Leonard Woolf and Mary Agnes Hamilton. *Foreign Affairs*, Sept. 1924, p. 62.

52. Zimmern, "P.M. at Geneva," *Labour Magazine* 3 (Oct. 1924): 249–51.

53. See Marquand, *Ramsay MacDonald*, pp. 351–54, for MacDonald at Geneva. A somewhat different perspective is provided by Viscount Cecil in *All the Way*, p. 166, when he notes that MacDonald "misconceived the nature of the Assembly, and addressed the experienced international statesmen there assembled as if they were an English public meeting." MacDonald's speech to the Assembly was later published as a Labour party pamphlet, "Way to Peace." The full text of the British rejection, dated July 5, 1924, is in *League of Nations. Reduction of Armaments. Treaty of Mutual Assistance. Replies of Governments*, League of Nations Documents A.35.1924.9. See also the Labour party pamphlet, "Labour's Great Record," pp. 5–6.

54. Herriot's suggestion that an aggressor be defined as the party to a dispute who refused to submit to arbitration appears to have originated with a group of Americans chaired by James T. Shotwell. See Lyman, *First Labour Government*, p. 174.

55. Brailsford, "Arbitrate or Disarm: A New View of Security," *New Leader*, Sept. 12, 1924. On the other hand, it should be noted that Brailsford doubted the efficiency alike of arbitration and disarmament to solve the problem of war so long as the question of "economic imperialism" was not tackled.

56. Spender, "Mr. MacDonald at the Foreign Office," *Fortnightly Review* 116 (Dec. 1924): 782–92.

57. *New Statesman* 23 (Sept. 13, 1924): 663.

58. Laski, "Ramsay MacDonald," p. 748.

59. See my "Arthur Henderson," in Craig and Gilbert, *Diplomats*, esp. pp. 314–16.

60. Wrigley, *Arthur Henderson*, pp. 152–53. See also Parmoor, *Retrospect*, pp. 213–64; Cole, *Makers*, p. 261; Medlicott, *British Foreign Policy*, pp. 93–94.

61. *League of Nations. Fifth Assembly. Verbatim Record*, 26th and 27th Plenary Meetings, Oct. 1, 1924.

62. Chelmsford to Cabinet, Sept. 27, 1924, CAB 24/168/CP 456, and Oct. 27, 1924, CAB 24/168/CP 478.

63. Marquand, *Ramsay MacDonald*, pp. 355–56; Lyman, *First Labour Government*, pp. 179–80.

64. *Times*, Oct. 13, 1924, quoted in Wrigley, *Arthur Henderson*, p. 153. The speech was then published as a pamphlet by the Labour Publications Department, "New Peace Plan." Also *Parliamentary Debates*, 5s., Commons 182 (Mar. 24, 1925): 291–307.

65. *New Leader*, Oct. 10, 1924, quoted in Lyman, *First Labour Government*, p. 178.

66. *New Leader*, Sept. 26, 1924. For a cogent discussion of the issue of peaceful change and sanctions, see Wolfers, *Britain and France*, esp. pp. 349–54.

67. Buxton, "Labour's Work for Peace at Geneva," esp. pp. 7–8.

68. Buxton, "Geneva Protocol and the British Fleet," *New Leader*, Oct. 23, 1924; Swanwick, "Peace and the Protocol," *New Leader*, Dec. 19, 1924.

69. *LP Annual Conference Report* (1924), pp. 102–3, 108–11. MacDonald's address was reprinted as a Labour party pamphlet, "No Surrender!" The Labour party's fullest explanation of the government's actions appeared in another long pamphlet, "Towards a European Settlement."

70. *LP Annual Conference Report* (1924), pp. 16–29, 222–24.

71. See the letter of the Liberal Walter Runciman to E. D. Morel, Sept. 5, 1924, UDC Papers, DDC/26. Lyman cites *Blackwood's Magazine*, Mar. 1924, p. 441, as an example of the vilification in some of the extreme Tory journals.

72. Ponsonby to Morel, July 31, 1924, Morel Papers, F8/123. Cline, *E. D. Morel*, p. 142, notes Ponsonby's initiative.

73. Brailsford, "Russian Settlement: Victory Snatched from Defeat," *New Leader*, Aug. 8, 1924. See the leading articles of Aug. 1 and Aug. 29, 1924, as well as *Daily Herald*, July 28, Aug. 6, and Aug. 7, 1924.

74. Typescript statement by Purcell and Morel, "Workers and the Anglo-Russian Treaty," Morel Papers, bundle no. 21.

75. "Anglo-Russian Treaties," pp. 4–9; J. R. Clynes, *Memoirs* 2:52; Snowden, *Autobiography* 2:682–84.

76. Lyman, *First Labour Government*, pp. 184–207, 237–45; Marquand, *Ramsay MacDonald*, pp. 361–78.

77. Winkler, "Arthur Henderson," in Craig and Gilbert, *Diplomats*, p. 316.

78. Henderson, "Aims of Labour," p. 40.

CHAPTER 6

1. Naylor, *Labour's International Policy*.

2. According to Beatrice Webb, Henderson reported that there were about thirty Labour M.P.'s—representatives of the Clyde, as well as Lansbury, Wedgwood, Trevelyan—who had made up their minds to turn MacDonald out of the leadership and—he prophecied—they would succeed. Cole, *Beatrice Webb's Diaries, 1924–1932*, Aug. 8, 1925, pp. 62–63.

3. *LP Annual Conference Report* (1925), pp. 244–51; Bullock, *Life and Times of Ernest Bevin*, pp. 258–60.

4. *TUC Annual Meeting Report* (1925), pp. 542–44, 576.

5. Ibid. (1926), and (1928), pp. 68–69.

6. Dowse, *Left in the Centre*, pp. 124–26.

7. Marwick, *Clifford Allen*, pp. 84–85, credits him with bringing such men as Norman Angell, Hugh Dalton, J. A. Hobson, and F. W. Pethick Lawrence "within the ambit of the I.L.P." Even Allen agreed that MacDonald must be held to a bold socialist policy for home and foreign affairs. Writing to Arthur Ponsonby early in the year, he admitted that if the same failings again appeared, "we must speak our minds with regard to the man himself, and meantime advocate in the party councils, in our papers and on the platform the bold policy we believe in. No sense of loyalty or political complication should prevent this from now onwards." Allen to Ponsonby, Feb. 2, 1925, Ponsonby Papers, fols. 48, 49, Bodleian Library, Oxford. See also Gilbert, *Plough My Own Furrow*, pp. 166–200.

8. Dowse, *Left in the Centre*, p. 122.

9. "I.L.P. Weekly Notes for Speakers," no. 283, Dec. 11, 1924.

10. MacDonald to Arthur Greenwood, Mar. 4, 1925, Leonard Woolf Papers, Part 1.D.1.a., University of Sussex Library. Later, MacDonald commended Woolf's memorandum on the CID for steering a very good middle course, although he believed that Woolf was still too frightened of the CID. MacDonald to Woolf, Feb. 8, 1926, Woolf Papers.

11. Marquand, *Ramsay MacDonald*, pp. 416–18; Young, "Foreign Office and Labour

Governments," Advisory Committee (1925); Noel-Baker and Ponsonby, "Note on the Committee of Imperial Defense," Advisory Committee (1925).

12. Advisory Committee, Minutes, Feb. 11, 1925; "Amendments to the Protocol by W. Gillies," Advisory Committee (1925).

13. Orde, *Great Britain and International Security*, pp. 68–154.

14. 179 HC Deb., 5s. (Dec. 9, 1924): 63–64; 185 HC Deb., 5s. (June 24, 1925): 1570–84.

15. 182 HC Deb., 5s. (Mar. 24, 1924): 338–47. MacDonald developed his position more fully in an article in *Labour Magazine* 3 (Apr. 1925): 531–34, which the Labour party then reprinted as a pamphlet, "Protocol or Pact."

16. Tucker, *Attitude*, pp. 106–7.

17. 182 HC Deb., 5s. (Mar. 24, 1925): 291–301. Henderson's speech was subsequently published as a pamphlet, "Labour and the Geneva Protocol."

18. 182 HC Deb., 5s. (Mar. 24, 1925): 367–72.

19. Barnes, "Geneva Protocol," *Labour Magazine* 3 (Jan. 1925): 391–93.

20. Noel-Baker, "Protocol and the *Status Quo*," *Labour Magazine* 3 (Apr. 1925): 497–500.

21. Noel-Baker, *Geneva Protocol*, esp. pp. 64–92, 132–42, 193–94.

22. Zimmern, "Europe First: A Defence of the Geneva Protocol," *Daily Herald*, Nov. 24, 1924.

23. *Clarion*, Jan. 16, 30, July 3, 1925; *New Statesman* 24 (Jan. 3, 1925): 355, and 24 (Mar. 14, 1925): 645.

24. *Lansbury's Labour Weekly*, Feb. 28, Mar. 21, 28, Sept. 26, 1925.

25. *Bradford Pioneer*, May 22, June 12, Oct. 9, 1925.

26. *Forward*, Jan. 17, 31, 1925.

27. *Socialist Review* 25, no. 135 (Jan. 1925): 4.

28. *New Leader*, Jan. 30, Feb. 13, 1925.

29. Ibid., Mar. 6, 1925.

30. Marquand, *Ramsay MacDonald*, pp. 368–69; MacDonald Diary, Sept. 14, 1927, PRO 30/69/1753, p. 250.

31. "Memorandum on Security Pact," Advisory Committee (1925).

32. "Report of Sub-Committee on the Security Pact," ibid.

33. Noel-Baker to MacDonald, July 3, 1925, MacDonald Papers, PRO 30/69/1170, files 45–48.

34. 188 HC Deb., 5s. (Nov. 18, 1925): 507–10.

35. Ibid., 434–46.

36. MacDonald to Ponsonby, Nov. 10, 1925, Ponsonby Papers, fol. 63.

37. In a letter to Beatrice, Sidney Webb describes the party meeting at which the group tried to persuade the majority to condemn the Locarno Pact. Passfield Papers, Nov. 25, 1924.

38. Joint Meeting of the LSI and IFTU, Bureaux, Brussels, January 3–4, 1925, *LP Annual Conference Report* (1925), Appendix 11, p. 342; *ILP Annual Conference Report* (1925), Appendix 10, p. 77. A few months later, the LSI Bureau, meeting in London, passed another resolution that incorporated the British insistence upon calling for the admission of Germany and Russia into the League on conditions of full equality. But, in a bow to the "partial pacts" such as the Locarno agreements, the LSI called upon its affiliated bodies to be vigilant to see that no such pacts should be concluded in opposition to the Geneva

Protocol principles of universal arbitration and the fullest "realization" of the covenant of the League. "Meeting of L.S.I. Bureau, London, July 4, 1925. Resolutions Adopted," *Labour Party Conference* (1925), Appendix 13, p. 345. See also Ernest E. Hunter, *New Leader*, Jan. 16, 1925, quoted in Miller, *Socialism and Foreign Policy*, p. 147. Hunter was a member of the ILP.

39. *ILP Annual Conference Report* (1925), pp. 53, 133–34, 162–64.

40. *New Statesman* 25 (Oct. 24, 1925): 35, and 25 (Nov. 21, 1925): 61.

41. See, for example, Tom Shaw in *Clarion*, Oct. 30, Nov. 27, 1925, and MacDonald in *Forward*, Nov. 7, 1925.

42. Dalton, *Call Back*, p. 170.

43. 183 HC Deb., 5s. (Mar. 23, 1926): 1085–99.

44. *Socialist Review* 27, n.s., no. 3 (Apr. 1926): 7.

45. MacDonald to Ponsonby, Nov. 18, 1927, Ponsonby Papers, fol. 50.

46. *Forward*, Nov. 7, 1925; *New Leader*, Dec. 4, 1925, Mar. 12, Feb. 26, Aug. 20, 1926. See also Buxton, "Britain versus the League" (Oct. 1925): pp. 103–4; Arnold-Forster, "British Government and Arbitration" (Nov. 1925): 129–30; Swanwick, "Labour's Neglect of the League" (Feb. 1926): 221–24; Ponsonby, "Mr. Chamberlain's Failure" (Apr. 1926): 289–90; Dalton, "League, Disarmament, and Arbitration" (May 1926): 336–37, all in *Foreign Affairs* 7.

47. See among others Wheeler-Bennett, *Disarmament and Security*; Chaput, *Disarmament in British Foreign Policy*; Jacobson, *Locarno Diplomacy*.

48. MacDonald Diary, June 20, 1926, PRO 30/69/1753, p. 233.

49. *Forward*, Mar. 13, Aug. 14, 1926; *Lansbury's Labour Weekly*, Mar. 20, July 17, Sept. 11, 1926; *Bradford Pioneer*, Feb. 26, Mar. 5, Sept. 11, 1926.

50. See *New Leader*, Nov. 5, 1926.

51. *ILP Annual Conference Report* (1926), pp. 70–72, 90–92.

52. *LP Annual Conference Report* (1926), pp. 253–57.

53. Ibid. (1928), p. 155.

54. "Why We Will Not Fight!," MacDonald Papers, PRO 30/69/1833.

55. Lord Parmoor to Ponsonby, Dec. 30, 1926, Ponsonby Papers, fol. 108–9, and Max Montgelas to Ponsonby, Ponsonby Papers, fol. 67–68.

56. "Disarmament by Example," *Journal of the Royal Institute of International Affairs* 7, no. 4 (July 1928): 225–40. Miller, *Socialism and Foreign Policy*, pp. 162–63, also cites Ponsonby's article, "Now Is the Time: 'Disarmament by Example,'" *Contemporary Review* 132, no. 6 (Dec. 1927): 687–93, and his speech at the 1929 ILP Conference to conclude that his stand undoubtedly ruined any prospect he might have had to be the next Labour foreign secretary, "a position to which his experience and ability might well have given him a claim." But while Ponsonby's relations with MacDonald remained cordial for some time, the tone of the latter's letters to his former colleague made clear that he regarded him as a subordinate rather than a major player. See, for example, MacDonald to Ponsonby, Mar. 22, 1927, Ponsonby Papers, fol. 16.

57. *Foreign Affairs* 9 (Apr. 1928): 317.

58. His letter of resignation to the Executive, June 14, 1928, is in UDC Papers, DDC 4/10, and J. A. Hobson's letter of June 27, 1928, asking him to reconsider is in the Ponsonby Papers, fol. 114.

59. *Foreign Affairs* 8 (May 1927): 295–96; 9 (Jan. 1928): 199–202; 9 (Apr. 1928): 291–92, 317–18.

60. 208 HC Deb., 5s. (July 11, 1927): 1761–73.

61. Letters to and from Ponsonby by B. Rawson [1929], Ponsonby Papers, fol. 58–59.

62. *New Leader*, Apr. 15, Sept. 23, 1927, Mar. 30, 1928; *Bradford Pioneer*, Sept. 16, 1927, Mar. 30, 1928.

63. *ILP Annual Conference Report* (1927), pp. 67–68, 84–85. The ILP Weekly Notes for Speakers, no. 419, July 21, 1927, issued in conjunction with the "No More War" movement and designed for use at meetings held in connection with "War Resistance Week-End," pointed out that war resistance resolutions had been endorsed since 1918 by the Women's Co-operative Guild, Primitive Methodist Assembly, Co-operative Congress, Labour Women's Conference, Labour party, Independent Labour party, Congregational Ministers' Peace Crusade, International Textile Workers, International Transport Workers' Federation, and Miners' International Federation. A pamphlet written for the "No More War" movement by F. Seymour Cocks, who was also active in ILP circles, looked back with regret to the jettisoning of the Geneva Protocol and the reintroduction of another era of secret diplomacy. Cocks, "War Danger," UDC Papers, DDC 5/174.

64. *ILP Annual Conference Report* (1928), pp. 75–78.

65. The judgment is from Medlicott, *British Foreign Policy*, p. 84.

66. From a steady stream of critical commentary, a few may be noted as representative: *New Statesman* 26 (Mar. 13, 1926): 665; *New Leader*, Apr. 15, 1927, Feb. 14, Aug. 17, 1928; *Clarion*, June, Aug., Oct. 1927; *Forward*, Apr. 28, 1928; *Daily Herald*, Feb. 20, Sept. 3, 26, Oct. 25, 1928, Apr. 27, 1929; *Bradford Pioneer*, Feb. 26, 1926, Sept. 16, 1927, Mar. 30, 1928.

67. 210 HC Deb., 5s. (Nov. 24, 1927): 2132.

68. Ibid., 2089–2186. The same surface agreement on criticizing the government was evident in a long special resolution on foreign policy presented to the party conference in October 1927 by the National Executive. It was introduced by the trade unionist C. T. Cramp and seconded by R. C. Wallhead of the ILP, one of the thirteen Labour M.P.'s who had voted against ratification of the Locarno Pacts. See *LP Annual Conference Report* (1927), pp. 236–44.

69. 222 HC Deb., 5s. (Nov. 13, 1928): 763–64.

70. McKercher, "British Diplomatic Service," pp. 220–22. See also his *Second Baldwin Government*.

71. A few examples can be found in *Daily Herald*, Dec. 8, 1927, Sept. 1, Nov. 13, 1928, and *Foreign Affairs* 10 (Dec. 1928): 38–39, (Jan. 1929): 55, (May 1929): 127.

72. Charles Ammon to MacDonald, Nov. 1, 1927, MacDonald Papers, PRO 30/69/1172, file 23.

73. Arnold-Forster, "Freedom of the Seas" and "Freedom of the Seas Old and New," Advisory Committee (1928). See also the pamphlets published separately by Noel-Baker, "Disarmament and the Coolidge Conference," and Arnold-Forster, *Free Seas*.

74. "Freedom of the Seas Old and New," esp. p. 19.

75. 217 HC Deb., 5s. (May 10, 1928): 431–58.

76. Woolf, "Proposals for the 'Outlawry of War,'" Advisory Committee (1927); Kenworthy, "Memorandum on Outlawry of War," and revised memoranda, Advisory Committee (1928). The Kenworthy and Woolf memos, unmarked [1928], are in the Noel-Baker Papers, NBKR 2/9.

77. Advisory Committee (1928), nos. 379d, 383, 383a, and finally, 389 ("American Peace Offer").

78. Exchange of corespondence between Cecil and MacDonald between Mar. 6 and Mar. 14, 1928, including an agreement by Lloyd George to sign document supporting an informal approach to the Foreign Office, MacDonald Papers, PRO 30/69/1173.

79. *New Leader*, Jan. 11, 13, 1928; *Daily Herald*, Dec. 1, 1927, Feb. 24, 1928; *Clarion*, Jan., May 1928.

80. "British Reply to Mr. Kellogg," Advisory Committee (1928); "American Peace Pact and the British Reply," Advisory Committee (1928); *ILP Annual Conference Report* (1929), pp. 83–84; "L.P. Weekly Notes for Speakers," no. 471, July 26, 1928, and no. 474, Aug. 16, 1928; *LP Annual Conference Report* (1928), pp. 183–84; 220 HC Deb., 5s. (July 30, 1938): 1803–61, and 222 HC Deb., 5s. (Nov. 6, 1928): 18–47.

81. *Bradford Pioneer*, Apr. 20, May 25, 1928.

82. *New Leader*, May 25, Aug. 10, 1928.

83. *Forward*, Sept. 1, 1928. See also *Daily Herald*, Nov. 7, Dec. 1, 1928, and Jan. 17, 1929.

84. *Foreign Affairs* 10 (Sept. 1928).

85. Noel-Baker, *Disarmament*, esp. pp. 325–28. See also his *League of Nations at Work*; "Locarno or the League? Sir Austen's Collapse and Its Lessons," *Socialist Review* 27, n.s., no. 4 (May 1926): 18–27; and his Advisory Committee memos, [Disarmament] (1926).

86. Arnold-Forster, "Victory of Reason," esp. pp. 83–84.

87. Dalton, *Towards the Peace of Nations*, pp. 7–23, 45–46, 87–90, 210–17, 235.

88. E.g., Norman Angell, *Human Nature and the Peace Problem*.

89. Arnold-Forster, "All-Inclusive Arbitration," p. 10.

90. "Arbitrate! Arbitrate! Arbitrate!," p. 12.

91. "A Year of Tory Mismanagement."

92. "Commentary on the British Government's Observations," Advisory Committee (1928), pp. 1–8.

93. "League's Model Arbitration Treaty," ibid., pp. 1–9.

94. Buxton, "Sanctions in the Covenant," ibid. (1927), pp. 1–3.

95. Mitrany, "A Labour Policy on Sanctions," ibid., pp. 1–9.

96. Arnold-Forster, "Sanctions (Commentary on Mr. Buxton's Paper)," ibid., pp. 1–9.

97. Henderson, "Principles of the Protocol," *Labour Magazine* 6 (Nov. 1927): 298–300.

98. Marquand, *Ramsay MacDonald*, p. 470.

99. Jordan, *Great Britain*, pp. 206–7.

100. Marquand, *Ramsay MacDonald*, p. 478.

101. *LP Annual Conference Report* (1928), p. 265.

102. "Labour and the Nation," esp. pp. 41–42, 49.

103. Sidney Webb to Beatrice Webb, Feb. 24, 1928, Passfield Papers.

104. "Suggested First Measures," Advisory Committee (1929), pp. 1–3.

CONCLUSION

1. See also my "Arthur Henderson," in Craig and Gilbert, *Diplomats*, esp. pp. 327–34.

2. See his memorandum replying to criticisms in CID paper 970-B, Nov. 19, 1929, CAB 4/19 and Cmd. 3803, submitted Feb. 23, 1931, PREM 1/98.

3. Philip Kerr to MacDonald, Feb. 26, 1930, PREM 1/84.

4. MacDonald's diary is dotted with criticisms of Henderson's "pomposity" and his "vanity." MacDonald Diary, entries for Nov. 20, 1929, and July 16, 1930, PRO 30/69/1753. Henderson's resentment of MacDonald's treatment of him appears in the papers of various colleagues. Henderson to George Lansbury, Feb. 22, 1929, Lansbury Papers, Vol. 9, fol. 22; Beatrice Webb Manuscript Diary, Dec. 2, 1929; Hugh Dalton's Diary, July 20, 1931, Dalton Papers, Part 1, file 14a.

5. But he often used the term of himself. See, for example, a letter to Senator William Borah of the United States in which he emphasizes the "psychological" differences between their two countries, identifying himself as an idealist born out of due time and concluding that it "is the lot of the pacifist." MacDonald to Borah, Aug. 26, 1929, MacDonald Papers, PRO 30/69/673 (Part 1)/4–5.

6. It was no mere coincidence that Clement Attlee should have referred to the "policy of Arthur Henderson" in his election day address in 1945.

BIBLIOGRAPHY

MANUSCRIPTS AND OFFICIAL DOCUMENTS

Cambridge, England
Churchill College Archive Centre
   Philip Noel-Baker Papers

Hull, England
University of Hull, Brynmor Jones Library
   Union of Democratic Control Papers

London, England
British Library
   Cecil of Chelwood Papers
Labour Party Archives
   Labour and Socialist International Collection
   Labour Party National Executive Committee Minutes and Agenda
   Reports of the Annual Conference of the Independent Labour Party
   Reports of the Annual Conference of the Labour Party
   Reports of the Annual Meeting of the Trades Union Congress
London School of Economics, British Library of Political and Economic Sciences
   George Lansbury Papers
   E. D. Morel Papers
   Passfield Papers
   Beatrice Webb Manuscript Diary
Public Record Office
   Cabinet Papers and Memoranda
   Conclusions of Cabinet Meetings
   Foreign Office Confidential Print and General Correspondence
   Ramsay MacDonald Papers
   Records of the Prime Minister's Office

Oxford, England
Oxford University, Bodleian Library
   Arthur Ponsonby Papers

Sussex, England
University of Sussex Library
   Leonard Woolf Papers

PRINTED MATERIALS

Cole, Margaret, ed. *Beatrice Webb's Diaries, 1912–24*. London, 1952.
——. *Beatrice Webb's Diaries, 1923–32*. London, 1956.
League of Nations. *Verbatim Record*, 1919–31.
Mackenzie, Norman, ed. *The Letters of Sidney and Beatrice Webb*. 3 vols. London, 1978.
Parliamentary Debates. Fifth series. House of Commons (1911–31).

**MINUTES AND MEMORANDA OF THE ADVISORY
COMMITTEE ON INTERNATIONAL QUESTIONS**

1918
"Colonies."
"The Freedom of the Seas."
"Intervention in Russia."
"A League of Nations."
"Notes on Procedure at the International Labour Conference Proposed to be Held at the
    Same Time and Place as the Official Peace Conference."
"Reform of the Foreign Services."

1919
Angell, Norman. "Peace Terms."
Brailsford, H. N. "A Parliament of the League of Nations," no. 44.
"Draft Memorandum on the Proposed Alliance with France," no. 112.
"Labour and the Proposed Alliance. An Interview with Mr. Arthur Henderson," no. 114.
"Policy towards Germany" [1919].

1920
B[urns], C. D[elisle]. "Notes on the League," no. 143.
"Draft Notes on European Federation. By X," no. 158.
"Interview [with W. H. Hutchinson]," no. 140.
"Letter from Henderson to Prime Ministers," no. 119.
"Letter to the Executive Committee," no. 149a.
Toynbee, A. J. "Draft Memorandum on the Draft Treaty Presented by the Allied Powers to
    Turkey, and on the Assignment of Mandates by the Supreme Council at San Remo,"
    nos. 141 and 141a.

1921
"Draft Pamphlet on Foreign Policy," no. 228a [1921].
"Draft Pamphlet on 'Labour and the League of Nations,'" no. 207a [1921].

1922
"Anglo-French Agreement," no. 232.
"Draft Report for the International Socialist Conference. The League of Nations and Dis-
    armament," no. 251a [1922].
"Resolutions for Submission to the Executive Committee," no. 233a.

1923
"Draft Manifesto," no. 270.
"Labour and the League of Nations. The Need for a League Foreign Policy."

"Memorandum on Ruhr Situation," no. 271a.
"Principles of a Disarmament Policy," nos. 278a and 284a.
[Reply to Baldwin Statement on Ruhr Situation], no. 289.

1924
"Draft Memorandum Prepared by the Special Sub-Committee on the Draft Treaty of Mutual Assistance," no. 323.
"The Draft Treaty of Mutual Assistance," no. 327.
"Labour, the League and Reparations," no. 310.
"Memorandum on the League and Disarmament by Prof. Shotwell," no. 322.
Morel, E. D., and G. Lowes Dickinson. "An Alternative Policy for a British Labour Government to the Policy Embodied in the 'Draft Treaty of Mutual Assistance,'" no. 318.
"Permanent Court of International Justice. Adherence of Great Britain to Optional Clause," no. 324.
"Report on Memorandum No. 310," no. 319.

1925
Gillies, W. "Amendments to the Protocol," no. 334.
"Memorandum on Security Pact," no. 339.
Noel-Baker, P., and A. A. Ponsonby. "Note on the Committee of Imperial Defense," no. 336.
"Report of Sub-Committee on Security Pact," no. 339a.
Young, George. "The Foreign Office and Labour Governments," nos. 333a–d.

1926
Arnold-Forster, Will. "All-Inclusive Arbitration," no. 346.
Noel-Baker, Philip. [Disarmament], nos. 345 and 345a.

1927
Arnold-Forster, Will. "Sanctions (commentary on Mr. Buxton's Paper)," no. 365.
Buxton, C. R. "Sanctions in the Covenant and the Protocol," no. 358.
Mitrany, David. "A Labour Policy on Sanctions," no. 366.
Woolf, Leonard. "Proposals for the 'Outlawry of War,'" no. 379a.

1928
"The American Peace Offer," no. 389.
"The American Peace Pact and the British Reply," no. 391.
Arnold-Forster, Will. "Freedom of the Seas," nos. 380 and 380a.
"The British Reply to Mr. Kellogg," no. 390a.
"Commentary on the British Government's Observations on Arbitration and Security," no. 386.
"Freedom of the Seas Old and New," no. 399b.
Kenworthy, J. M. "Memorandum on Outlawry of War," no. 379b and revised nos. 379c and 379d, 383 and 383a.
"The League's Model Arbitration Treaty and the Labour Party's Draft," no. 396.

1929
"Suggested First Measures in Foreign Affairs Which Might Be Taken by a Labour Government," no. 394b.

MEMOIRS AND AUTOBIOGRAPHIES

Angell, Norman. *After All: The Autobiography of Norman Angell.* London, 1952.

Brockway, A. Fenner. *Inside the Left.* London, 1942.

Cecil, Robert. *All the Way.* London, 1949.

——. *A Great Experiment.* London, 1941.

Clynes, J. R. *Memoirs.* 2 vols. London, 1937.

Dalton, Hugh. *Call Back Yesterday: Memoirs 1887–1932.* London, 1953.

Gallacher, William. *The Rolling of the Thunder.* London, 1947.

Haldane, Richard Burdon. *An Autobiography.* London, 1929.

Hamilton, Mary Agnes. *Remembering My Good Friends.* London, 1944.

Hobson, J. A. *Confessions of an Economic Heretic.* London, 1938.

Parmoor, Lord. *A Retrospect: Looking Back over a Life of More than Eighty Years.* London, 1936.

Snowden, Philip. *An Autobiography.* 2 vols. London, 1934.

Swanwick, H. M. *I Have Been Young.* London, 1935.

Woolf, Leonard. *Downhill All the Way: An Autobiography of the Years 1919 to 1939.* New York, 1975.

CONTEMPORARY WRITINGS

Angell, Norman. *Human Nature and the Peace Problem.* London, 1925.

——. *The Peace Treaty and the Economic Chaos of Europe.* London, 1919.

Arnold-Forster, Will. *The Free Seas (for the National Council for the Prevention of War).* London, 1929.

——. "The Victory of Reason. A Pamphlet on Arbitration." London, 1926.

Brailsford, H. N. *After the Peace.* London, 1920.

——. *A League of Nations.* London, 1917.

——. *The War of Steel and Gold: A Study of the Armed Peace.* London, 1914.

Dalton, Hugh. *Towards the Peace of Nations.* London, 1928.

Henderson, Arthur. "War against War." *Labour Magazine* 1 (Jan. 1923): 392–93.

Morel, E. D. *The Horror on the Rhine.* London, 1920.

Noel-Baker, Philip. *Disarmament.* London, 1926.

——. *Disarmament and the Coolidge Conference.* London, 1927.

——. *The Geneva Protocol for the Pacific Settlement of International Disputes.* London, 1925.

——. "The Growth of International Society." *Economica* 4 (Nov. 1924): 262–77.

——. *The League of Nations at Work.* London, 1926.

——. "The Obligatory Jurisdiction of the Permanent Court of International Justice." *The British Year Book of International Law.* London, 1924.

Ponsonby, Arthur. "Disarmament by Example." *Journal of the Royal Institute of International Affairs* 7, no. 4 (July 1928): 225–40.

Swanwick, H. M. *Builders of Peace: Being Ten Years' History of the Union of Democratic Control.* London, 1924.

Trevelyan, Charles. *The Union of Democratic Control (an Organization Created to Secure the Control over Their Foreign Policy by the British People, and for the Promotion of International Understanding), Founded in November, 1914, Its History and Its Policy.* 3rd and rev. ed. London, 1921.

Woolf, Leonard. *International Government.* London, 1916.

LABOUR PARTY PAMPHLETS, LEAFLETS, AND REPORTS

"Agenda for National Conference of Labour Women." London, 1921.

"The Anglo-Russian Treaties" (Can Labour Rule? series, no. 6). London, 1924.

"Arbitrate! Arbitrate! Arbitrate! The Case for All-Inclusive Pacific Settlement of International Disputes." London, 1927.

Bowerman, C. W., and Arthur Henderson. "The International Situation." London, 1923.

Buxton, C. R. "Labour's Work for Peace at Geneva." London, 1924.

"Control of Foreign Policy." London, [1921].

"The Empire in Africa. Labour's Policy." London, [1920].

"Freedom of the Seas Old and New." London, 1929.

Henderson, Arthur. "The Aims of Labour." London, [1917].

——. "Labour and Foreign Affairs." London, 1922.

——. "Labour and the Geneva Protocol." London, 1925.

——. "The Peace Terms." London, 1919.

"International Labour and Peace." London, 1919.

"Labour and the Nation." London, 1928.

"Labour and the Peace Treaty." London, 1919.

"Labour and the Peace Treaty. An Examination of Labour Declarations and the Treaty Terms." London, 1919.

"Labour and the Ruhr." London, 1923.

"Labour's Great Record. An Outline of the First Six Months' Work of the Labour Government." London, 1924.

"The Labour Party." [Unnumbered leaflet, London], 1918.

MacDonald, J. R. "The Foreign Policy of the Labour Party." London, 1923.

——. "No Surrender!" London, 1924.

——. "A Policy for the Labour Party." London, 1920.

——. "Protocol or Pact." London, 1925.

"The New Peace Plan: Labour's Work at the League of Nations Assembly." London, 1924.

"Towards a European Settlement: Reparations. An Exposition of the Dawes Report and the London Agreement." London, 1924.

"Why I Shall Vote Labour: A Working Woman's Letter from 'Blighty.'" Leaflet no. 26, new series. [London], 1918.

"Why Labour Supports a League of Nations." Leaflet no. 17, new series. [London], 1918.

"Why Women Should Join the Labour Party and Vote for the Labour Candidates." Leaflet no. 3, new series. [London], 1918.

Woolf, Leonard. "International Economic Policy." London, 1920.

——. "Mandates and Empire." London, 1920.

"A Year of Tory Mismanagement." London, 1926.

Young, George. "The Reform of Diplomacy: A Practical Programme." London, [1921].

OTHER PAMPHLETS, LEAFLETS, AND REPORTS

"Amendments to the Covenant of the League of Nations." [Trades Union Congress and
     Labour Party]. London, 1919.
Arnold-Forster, Will. "France, Ourselves and the Future." [Union of Democratic Con-
     trol]. London, 1922.
Brockway, F. "How To End War." [Independent Labour Party Programme Pamphlet, no.
     2]. [London, 1922].
Cocks, Seymour. "The War Danger." [Union of Democratic Control]. London, 1927.
"I.L.P. Weekly Notes for Speakers." 1919–1931.
"International Socialism and World Peace." [Independent Labour Party Pamphlet], new
     series, no. 1. London, 1919.
King, Joseph. "Political Crooks at the Peace Conference." [Independent Labour Party
     Pamphlet, no. 29]. [London], 1920.
"Labour and the European Situation." [Trades Union Congress and Labour Party].
     London, 1923.
"Why We Will Not Fight!" [Independent Labour Party]. London, 1927.

PERIODICALS AND NEWSPAPERS

Bradford Pioneer, 1918–1929
British Citizen and Empire Worker, 1918–1920
Clarion, 1918–1929
Contemporary Review, 1918–1929
Daily Herald, 1918–1929 (weekly until March 31, 1919)
Foreign Affairs, 1920–1929
Fortnightly Review, 1919–1929
Forward, 1918–1929
Labour, 1937
Labour Leader, 1918–1922
Labour Magazine, 1922–1929
Lansbury's Labour Weekly, 1925–1926
Nation, 1919–1920
New Leader, 1922–1929
New Statesman and Nation, 1918–1956
Railway Review, 1919
Socialist Review, 1918–1929
The U.D.C., 1919–1920

SECONDARY WORKS

Anderson, Mosa. *Noel Buxton*. London, 1952.
Bealey, Frank. "The Electoral Arrangement between the Labour Representation Com-
     mittee and the Liberal Party." *Journal of Modern History* 28 (Dec. 1956): 353–73.
Bealey, Frank, and Henry Pelling. *Labour and Politics, 1900–1906: A History of the La-
     bour Representation Committee*. London, 1958.

Brand, Carl F. *The British Labour Party: A Short History*. Stanford, 1941. Rev. ed. 1974.

——. *British Labour's Rise to Power*. Stanford, 1941.

Bullock, Alan. *The Life and Times of Ernest Bevin*. Volume 1. *Trade Union Leader, 1881–1940*. London, 1960.

Bullock, Alan, and M. Shock. *The Liberal Tradition from Fox to Keynes*. London, 1956.

Chaput, R. A. *Disarmament in British Foreign Policy*. London, 1935.

Cline, Catherine A. *E. D. Morel, 1873–1924: The Strategies of Protest*. Belfast, 1980.

——. *Recruits to Labour*. Syracuse, N.Y., 1963.

Cocks, F. Seymour. *E. D. Morel: The Man and His Work*. London, 1920.

Cole, G. D. H. *The Second International 1889–1914: Parts I and II*. Vol. 3 of *A History of Socialist Thought*. New York, 1956.

Cole, Margaret. *Makers of the Labour Movement*. London, 1940.

Cowling, Maurice. *The Impact of Labour 1920–1924: The Beginning of Modern British Politics*. Cambridge, 1971.

Cross, Colin. *Philip Snowden*. London, 1966.

Dowse, Robert E. *Left in the Centre: The Independent Labour Party 1893–1940*. Evanston, Ill., 1966.

Garratt, G. T. *The Mugwumps and the Labour Party*. London, 1932.

Gathorne-Hardy, G. M. *A Short History of International Affairs, 1920–1939*. 3rd rev. ed. London, 1942.

Gilbert, Martin. *Plough My Own Furrow: The Story of Lord Allen of Hurtwood as Told through his Writings and Correspondence*. London, 1965.

Graubard, Stephen R. *British Labour and the Russian Revolution*. Cambridge, Mass., 1956.

Grun, George A. "Locarno: Idea and Reality." *International Affairs* 31 (1955): 477–85.

Hamilton, Mary Agnes. *Arthur Henderson*. London, 1938.

Hirsch, Felix. "Locarno: Twenty-Five Years After." *Contemporary Review* 178 (1950): 279–85.

Jacobson, J. *Locarno Diplomacy, Germany and the West, 1925–1929*. Princeton, N.J., 1972.

Jordan, W. M. *Great Britain, France and the German Problem*. London, 1943.

Koss, Stephen. *The Rise and Fall of the Political Press in Britain*. Vol. 2: *The Twentieth Century*. Chapel Hill, N.C., 1984.

Laski, Harold. "Ramsay MacDonald." *Harper's* 164 (May 1932): 746–56.

Leventhal, F. M. *Arthur Henderson*. Manchester, 1989.

——. *The Last Dissenter: H. N. Brailsford and His World*. Oxford, 1985.

Lyman, Richard W. *The First Labour Government, 1924*. London, 1957.

McBriar, A. M. *Fabian Socialism and English Politics, 1884–1918*. London, 1950.

McDougall, Walter A. *France's Rhineland Diplomacy, 1914–1924: The Last Bid for a Balance of Power in Europe*. Princeton, N.J., 1978.

McKercher, B. J. C. "The British Diplomatic Service in the United States and the Chamberlain Foreign Office's Perceptions of Domestic America, 1924–1927: Images. Reality, and Diplomacy." In *Shadow and Substance in British Foreign Policy; Memorial Essays Honouring C. J. Lowe*, edited by B. J. C. McKercher and D. J. Moss. Edmonton, 1984.

——. *The Second Baldwin Government and the United States, 1924–1929: Attitudes and Diplomacy*. Cambridge, 1984.

Maddox, William P. *Foreign Relations in British Labour Politics, 1900–1924*. Cambridge, Mass., 1950.

Marks, Sally. *The Illusion of Peace: International Relations 1918–1933*. New York, 1976.

Marquand, David. *Ramsay MacDonald*. London, 1977.

Marwick, Arthur. *Clifford Allen: The Open Conspirator*. Edinburgh, 1964.

Medlicott, W. N. *British Foreign Policy since Versailles*. London, 1940.

Meyerowitz, Selma S. *Leonard Woolf*. Boston, [1982].

Miller, Kenneth E. *Socialism and Foreign Policy: Theory and Practice in Britain to 1931*. The Hague, 1967.

Morgan, Kenneth O. *Keir Hardie: Radical and Socialist*. London, 1984.

Morris, A. J. A. *C. P. Trevelyan, 1870–1958*. Belfast, 1977.

Namier, L. B. "Diplomacy in the Interwar Period." *World Politics* 7 (Oct. 1954): 102–18.

Naylor, J. F. *Labour's International Policy: The Labour Party in the 1930s*. London, 1969.

Nelson, Keith L. *Victors Divided: America and the Allies in Germany, 1918– 1923*. Berkeley, Calif., 1975.

Northedge, F. S. *The Troubled Giant: Britain among the Great Powers, 1919– 1939*. New York, 1966.

Orde, Anne. *Great Britain and International Security 1920–1926*. London, 1978.

Pelling, Henry. *The Origins of the Labour Party, 1880–1900*. London, 1954.

Pimlott, Ben. *Hugh Dalton*. London, 1985.

Poirier, Philip P. *The Advent of the British Labour Party*. New York, 1958.

Postgate, Raymond. *The Life of George Lansbury*. London, 1951.

Reid, J. H. Stewart. *The Origins of the British Labour Party*. Minneapolis, 1955.

Reynolds, P. A. *British Foreign Policy in the Inter-War Years*. London, 1954.

Sacks, Benjamin. *J. Ramsay MacDonald in Thought and Action*. Albuquerque, 1952.

Schneer, Jonathan. *George Lansbury*. Manchester, 1990.

Schuker, Stephen A. *The End of French Predominance in Europe. The Financial Crisis of 1924 and the Adoption of the Dawes Plan*. Chapel Hill, N.C., 1976.

Seymour, Charles, ed. *The Intimate Papers of Colonel House*. 4 vols. Boston, 1928.

Swartz, Marvin. *The Union of Democratic Control in British Politics during the First World War*. Oxford, 1971.

Taylor, A. J. P. *The Trouble Makers: Dissent over Foreign Policy 1792–1939*. London, 1957.

Tiltman, H. Hessell. *J. Ramsay MacDonald: Labour's Man of Destiny*. New York, 1929.

Tracey, Herbert, ed. *The Book of the Labour Party: Its History, Growth, Policy and Leaders*. 3 vols. London, 1925.

Tucker, William R. *The Attitude of the British Labour Party towards European and Collective Security Problems, 1920–1939*. Geneva, 1950.

Van Der Slice, Austin. *International Labour, Diplomacy, and Peace 1914– 1919*. Philadelphia, 1941.

Walters, F. P. *A History of the League of Nations*. 2 vols. London, 1952.

Webb, Sidney. "The First Labour Government." *Political Quarterly* 32 (Jan.– Mar. 1961): 9–18.

Wedgwood, C. V. *The Last of the Radicals, Josiah Wedgwood, M.P.* London, 1951.

Wheeler-Bennett, J. W. *Disarmament and Security since Locarno, 1925–1931*. London, 1932.

Williams, Francis. *Fifty Years' March: The Rise of the Labour Party*. London, 1950.

Wilson, Duncan (assisted by J. Eisenberg). *Leonard Woolf: A Political Biography*. New York, 1978.

Windrich, Elaine. *British Labour's Foreign Policy*. Stanford, 1952.

Winkler, Henry R. "Arthur Henderson." In *The Diplomats 1919–1939*, edited by Gordon Craig and Felix Gilbert. Princeton, N.J., 1953.

——. "British Labor and the Origins of the Idea of Colonial Trusteeship, 1914–1919." *The Historian* 13 (Spring 1951): 154–72.

——. "The British Labour Party and the Paris Settlement." In *Some Pathways in Twentieth-Century History: Essays in Honor of Reginald Charles McGrane*, edited by Daniel R. Beaver. Detroit, 1969.

——. "The Emergence of a Labor Foreign Policy in Great Britain, 1918–1929." *Journal of Modern History* 28 (Sept. 1956): 247–58.

——. *The League of Nations Movement in Great Britain, 1914–1919*. New Brunswick, N.J., 1952.

Wolfers, Arnold. *Britain and France between the Wars*. New York, 1940.

Woolf, Leonard. "Labour's Foreign Policy." *Political Quarterly* 4 (1933): 504–24.

Wrigley, Chris. *Arthur Henderson*. Cardiff, 1990.

Wuliger, R. *The Idea of Economic Imperialism, with Special Reference to the Life and Work of E. D. Morel*. Ph.D. thesis, University of London, 1953.

Zimmern, Alfred. *The League of Nations and the Rule of Law 1918–1935*. London, 1939.

INDEX

Adamson, Will, 20, 52, 105
Advisory Committee on International
  Questions, 15, 21–22, 24–25, 124,
  155, 158–60, 195–96; and League of
  Nations policy, 2; on need for military
  sanctions, 28; analyzes peace goals,
  28–29; cautious about disarmament,
  28–29; and Berne Conference, 31–33;
  on modifications of Draft Covenant,
  38; memorandum on proposed peace
  treaty, 46–47; opposes strict policy
  toward Germany, 47–48; on American
  defection from League, 66–67; opposes French alliance, 67, 86–87; limited role of, 78–79; on support for
  League, 89–90, 115–16; memorandums
  on Ruhr policy and reparations, 102–3,
  129–31; on disarmament and sanctions,
  114–16; diminished role of, 129; con-
  siders Draft Treaty of Mutual Assistance, 139–42; supports Geneva Protocol, 159–60; on proposed Locarno
  Pact, 165–66; pamphlet on freedom of
  the seas, 177; and American antiwar
  proposals, 177–79; advice to Labour
  party Executive, 184; and model arbitration treaty, 185; refutes opposition to
  international arbitration, 185; proposes
  strategy for new Labour government,
  190
Allen, Clifford, 33, 157, 167; recognizes
  MacDonald's faults, 220 (n. 7)
Amalgamated Marine Workers, 100
Angell, Norman, 59, 104, 121, 183; advocates collective security, 15; member of
  International Advisory Committee, 15;
  authors memorandum denouncing

peace treaty, 46–47; publishes *The
  Peace Treaty and the Economic Chaos
  of Europe,* 59–61; on need for forcible
  sanctions, 128
Anglo-French pact: Labour's opposition
  to, 81–82
Anticapitalism: erosion in Labour circles,
  192
Anti-imperialism: decrease in Labour
  propaganda, 193
Arnold-Forster, Will, 25, 121, 158, 196;
  authors UDC pamphlet, 100–102;
  opposes Ponsonby's pacifism, 172;
  drafts document of free seas, 177; on
  use of force, 180–82, 186–87; on disarmament issues, 181; on arbitration, 184
Asquith, Herbert, 8
Attlee, Clement, 6

Baldwin, Stanley, 6, 80, 124, 132, 158, 175
Balfour, Arthur, 80
Balkan Committee, 15
Barnes, G. N.: supports Geneva Protocol
  and sanctions, 162
Beacham, V., 84
Beatty, Admiral David, 147
Bees, Edouard, 145
Berne Conference, 31–32; strength of
  British delegation, 33; British proposals
  for international organization, 33–35;
  on self-determination, 35
Bevin, Ernest, 196; opposition to Mac-
  Donald, 155
Blatchford, Robert: supports Allied
  League of Nations, 26–27; approves
  Draft Covenant, 37; on outlawry of war,
  179

Body of Delegates: proposed for League by Labour, 39

Bonar Law, Andrew, 96, 106

Borah, Senator William E.: and outlawry of war, 178

Bradford Pioneer, 46, 109, 143, 175; on Geneva Protocol, 164; opposes Locarno Pacts, 169; on failure of real disarmament conference, 174; denounces British reservations to Kellogg proposals, 179

Brailsford, H. N., 25; and *New Leader*, 19; as spokesman for ILP views on foreign affairs, 19; attacks Clemenceau's alliance system, 30–31; criticizes Wilson, 31; advocates a "Deliberative International Parliament," 32–33; denounces French policy at peace conference, 54; rejects peace settlement, 71; suggests an "Economic League of Nations," 71–72; authors Labour party pamphlet, 85; on French capitalism and the Ruhr, 98–99, 104; supports Labour government's foreign policy, 127; opposes Dawes Report, 135; praises MacDonald's Geneva speech, 145; analyzes Geneva Protocol, 148, 164–65; dismissed as editor of *New Leader*, 157; doubtful about Locarno, 169; on failure to deal with economic imperialism, 219 (n. 55)

Briand, Aristide, 80

Bridge, Cyprian: on Anglo-Saxon plan for world hegemony, 37

Bright, John, 13

British Citizen and Empire Worker: calls League a sop to Wilson's domestic needs, 37–38; supports punitive peace, 38; criticizes Labour's leaders, 203–4 (n. 29)

Brockway, A. Fenner, 171, 172

Bromley, John, 86

Burns, C. Delisle: opposes Ponsonby's pacifism, 172

Buxton, Charles Roden, 157, 185; pacifism and opposition to sanctions, 15–16,

185–86; on Draft Covenant, 38; denounces Ruhr occupation, 96; on delegation to Ruhr, 104–5, 112; supports Geneva Protocol, 148–49

Buxton, Noel, 44, 95, 104; influence in moderating Labour extremism, 15–16; deplores slow pace of disarmament, 176

Buxton, Sir Thomas Fowell, 15

Campbell case, 150, 152–53

Capper, Senator Arthur: and outlawry of war, 178–79

Carlton Club: Conservative revolt at, 95

Cecil, Lord Robert, 21, 162; supports outlawry of war, 179; berates Tory neglect of League, 210 (n. 50); faults Mac-Donald's visit to Geneva, 219 (n. 53)

Chamberlain, Sir Austen, 6, 160, 165; handling of Germany's entry into League, 168–69; challenges Mac-Donald's peace proposals, 176; welcomes Kellogg initiative, 178

Chelmsford, Viscount, 147

Churchill, Sir Winston, 6, 18

Clarion: supports Draft Covenant, 37; urges U.S. participation in League, 37; accepts peace terms, 50; joins disapproval of peace settlement, 76; criticizes Geneva Protocol, 163; cites failures of Baldwin government, 175; reluctantly supports outlawry of war, 179

Clemenceau, Georges: insists on alliances and strategic frontiers, 29

Clynes, J. R., 18, 20, 95, 121, 152; early supporter of League machinery, 20; on use of League to repair peace treaty, 51; on Ruhr issue, 106; Beatrice Webb's assessment of, 201 (n. 38)

Cocks, Seymour, 113

Committee of Action: organized by International, 44–46; British Labour's role in denouncing peace preliminaries, 45

Committee of Imperial Defense (CID), 159; opposes Draft Treaty of Mutual Assistance, 142–43

Conscription: opposed by Labour party and TUC, 39

Conservative party, 10

Contemporary Review, 129

Cook, A. J.: denounces reparation settlement, 156

Cook-Maxton Manifesto: effect on foreign policy debate, 180

"Coolidge" negotiations: conflicting British and American views, 177

Coupon election, 8

Cramp, C. T., 108

Crossman, R. H. S., 12

Curzon, Lord, 133; unbending posture toward Turks, 95

Daily Herald, 19, 73–75, 82, 98, 99, 109, 163, 172, 175; indifference to League reform, 64; early support of Labour government's foreign policy, 127–28; criticizes German government, 128; praises "pacifism" of MacDonald and Leach, 128; early acceptance of Dawes Plan, 134; weak support for outlawry of war, 179

Dalton, Hugh, 25, 43, 158, 168, 196; increasing influence on foreign affairs, 22; realism about sanctions, 180, 183; opposes frontier revision campaign, 182–83; publishes *Towards the Peace of Nations*, 182–84; defends principles of Geneva Protocol, 183

Dawes Plan, 124, 134

Dickinson, G. Lowes, 104; criticizes Draft Treaty of Mutual Assistance, 139–40

Disarmament, 39; and labor movement, 170; ILP and unilateral disarmament, 170–72, 174–75; ILP and disarmament by example, 175

Disarmament Conference: endorsed by Labour, 171; slow progress of, 175; Preparatory Commission for, 181

Divisional Labour parties, 8

Draft Treaty of Mutual Assistance, 139–40

Economic Consequences of the Peace, 50

Ewer, W. N., 74

Ex-Liberals: aggressive critics of international policy, 95

Fabian Society, 8; silence on international questions, 11

Federation of League of Nations Societies, 184

Foreign Affairs, 17–18, 54–55, 64, 72, 97–98, 109–10, 126, 136, 173; opposes Locarno Pact, 169–70; minimizes value of Kellogg Pact, 179–80

Foreign Office: opposes Optional Clause, 131

Forward, 38, 50, 109, 175; denounces Draft Covenant, 36; spurns Geneva Protocol, 164; rejects Locarno agreements, 169; scoffs at outlawry of war, 179

France, 6, 9, 17; Labour's suspicion of, 1

Freedom of the seas, 190; conflicting views concerning, 177

General Act of Conciliation, Arbitration, and Judicial Settlement, 185, 193

General Election of 1918: Labour's position on foreign issues, 27; Lloyd George's campaign, 27; rejection of Labour's leaders, 27–28

General Election of 1922, 95

General strike: intensifies TUC indifference to foreign affairs, 156–57

Geneva Protocol, 145–47; opposed by service departments, 147; abandoned by Labour, 170

German Social Democrats, 7

Germany, 6, 9, 11, 17, 68–70; as aggrieved nation, 2; and League "Executive Council," 39; defaults on reparation payments, 95–96; welcomed into League, 171

Gillies, William, 66, 108

Great Depression, 5, 191

Greco-Turkish war, 79

Haldane, Viscount: advises against signing Optional Clause, 131–32; growing sympathy for Labour's views, 200 (n. 18)

Hardie, Keir, 3, 11, 12

Hastings, Sir Patrick, 152

Henderson, Arthur, 5, 40, 43, 61, 92, 159, 190–91; and use of international force, 2, 3; League of Nations policy of, 3; and 1918 constitution, 8; supports war effort, 24; understands need for compromise and negotiation, 24; use of Advisory Committee, 24–25, 67–68, 155; authors pamphlet on peace terms, 48–49; denounces Versailles Treaty, 55; early acceptance of League, 66–67; begins to reorient Labour policy, 90–91; champions compromise in international affairs, 94; on Ruhr issue, 107–8; realism of, 122–23; and collective security, 124; treatment by MacDonald, 125; and Burnley by-election, 133; role in drafting Geneva Protocol, 145–47; growing importance in shaping foreign policy positions, 153–54; frustrates attempt to dump MacDonald, 155; continued advocacy of Geneva Protocol, 161; influence of advisors on, 181; argues for compulsory arbitration and sanctions, 187–88; opposes service departments, 193; assessment of his policy, 195–96

Herald, 38; criticizes Draft Covenant, 36; publishes Will Dyson's famous cartoon, 50

Herriot, Edouard, 134, 143, 145

Hitler, Adolf, 5

Hobson, J. A.: finds fault with Draft Covenant, 37; rejects Ponsonby's pacifism, 172

Hodges, Frank, 75

Hudson, J. H., 85, 172

Hutchinson, W. H.: disapproves Supreme Council, 75

Independent Labour party (ILP), 3, 8, 12, 18–20, 23, 64, 65–66, 72, 89, 109, 110, 121, 168; early plans for international organization, 4; isolation on foreign policy issues, 5; indifference to foreign affairs, 10–11; left-wing radical recruits, 14–15; importance after 1918, 19; alienation from Labour party, 18, 157, 180; denounces peace preliminaries, 43; criticizes Allied support of Poland, 69; regards Germany as victim, 69; damns French vindictiveness, 69–70; resolutions at 1921 conference of, 82; "No More War" resolution of, 83; rejects use of League in Ruhr issue, 111–12; widens breach with Parliamentary party, 112; differences at 1923 conference of, 112–14; on use of force, 113; early support of Labour government's foreign policy, 127; suspicion of MacDonald, 135; on democratic control of foreign policy, 137–39; loss of middle-class element, 157; effort to censure Parliamentary party, 170–71; and disarmament by example, 172, 174–75; materials in support of "No More War" movement, 223 (n. 63)

International Bureau of Labor: supported by Labour party and TUC, 39

International Conference of Disabled and Ex-Service Men, 184

International Federation of Trade Unions, 108

International Government, 21

International Labor Organization, 2

International Socialist Conference: held at Hamburg in 1923, 118; reunites Vienna Union with Second International, 118; British preparatory materials for, 118–19; controversies at, 120

Inter-Parliamentary Conference: held at Paris in 1923, 108–9

Kellogg, Frank, 179; and elimination of war, 177–78

Kellogg treaty, 177–78

Kennedy, Tom, 88

Kenworthy, J. M.: urges rejection of peace

terms, 53; condemns slow pace of disarmament, 176; welcomes outlawry of war, 178

Keynes, J. M., 59, 90

Kirkwood, James, 85

Labor movement: frustration after World War I, 4

Labor press: importance despite small circulation, 38

Labour and Foreign Affairs: on strengthening League machinery, 90. *See also* Henderson, Arthur

Labour and Socialist International, 20, 108, 185; presents Berne resolutions to Clemenceau, 40; Permanent Commission of, 40, 110; Amsterdam resolutions of, 40–43; critique of peace conference, 40–43; Lucerne meeting, 61–64; split over Bolshevik Russia, 62; ambivalence about League, 62–64; minority views supported by British Left, 64; resolutions at Berne Conference, 204 (n. 31); resolution on Locarno, 221–22 (n. 38)

"Labour and the Nation," 192; outlines foreign policy positions of Labour party, 189–90

Labour and the Peace Treaty: handbook for Labour speakers, 55–56; critical of peace treaty and League, 55–58

Labour and the Ruhr, 104–5

Labour Leader, 19, 38, 66, 82

Labour Magazine, 187–88; promotes discussion of Geneva Protocol, 162

Labour party, 84; plans for international organization, 4; 1918 constitution, 8; changing views on international affairs, 10; and Second International, 11–12; demands a "Wilson peace," 30; proposes amendments to Draft Covenant, 38–39; rejects May preliminaries of peace, 43–44; Southport conference of, 51–52; conference (1920 and 1921) resolutions, 77, 85–87; passes "No More War" resolution (1922), 88–89

Labour Representation Committee, 7, 11

"Labour, the League and Reparations," 130–31

Lansbury, George, 99, 121, 134, 150, 164, 172, 194–95, 196; pacifism of, 13; supports Wilson, 30; uncritical of Bolshevik excesses, 31; damns Versailles Treaty, 54; upholds Bolsheviks, 74; discounts League, 75; opposes Locarno, 167

Lansbury's Labour Weekly: grudgingly supports Geneva Protocol, 163–64; protests Locarno Pact, 164

Leach, William, 128

League of Nations, 1, 2, 5, 6, 117, 192–93; as capitalist instrument, 2; and Draft Covenant, 36; Labour demands representative body, 56; passivity during Ruhr occupation, 96; analyzed by Dalton, 182–83; gap in covenant of, 185; support for General Act of, 185; MacDonald's lukewarm support of, 194; views of, 199 (n. 2); considered a farce by ILP, 203–4 (n. 29)

League of Nations covenant, 193; Labour demands inclusion in peace treaty, 39

League of Nations policy: as alternative to class warfare, 14

League of Nations Union, 179, 184

Lees Smith, H. B., 95, 176

Liberal party, 7, 8, 14; pre-1914 dissidents in, 12–13

Lloyd George, David, 4, 6, 8, 81, 152; intransigence during election campaign, 29; meets with Labour representatives, 40; pro-Greek policy of, 95; condemns Preparatory Commission, 176

Locarno treaties, 10, 160

MacDonald, James Ramsay, 2, 5, 11, 18, 20, 34, 36, 40, 43, 50, 70, 92–94, 125, 128, 137, 180, 190; relies upon spirit of goodwill, 2; controls American policy, 3; on growth of international spirit, 23; opposes British entry into war, 23; success as foreign secretary, 23–24; on general disarmament at Berne, 34; demands self-determination for all nations, 35; denounces Draft Covenant, 36; urges acceptance and reform of League, 51; ambivalence on peace treaty and League, 55; disenchantment with Labour party colleagues, 65; relations with ILP, 70; at 1922 Labour party conference, 87; hedges on opposition to League, 93–94; at 1922 UDC conference, 96–97; on Ruhr policy, 105–6, 107; vagueness on use of force, 121–22; acceptance of Dawes Plan, 124; treatment of Henderson, 125; advice on Optional Clause and reparations, 131–32; on Franco-German balance of power, 132; and Burnley by-election, 133; negotiations on Dawes Plan and Ruhr, 133–34; frustration with Labour press, 135; rejects Draft Treaty of Mutual Assistance, 144; at 1924 League Assembly, 144–45; at 1924 Labour party conference, 149–50; mishandles Campbell case, 152–53; leadership in first Labour government, 153; breaks with ILP, 157, 218 (n. 32); attitude to reform of Foreign Office, 159; ambivalence toward Geneva Protocol, 160–61; second thoughts on Locarno, 166–67; sees Locarno as possible opportunity, 166–67; criticizes ILP activists, 170; on 1927 resolution on disarmament, 176; and freedom of the seas, 177; supports Kellogg proposals, 178; suspicious of sanctions, 180–81; views on disarmament, 188–89, 194; and "Labour and the Nation," 189; influenced by military leaders, 193; lukewarm support of League, 193; comparison with Lansbury, 194; attempts to control Morel, 214–15 (n. 36); assesses the political parties, 218 (n. 32); diary criticisms of Henderson, 225 (n. 4)

McGurk, J. M.: sees League as hope for future, 51

Manchester Guardian, 165, 172

Mandates (League of Nations), 2, 38–39

Marquand, David, 8, 93

Maxton, James, 113; as militant anticapitalist, 13; advocates disarmament by example, 174–75

Mellor, William, 74

Memorandum on War Aims, 26

Meynall, Francis, 74

Mitrany, David, 196; suggests compromise on sanctions, 186

Montgelas, Count Max: supplies Morel with information, 79

Morel, E. D., 15, 17; campaigns against secret diplomacy, 17; supports revision of Versailles Treaty, 17; leads UDC campaign to revise German settlement, 49–50; consistently opposes peace treaty, 54–55; views League as instrument of oppression, 65; campaigns to redress German grievances, 72–73, 79–80; caricatures French use of black troops in Rhineland, 73; condemns occupation of Ruhr, 73; on Germany and France, 97–98, 104; on Ruhr, 106–7, 109–11; as possible foreign secretary, 125, 126; briefly supports Labour government's foreign policy, 127; opposes Dawes Plan, 135–36; and democratic control of foreign policy, 137–39; criticizes Draft Treaty of Mutual Assistance, 139–40; and Russian treaty, 150–51; death of, 169; berates British foreign policy, 208–9 (n. 32); rhetoric of criticized, 209 (n. 34); attacks Labour colleagues, 210 (n. 56); connections with Max Montgelas, 211 (n. 57)

Mosley, Oswald, 189; deplores "miniature Napoleons," 209–10 (n. 49)

Namier, L. B., 25

Nansen, Fridtjof: submits arbitration treaty to League Assembly, 185

Nation, 109

National Council for the Prevention of War, 184

National Executives (TUC and Labour party): manifesto on Ruhr, 120

National government, 194

National Joint Committee (TUC and Labour party), 103

National Union of Agricultural Workers, 99

New Leader, 19, 98, 105, 109, 148, 175; briefly supports Labour government's foreign policy, 127; credits Dawes Plan with progress, 134; increasingly opposes Dawes Report, 135; hopes for alternative to Draft Treaty of Mutual Assistance, 143–44; and Geneva Protocol, 164–65; opposes Locarno agreements, 169; criticizes disarmament talks, 174; denounces British reservations in Kellogg Pact, 179; reluctantly supports outlawry of war, 179

New Statesman, 50, 53, 109, 175; denounces Draft Covenant, 49; shares views with Left, 76; applauds Washington Conference, 81; argues for moderation, 126–27; grudgingly supports Dawes Plan, 134; backs MacDonald, 143; rejects Geneva Protocol, 163; approves Locarno agreements, 168

New unionism, 10

Noel-Baker, Philip, 158, 183, 196; advisor to Henderson, 21–22; on League as parliament of man, 131; proposes reform of CID, 159; leading advocate of Geneva Protocol, 162–63; realism on sanctions, 162–63, 180–81; on disarmament issues, 166, 181

Norwich amendment: at 1923 ILP conference, 113–14

Optional Clause, 131, 190; supported by Arnold Forster, 181; relation to Geneva Protocol, 184–85; championed by International Advisory Committee, 185

Outlawry of war: reception of American initiative on, 178–80

Pacifism: in labor ranks, 13

Palme Dutt, R., 104

Parliamentary Labour party, 11, 20, 124–25; denounces preliminary peace, 46; minimal discussion of peace treaty by, 52–53; passivity in early twenties, 77; on Ruhr, 106–7; divided on Dawes Plan, 135–36; on democratic control of foreign policy, 137–39; reluctantly supports Locarno, 166, 168

Parmoor, Lord, 145–47

Peace settlement: disillusion of trade union leaders with, 206 (n. 87)

Permanent Court of International Justice, 130

Poincaré, Raymond, 81, 132, 133

Politis, Nicolas, 145

Pollitt, Harry, 117

Ponsonby, Arthur, 15, 16, 18, 72, 95, 121, 147, 150–51, 170, 173–74, 187; pacifism of, 16–17, 172–74; supports unilateral disarmament, 17, 175; endorses passive resistance in Ruhr, 111; as undersecretary for foreign affairs, 125; and democratic control of foreign policy, 138–39; opposes Locarno, 167; gives reasons for formal support of Labour's foreign policy, 173–74

Protocol for the Pacific Settlement of International Disputes. *See* Geneva Protocol

Purcell, A. A., 151; attacks Dawes scheme, 137

Rakovsky, Christian, 151

Reparation Commission, 96

Reparations: figures set, 79

Rowlinson, E. D., 87–88

Ruhr: occupation of, 96, 124; and the Labour press, 126–28

Russia, 20, 35, 68–69; admission to a League "Executive Council" urged by Labour, 39; Labour and intervention in, 68; diplomatic relations with, 190

Russian treaty: negotiations for, 150–52

Russo-Polish war, 79

Sanctions: UDC opposes, 37

Second International, 11–12

Shaw, Tom, 104, 166

Shinwell, Emanuel: advocates international cancellation of debts, 100

Shotwell, James T., 25; analyzes Draft Treaty of Mutual Assistance, 140

Singapore naval base: opposed by Advisory Committee, 190

Smillie, Robert, 75, 89

Snowden, Ethel, 33

Snowden, Philip, 20, 94, 95, 147, 152; as ILP voice in foreign affairs, 19–20; doubts Wilson's effectiveness, 31; denounces Draft Covenant, 36; applauds American rejection of covenant, 66; spurns peace settlement, 70; begins to accept League, 93; splits with ILP, 93; on Ruhr issue, 106; criticizes Dawes Plan, 134–35; attacks supporters of Geneva Protocol, 165

Social Democratic Federation, 88; indifference to foreign affairs, 10

Socialism in Our Time: outlines ILP views, 158

Socialist Review, 94, 121; criticizes Parliamentary party, 164

Stuart-Bunning, G. H., 40, 43

Swanwick, Helena, 169, 173; opposes Draft Treaty of Mutual Assistance, 144; briefly accepts Geneva Protocol, 149

Taff Vale decision, 11

Tawney, R. H., 189

Thomas, J. H., 34, 75, 108, 117, 156; influence within trade union movement, 20; contrasts League with International, 75; at 1922 TUC conference, 100

Thompson, Alexander M.: supports Draft Covenant, 37

Thomson, Brigadier General C. B., 104

Tillett, Ben, 137

Toynbee, Arnold, 25, 104

Trades Union Congress (TUC), 8, 10, 20–21, 99–100, 117; and Second International, 12; demands a "Wilson" peace, 30; proposes fundamental amendments to Draft Covenant, 38–71; gives scant attention to international issues, 83–84; suspects Dawes proposals, 137; opposes Dawes plan, 156

Trade unions, 8

Transfer problem: emphasized by Keynes and Angell, 207 (n. 4)

Trevelyan, Sir Charles, 15–18, 95, 157; disillusionment and retirement, 16

Turner, Ben: TUC presidential address, 157

Unilateral disarmament: and ILP, 170–71, 174–75; rejected by UDC, 172–73; advocated by Maxton and Ponsonby, 174–75; opposed by Labour party leaders, 180–81

Union of Democratic Control (UDC), 14–17, 19, 91, 121, 184; offers advice to Wilson, 29–30; objects to covenant, 36–37, 64–65, 72; denounces proposed German treaty, 49; 1922 conference of, 96–97; position on the Ruhr, 110–11; endorses Dawes Plan, 136; advocates democratic control of foreign policy, 137–39; favors Optional Clause, 144; opposes Draft Treaty of Mutual Assistance, 144; rejects pacifist resolution, 172–73

United Kingdom: assumptions of ten-year rule, 9; weakened position after war, 9; hopes for disarmament, 9–10

Versailles settlement, 10, 17

Vienna Union, 108

Walker, R. B.: demands general strike against war, 84; TUC presidential address, 99

Wallhead, Richard C., 88; opposes ratification of Locarno, 167

War Office: opposes Optional Clause, 132; on strengthening League, 132

War resistance: resolution adopted by

ILP, 171; accepted by Labour party
conference, 171–72

Webb, Beatrice, 110, 135; calls peace
treaty intolerable, 48–49; recognizes
importance of International Advisory
Committee, 202 (n. 47); finds fault with
Lansbury, 209 (n. 36)

Webb, Sidney, 190; and constitution of
1918, 8; praises MacDonald's good
sense in Council, 206 (n. 72); comments on cabinet neglect of foreign
affairs, 216 (n. 10)

Wedgwood, Josiah, 95, 147; opposes ratification of Locarno, 167–68

Weimar Republic: revisionist nationalism
in, 2

Wheatley, John, 113

Wilkinson, Ellen, 189

Williams, Bob, 75, 108

Wilson, Woodrow, 4, 39; Labour's support
of, 28; skepticism about influence of,

29; and minority representation at
peace conference, 204 (n. 30)

Women's International League, 181, 184

Women's Peace Pilgrimage, 184

Woolf, Leonard, 21, 92–93, 104, 109, 121;
author of *International Government*,
21; secretary of International Advisory
Committee, 21; welcomes outlawry of
war proposals, 178

World Peace Congress, 94

World War I, 5, 7

Young, George, 129; disapproves government's organization for foreign affairs,
158–59

Zimmern, Alfred: supports Geneva Protocol, 163

Zinoviev letter: promotes criticism of foreign affairs machinery, 158–59